Musical Scores and the Eternal Present

Musical Scores and the Eternal Present

Theology, Time, and Tolkien

CHIARA BERTOGLIO

PICKWICK *Publications* • Eugene, Oregon

MUSICAL SCORES AND THE ETERNAL PRESENT
Theology, Time, and Tolkien

Pickwick Publications
An Imprint of Wipf and Stock Publishers
199 W. 8th Ave., Suite 3
Eugene, OR 97401

www.wipfandstock.com

PAPERBACK ISBN: 978-1-7252-9502-5
HARDCOVER ISBN: 978-1-7252-9503-2
EBOOK ISBN: 978-1-7252-9504-9

Cataloguing-in-Publication data:

Names: Bertoglio, Chiara, 1983–, author.

Title: Musical scores and the eternal present : theology, time, and Tolkien / Chiara Bertoglio.

Description: Eugene, OR : Pickwick Publications, 2021 | Includes bibliographical references and indexes.

Identifiers: ISBN 978-1-7252-9502-5 (paperback) | ISBN 978-1-7252-9503-2 (hardcover) | ISBN 978-1-7252-9504-9 (ebook)

Subjects: LCSH: Music. | Religious aspects. | Theology. | Time. | Time in music. | Tolkien, J. R. R. (John Ronald Reuel), 1892–1973—Criticism and interpretation.

Classification: ML3921 .B48 2021 (print) | ML3921 .B48 (ebook)

This book contains material reworked after previously published articles:

Bertoglio, Chiara. "Dante, Tolkien, and the Supreme Harmony." In *Tolkien and the Classics*, edited by Giampaolo Canzonieri et al., 83–96. Zürich; Jena: Walking Tree, 2019.

———. "Dissonant Harmonies: Tolkien's Musical Theodicy." *Tolkien Studies* 15 (2018) 93–114.

———. "High Scores: The Notation of Music, Time and the Eternal Present." *Logoi.ph* 5.14 (2019) 59–122.

———. "Polyphony, Collective Improvisation and the Gift of Creation." In *Music in Tolkien's Work and Beyond*, edited by J. Eilmann and F. Schneidewind, 3–28. Zürich; Jena: Walking Tree, 2019.

To my Mother,
who constantly helps me to see God's Providence in action

To Anna and Laure—
may the book of your lives be the score of a beautiful symphony

E Dio è lo scriuano
ch'à 'perta la mano
che 'l canto ha ensegnato.
[Jacopone da Todi, *Lauda LXIV*]

Table of Contents

Praeludium

> Du siehst, mein Sohn,
> zum Raum wird hier die Zeit.
> [Richard Wagner, *Parsifal*]

TIME AND SPACE, VISUAL and aural, are four of the fundamental coordinates through which we perceive and conceptualize our life. Seemingly, the members of each pair pertain to different, almost opposed domains: yet, the theory of relativity has taught us the possibility of conceiving Time as the fourth dimension of Space, and our bodily senses rarely work in isolation. Music is the art of sounds in time, but it is visually and spatially represented by musical scores. By observing them, time becomes space (as in Wagner's *Parsifal*), and can be viewed simultaneously in its unfolding. This experience may therefore become a symbol for the eternal present, i.e., the condition outside time, that transcends time, but which nonetheless embraces its totality.

This concept inspired the writing of the present book, which aims to demonstrate its theological fecundity. I will articulate my discourse in two Parts: each focuses on a distinct aspect and has a distinct approach, but both elaborate the same hypotheses and are deeply intertwined. Using a wide array of tools from a variety of disciplines, Part One discusses the implications of the idea that musical scores may by analogy symbolize the "eternal present." In Part Two, I will take the first pages of Tolkien's *The Silmarillion* as the starting point for a theological understanding in musical terms of the biblical Book of Genesis.

The topic I will be treating in Part One lies at the borders between theology and philosophy, music aesthetics and practice, but also touches upon such seemingly unrelated subjects as physics, history of art and the psychology of music, thus requiring a continuous shift in perspective. Though such shifts may challenge the reader's endurance, it is only by viewing the perspectives together that the concluding picture will emerge. Indeed, when consulting numerous sources on this topic, I realized that several scholars had, in their respective fields, provided the indispensable ground for my research, though—as far as I know—none had formulated it in these terms.[1]

In order to ease the task of reading Part One, I will briefly sketch *how* its various sections intertwine with each other and how they contribute to the point I wish to make. I begin with "Time and the Eternal Present," a brief summary of how Christian theologians and other thinkers have come to define the relationship between God and time as an "eternal present," and what such a concept can entail. I will also discuss the history of visual representations of Time and how this phenomenon came to be represented in spatial terms. In chapter 2, "Musical Scores and Temporality," I will turn to the history of musical notation, and to how the various forms of Western visualization of prescriptive or descriptive notations came to represent succession, duration, simultaneity and synchronicity. The aim of this discussion is to demonstrate how phenomena studied by psychologists of music and how the musicians' actual experience can provide a meaningful analogical representation of an "eternal present." In chapter 3, "Music as a Syntax of Time," I then argue that the structure of music, as represented by the score and/or as experienced by the musician or listener, is made intelligible through a system which renders musical events meaningful in their articulation in time. Special cases of musical notation will also be discussed, including graphic scores and some works by Iannis Xenakis. Subtly different views emerge from the subsequent discussion of Pierre Boulez's study of Paul Klee's paintings, which embody musical notation as a symbol for temporality, and from a distinctive but closely related view developed by Vasilij Kandinsky.

In chapter 4, "Observing the Score," I discuss the information which scores as visual objects may transmit. This is complemented by a brief

1. The only trace I have found of a statement similar to the view proposed here (though the idea is not developed, particularly in its theological implications, and it remains at the stage of a metaphor) is in Pickover, *Time*, 41–42: "An observer existing outside of time, in a region called 'hypertime', can see the past and future all at once. In a strange sense, when we scan back and forth over a musical score we are like a hyperbeing who lives outside of time. . . . A musical score makes time solid. A musician can see past, present, and future all at once."

survey of how the depiction of musical scores in visual art, particularly in the domain of *vanitas* and still-life painting, has represented the flowing of time, its fixation through art, eternity (or eternalization), and simultaneity. The observation of a score, and the capability to digest the information it contains in a multidimensional navigation of time characterizes the processes of musical performance. The relationship between score and interpretation reveals the complex concept of temporality experienced by musicians. This variety of approaches contributes to the surfacing of the main points of Part One: that music symbolizes the ordering of aural events in time; that musical scores allow the simultaneous visualization of these events; and that this experience is a powerful human analogue to the transcendent reality of the eternal present.

Part Two develops the theological implications of Part One, rehearsing their significance in a reinterpretation of the Christian understanding of Creation, as seen through the lens of Tolkien's *Ainulindalë*. Chapters 5 ("Beholding God") and 6 ("Polyphonic Improvisations") discuss the beginning of this imaginative literary work, where a divine being firstly creates a court of spiritual powers, similar to the angels of the Christian tradition. The Godhead then imparts "knowledge" to these creatures, in the form of a "theme of music," inviting them to "adorn" this music freely. Their singing is monodic at first, and when they later learn to know their brethren, it becomes a polyphony. By showing how Tolkien's myth intertwines with the writings of numerous Christian theologians, musicians, and authors, and with the history of music in the Western Middle Ages as known by Tolkien, I will discuss the implications of a "musical" concept of this imparted knowledge and of this polyphonic singing: it is in the contemplation of God that the intelligent beings discover the truth about themselves, about their brethren and about Him, and this enables their creative freedom to flourish in the encounter between God's will and a creature's liberty. This leads to my thesis that the contemplation of God may be likened to a musical score, "read" by the heavenly musicians, and, at the same time, enabling them to improvise freely and spontaneously.

Chapter 7, "Discord and Dissonance," discusses Tolkien's account of the rebellion of the greatest of the "angels," who disrupts the heavenly concert by attempting to replace the divine theme with one of his own. Here too the theological content of Tolkien's myth substantially coincides with the Christian interpretation of the Fall of Lucifer. By narrating it through music, however, its symbolic value is enriched: the diabolic music brings discord and breaks the musical relationships, but it nonetheless can be absorbed and transformed by the divine composer. While God neither wills nor justifies the dissonances in the music of history, his capability to encompass them in his redemptive song is a manifestation of his providence, i.e., of the loving care with which he sustains the life of the created world and saves us. By faith, Christians believe that their individual stories and the world's collective history do make a beautiful music, though our experience as mortal beings does not allow us to contemplate and to understand it in full. Outside of time, though, the blessed spirits already fix their gaze in God, and, in the contemplation of his eternal present, they can see, as if concentrated in a single point, the marvellous unfolding of the entire song. This mystical experience is wonderfully told by the Italian poet Dante, whose personal story is both visually contemplated, and aurally perceived, by his deceased ancestor Cacciaguida in the *Commedia*.

Temporal events are therefore symbolized by musical events, whose succession is not haphazard but rather corresponds to the Composer's creativity and artistry; mortal beings can believe in faith that the "notes" of their lives possess a meaning (and a beautiful one) in God's Music, contemplated outside time by the blessed (chapter 8, "Creation and Subcreation"). And so it follows that the act of making music represents an almost theological undertaking, as it posits the goodness, beauty, and intelligibility of the universe. Artists respond in a particularly clear fashion to the divine calling to creativity, which is foundational for human beings made in the image of their Creator; but they also encourage those who will listen to their music and read their books to weave their own individual stories as histories of salvation. Human creativity thus becomes a powerful form of announcement of the *euangelion*, of the good news of the Gospel, and allows us to glimpse, albeit for a fleeting moment, the full score of the symphony in God's Eternal Present.

By now it will be clear that I am writing from a perspective grounded in Christian theology. Although my main conclusions will be based on this religious perspective, I hope that the journey will enrich readers who do not share my Christian worldview, but who may find such a perspective culturally interesting. I have cited from and made use of a variety of disciplines, with a rather synchronistic approach which would be inadmissible in a historical work or in an essay in literary criticism; however, since each approach seemed to shed a particular light on one of the topics I wished to discuss, their causal connections are frequently less relevant than the perspectives they offer. At the same time, and for the same reason, I have not aimed at a systematic thoroughness in the treatment of the sources: I have chosen selectively, drawing from the inexhaustible well of Christian culture in order to let my argument appear more clearly.

The primary aim of this book is to contribute to a theological understanding of music and of its notation as a powerful symbol for a transcendent and consoling reality: the supreme beauty of God, his providence, and our final destiny as singers in His eternal symphony.

Acknowledgments

I WOULD LIKE TO thank Walking Tree Publishers and the publishers of *Logoi.ph* and *Tolkien Studies* for kindly allowing me to rework sections from previously published articles in this book.

I wish to express my gratitude to a number of friends and colleagues who have read and commented upon earlier drafts of this book, providing me with helpful suggestions and valuable stimuli and ideas. My heartfelt thanks to Fabio Alessi, Richard Bell, Giovanni Carmine Constabile, Paolo Gozza, Pier Francesco Micciché, Nils Holger Petersen, Alessandra Ruffino, Giuseppe Scattolini, László Stachó. Particular thanks to Ruth Tatlow, who is not only a great scholar and a formidable editor, but, even most importantly, is a true friend.

Abbreviations

PL	Migne, J.-P., ed. *Patrologia Latina. Cursus completus.* Online. http://patristica.net/latina.
I Sent.	Bonaventure of Bagnoregio. *Commentaria in IV libros sententiarum.* 1934.
ST	Thomas Aquinas. *Summa Theologiae.* 1920.

PART ONE

1

Time and the Eternal Present

> The actual infinite, a nonsense for philosophy, is the reality, the very essence of music.
> (Emil Cioran, *Syllogismes de l'amertume*)[1]

TIME IS THE SHAPE of every experience of the human being. We have no memory, no project, no knowledge outside time. The first instants of our life are punctuated by our mother's heartbeats; later, our identity is framed and given intelligible form by the intertwining rhythms of our bodies, of our breathing, walking, dancing, and by those of the day, of the year, of life.

And yet, the very definition of time is one which continuously eludes our grasp. As St. Augustine memorably wrote,

> What, then, is time? If no one ask of me, I know; if I wish to explain to him who asks, I know not. Yet I say with confidence, that I know that if nothing passed away, there would not be past time; and if nothing were coming, there would not be future time; and if nothing were, there would not be present time.[2]

The concepts of past, present and future are among the first with which we become acquainted in our infancy, as we learn to expect the satisfaction of our needs, to reclaim it, and to obtain it. However, we are also keenly aware that time past is irremediably lost, that the future is still to come and therefore it exists only in potency, and that present, the only actual and

1. Cioran, *Syllogismes de l'amertume*, 146.
2. Augustine, *Confessiones* 11.14 (244).

"real" moment of our being, is a point in time with virtually no extension, and therefore, seemingly, as elusive as past and future.

Sometimes, we perceive Time as the Chronos of the ancients, as a devourer of his progeny; we long to fix the moments of happiness and beatitude, as did Goethe's Faust ("Then to the moment I might say: / Beautiful moment, do not pass away!"[3]); we are continuously hoping for and expecting some bliss to come, and we acutely feel that no memory, happy as it may be, will ever be comparable to the original experience.

If, then, the past has dissolved into memory, the future is in the mist of possibility, and the present is a continuously moving point, what is Time really? We realize that the perfection of Being must not be ruled by Time's voracious processes of becoming and dissolution, and that God must possess a mode of existence beyond, above and outside Time, and yet be able to rule Time, to intervene in those processes which take place in Time, and to encompass temporality itself. Thus, the concepts of eternity, of eternal present, of timelessness (which are, of course, very different from one another) have attempted to explain this mode of being.

In philosophical and non-religious terms (though in terms which can easily be appropriated and understood by theology), Henri Bergson conceptualized an analogous idea:

> Now, it is very true that common sense and science itself until now have, a priori, extended this conception of simultaneity to events separated by any distance. They no doubt imagined . . . a consciousness coextensive with the universe, capable of embracing the two events in a unique and instantaneous perception.[4]

This experience was linked by Bergson himself to the idea of a four-dimensional representation of the Space-Time in which Einstein's theory of relativity was understood and framed in philosophical terms: "Immanent in our measurement of time, therefore, is the tendency to empty its content into a space of four dimensions in which past, present and future are juxtaposed or superimposed for all eternity."[5] This view has fascinating points of intersection with that maintained by Ludwig Wittgenstein: "If by eternity is understood not endless temporal duration but timelessness, then he lives

3. Goethe, *Faust*, 224.
4. Bergson, *Durée*, 42 (55).
5. Bergson, *Durée*, 45 (60).

eternally who lives in the present. Our life is endless in the way our visual field is without limits."[6]

The idea of "eternal present," therefore, is both entirely alien to our daily experience, and subtly intriguing for musicians, philosophers, artists, and mathematicians. And, as we will see, some ideas derived from the theory and practice of Western classical music can become useful conceptual tools in the effort to express a reality which is clearly beyond our human intellect. I will proceed on the basis of *analogy*, a theological principle that has allowed many Christian thinkers to state meaningful truths about God and his mode of being. Such truths emerge in spite of our constant awareness that our limits and finiteness as created beings, and of the language we employ, will always and hopelessly fall short of any comprehensive understanding of the uncreated Being. This humbling knowledge has nonetheless been traditionally coupled with daring attempts to overcome the apophatic theology of denial, trusting that God's self-revelation in the history of salvation provides us with a language "capable of the infinite."

The Eternal Present in Boethius

The past which exists no more, the future which still does not exist and the present which passes in an instant seem all to be on the verge of non-existence. By way of contrast, God's mode of being has frequently been expressed as the divine encompassing of a simultaneous, actual, and non-ephemeral presence of past, present, and future. Though God's Being does not coincide with the conglomeration of Time, a long tradition of Christian theology has maintained that, *in Him*, all past, all present, and all future are coincident. This view has been called "the eternal present," and it has been beautifully described by some of the greatest thinkers of the first centuries of the Christian era.

One of the first to treat the subject of God's eternal present was Boethius. For him, in the eternal present, all things are known by God in his omniscience and prescience, and yet are not bound by necessity. A deliberate will "drives" even those actions which we are able to foresee, as in the case of a chariot driven by an *Auriga*: consequently, not everything foreseeable is necessary, and God is supremely free to act unconstrained

6. Wittgenstein, *Tractatus* 6.4311 (185). I am very grateful to my friend and colleague Pier Francesco Micciché for drawing my attention to this quote.

by necessity. Boethius famously contrasted the view of pagan philosophers with the mode of being of the Christian God:

> Eternity, then, is the complete, simultaneous and perfect possession of everlasting life; this will be clear from a comparison with creatures that exist in time. . . . For it is one thing to progress like the world in Plato's theory through everlasting life, and another thing to have embraced the whole of everlasting life in one simultaneous present.[7]

Boethius compares visual knowledge, which is capable of embracing an object as a whole ("*uno ictu mentis*," as he specifies), and tactile knowledge, which instead needs a space of time in order to be able to apprehend a physiognomy. Boethius then juxtaposes the visual to the aural: "*cum vel lux oculos ferit / vel vox auribus instrepit*" ("As when light strikes upon the eye / Or voices clatter in the ear / The active power of mind then roused / Calls forth the species from within / To motions of a similar kind"[8]). These lines encompass the main subjects of this book: textuality and writing, visual and aural, and the all-important connection between temporality, eternity, and prescience. In the sixth Prose of the *Consolation*, Boethius explicitly affirms the idea of the eternal present, in which God, as if from the summit of a mountain, can see and embrace all things:

> Since, therefore, all judgement comprehends those things that are subject to it according to its own nature, and since the state of God is ever that of eternal presence, His knowledge, too, transcends all temporal change and abides in the immediacy of His presence. It embraces all the infinite recesses of past and future and views them in the immediacy of its knowing as though they are happening in the present. If you wish to consider, then, the foreknowledge or prevision by which He discovers all things, it will be more correct to think of it not as a kind of foreknowledge of the future, but as the knowledge of a never-ending presence. So that it is better called providence or "looking forth" than prevision or "seeing beforehand." For it is far removed from matters below and looks forth at all things as though from a lofty peak above them.[9]

This "gaze from above" image will be used by several other authors, as the forthcoming pages will show.

7. Boethius, *Consolation* 5.6 (132).
8. Boethius, *Consolation* 5.4 (129).
9. Boethius, *Consolation* 5.5 (134).

Augustine's Songs: Time and Memory

Approximately a century earlier, St. Augustine had treated similar subjects, most famously in his *Confessions* and in the *City of God*. In the *Confessions* Augustine hinted at the concept of the eternal present:

> Nor dost Thou by time, precede time: else wouldest not Thou precede all times. But in the excellency of an ever-present eternity, Thou precedest all times past, and survivest all future times, because they are future, and when they have come they will be past; but "Thou art the same, and Thy years shall have no end."[10]

Later in the same Book, Augustine reflects on the measurability of time with reference to a sounding voice, arguing that a music which is yet to come cannot be "measured," nor it is possible to measure one which is no longer: "It was future before it sounded, and could not be measured, because as yet it was not; and now it cannot, because it no longer is. Then, therefore, while it was sounding, it might, because there was then that which might be measured. But even then it did not stand still, for it was going and passing away."[11] It is significant to note that, within this context, Augustine employs a spatial term: "*spatium temporis*," translated as "a space of time."[12]

> Should any one wish to utter a lengthened sound, and had with forethought determined how long it should be, that man hath in silence verily gone through a space of time, and committing

10. Augustine, *Confessiones* 11.13.16 (243).

11. Augustine, *Confessiones* 11.27.34 (254–55).

12. On numbers, space, time and performing arts in Augustine, see also Augustine, *De libero arbitrio*, II.16.42 (Augustine, *On Free Choice of the Will*, 61). On the relationship between time (present), space and memory, cf. the perceptive commentary by Løgstrup on Augustine's thought: "Without the timelessness of the spatial we would have no consciousness of time. . . . The present is a liminal concept, at least when it is considered as a moment without extension, but not otherwise. Otherwise, my present has extension. We are used to reserving the word extension for space, but also the present has extension. It extends back into what has passed and forward to what will immediately arrive. . . . But what is perceived does exist in another way. It is not given extension by the *memoria* of the soul. Rather, it already has extension because of its immutability as spatial" (Løgstrup, *Skabelse*, 34–35, in Petersen, "Time and Space," 305–6). (I am very grateful to my friend and colleague Nils Holger Petersen for drawing my attention on Løgstrup's thought. As summarized by Petersen himself, "It can then be said that for Løgstrup the possibility of retaining a melody in our memory is explained through the importance of space for our perception of time," and it is therefore crucial that "the melody has character, form, something that makes possible the perception of the melody as a totality, the remembered totality" [Petersen, "Time and Space," 307].)

> it to memory, he begins to utter that speech, which sounds until it be extended to the end proposed; truly it hath sounded, and will sound. For what of it is already finished hath verily sounded, but what remains will sound; and thus does it pass on, until the present intention carry over the future into the past; the past increasing by diminution of the future, until, by consumption of the future, all be past.[13]

The visualization of time as space compels the thinker to imagine the present as a (geometrical) point. Augustine's conclusion is that memory and imagination are where humans can measure time: "In thee, O my mind, I measure times"; "for when both the voice and tongue are still, we go over in thought poems and verses, and any discourse, or dimensions of motions."[14]

Still later, Augustine employed the example of a known psalm (which was normally sung) in order to demonstrate a point which is highly relevant here:

> I am about to repeat a psalm that I know. Before I begin, my attention is extended to the whole; but when I have begun, as much of it as becomes past by my saying it is extended in my memory; and the life of this action of mine is divided between my memory, on account of what I have repeated, and my expectation, on account of what I am about to repeat; yet my consideration is present with me, through which that which was future may be carried over so that it may become past. Which the more it is done and repeated, by so much (expectation being shortened) the memory is enlarged, until the whole expectation be exhausted, when that whole action being ended shall have passed into memory. And what takes place in the entire psalm, takes place also in each individual part of it, and in each individual syllable: this holds in the longer action, of which that psalm is perchance a portion; the same holds in the whole life of man, of which all the actions of man are parts; the same holds in the whole age of the sons of men, of which all the lives of men are parts.[15]

This excerpt from the *Confessions* invites us to consider a few elements: firstly, the use of a song as a tool for putting memory and time in dialogue

13. Augustine, *Confessiones* 11.27.36 (256–57).

14. Augustine, *Confessiones* 11.27.36 (256).

15. Augustine, *Confessiones* 11.28.38 (257). Interestingly, Bjerstedt et al. connect Augustine's view with that proposed by Ricoeur for the understanding of literary narratives in a threefold mimesis of "prefiguration, configuration and refiguration." See Bjerstedt et al., "Musical Present," 27–28; Ricoeur, *Time and Narrative*, 1:52–87.

with each other; secondly, the capability of "navigating" time, recalling and imagining different temporalities in a simultaneous fashion; thirdly, the fact that Augustine adds a reference both to the "whole life of man," which is therefore seen as unfolding in time much in the same way as a song, and to "the whole age of the sons of men." The metaphor or symbol is further explored slightly later, where the sung aspect is still further stressed:

> If there be a mind, so greatly abounding in knowledge and foreknowledge, to which all things past and future are so known as one psalm is well known to me, that mind is exceedingly wonderful, and very astonishing: because whatever is so past, and whatever is to come of after ages, is no more concealed from Him than was it hidden from me when singing that psalm, what and how much of it had been sung from the beginning, what and how much remained unto the end. But far be it that Thou, the Creator of the universe, the Creator of souls and bodies,—far be it that Thou shouldest know all things future and past. Far, far more wonderfully, and far more mysteriously, Thou knowest them. For it is not as the feelings of one singing known things, or hearing a known song, are—through expectation of future words, and in remembrance of those that are past—varied, and his senses divided, that anything happeneth unto Thee, unchangeably eternal, that is, the truly eternal Creator of mind. As, then Thou in the Beginning knewest the heaven and the earth without any change of Thy knowledge, so in the Beginning didst Thou make heaven and earth without any distraction of Thy action.[16]

We may therefore see that Augustine discussed the problem of Time in its mysterious flowing on the ridge between past and future; the point-like, elusive form of present stipulates that the measurement of Time can happen only in memory.[17] This measurement is exemplified at first through the comparison of the durations of a written verbal text, and later through the concept (in anticipation and in memory) of a "well known song." The mind's capability to imagine, almost simultaneously, the temporal development of a song in its unfolding is seen in a fashion similar to God's prescience. Interestingly, however, Augustine's discussion is grounded on the premise that the duration of the musical sounds cannot be written down;

16. Augustine, *Confessiones* 11.31.41 (259–60).

17. This intuition by St. Augustine would be developed in the twentieth century by Koechlin: "As concerns the measure of this (musical) duration, the role of musical memory possesses an importance that seems to escape many" (Koechlin, "Temps," in Carter, "Music and the Time Screen," 64).

indeed, it can only indirectly be established, through the lyrics' metrics. The first example used by Augustine in his discussion of the lengths of time is in fact that of a written verbal text ("*Deus creator omnium*," 11.27.35), the duration of whose syllables is examined by the author. Later, he argues by citing musical durations as a symbol of transience (precisely because they could not yet be notated in writing).

If here Augustine highlighted the radical temporality and elusive fleetingness of all things created, he was also acutely aware of the possibility of transcending time. As Teixeira and Ferraz put it, "Memory is the possibility of the past to make itself present, albeit as a past, but a past 'impelled' by the future that attracted it. Now, even eternity, finally, will be this present, but a present without a past or future, in a constant state of fullness."[18] St. Augustine in fact proclaimed:

> Before the world was, and indeed before all that can be called "before," Thou existest, and art the God and Lord of all Thy creatures; and with Thee fixedly abide the causes of all unstable things, the unchanging sources of all things changeable, and the eternal reasons of all things unreasoning and temporal.[19]

Aquinas: A Gaze from Above

On this subject, as happened with several other topics, the medieval theologian St. Thomas Aquinas resumed, subsumed, and developed Augustine's thought, while adding his own original insights. In his view, which he expressed in the *Summa*, "God knows future contingent things," and "although contingent things become actual successively, nevertheless God knows contingent things not successively, as they are in their own being, as we do, but simultaneously," since "His knowledge is measured by eternity, as is also His being; and eternity being simultaneously whole comprises all time," so that "His glance is carried from eternity over all things as they are in their presentiality."[20] Later (*ad* 3) Aquinas states that God's "understanding is in eternity above time"; echoing Boethius, Aquinas likens this knowledge to a gaze from above. He argues that our knowledge is like "he who goes along the road [and] does not see those who come after him; whereas

18. Teixeira and Ferraz, "Performance of Time," 498.

19. Augustine, *Confessiones* 1.6.9. (6).

20. *ST* Ia, q. 14, a. 13 co.

he who sees the whole road from a height, sees at once all travelling by the way." This image is intriguingly reminiscent of topography, i.e., of the visual mapping of a territory, reproduced in a bird's eye view: we will later see that both conceptually and practically there was a convergence of thought and experience in geographical, temporal, and musical representations of time and space.[21] God's eternal present is therefore understood by Aquinas as implying an all-embracing gaze, allowing him to "see" all times and places at a glance. Here we touch upon one of the focal points of our discussion, i.e., the intertwining of the visual and of the temporal in the experience of the eternal present. If Time itself, which informs and shapes all of our knowledge, proves to be such an elusive idea, how can we conceptualize the convergence of all Time into a simultaneity beyond duration? In order to reach the possibility of such a conceptualization, we need first to survey some of the ways in which Time has been "viewed" and described.

Viewing Time

Indeed, the very idea of "viewing" Time demonstrates our indebtedness to visual (and therefore spatial) models in our understanding of temporal phenomena. Many of the following examples are not mere "representations" of Time, being indeed *symbolic* images, which do not (primarily) aim at providing a visual (spatial) equivalent of an experience of Time. They rather aim at creating mental associations and links which allow a holistic form of thought, encompassing different dimensions of human knowledge. The *symbol*, by its very nature and according to the etymology of the word, "keeps together" what analysis may divide into different fields of the human experience; thus, visual symbolizations of Time are not the naïve efforts to express the unintelligible, but efficacious ways of putting symbols into action. Moreover, and at least since Plato theorized it, "conceptualization" and "visualization" are strictly bound to each other in the Western thought; in fact, the very term of *idea* comes from the semantic field related to visual phenomena. As Napolitano Valditara summarizes it, Plato realized a shift in the meaning of "terms connected to vision (*eidos, idea*)," and which had

21. Interestingly, Higgins cites the culture of certain Australian native tribes, who "employ musical metaphors to help them navigate the environment," correlating "the stream of a song with features of the physical environment. Their songs serve as literal maps, with contours and details that correspond to the shape of the land and its physical landmarks" (Higgins, "Visual Music," 487).

hitherto been used "in the common language to signify the sensible form of things"; they now acquired the power to signify "the determined and essential being [of the things], which can be reached by the intellect."[22]

Thus, to conceptualize Time meant to visualize it, albeit symbolically. The "idea" of Time needed to become a "vision" of time. However, as maintained by Henri Bergson, "The analogy between time and space is, in fact, wholly external and superficial. It is the result of our using space to measure and symbolize time";[23] and William J. T. Mitchell adds: "The fact is that spatial form is the perceptual basis of our notion of time, that we literally cannot 'tell time' without the mediation of space."[24] It might be argued that, at least in the symbolic fashion described above, this approach dates back to a period well before the first visual representations of time: Aristotle compared time "to a line on which a point makes a division but also constitutes continuity on the line,"[25] and various attempts have since been made to cross the boundary between space and time, sometimes succeeding in shaping the very vocabulary we use to discuss temporality. In turn, such concepts depend on our capability to discuss time by referring to visible changes and phenomena. A common example and perhaps one the first experiences through which we become aware of how space can represent time is the movement of a shadow on a sundial.

These problems and observations are clearly intrinsic to human nature and have elicited varied responses by the greatest minds regardless of historical period, religion, or culture. The Christian stress on the "eternal present" as God's relationship with Time, however, has proved particularly fruitful for the development of symbolic representations of Time and of the "eternal present" itself.

Syn-optic

It can be argued that the very structure of the Gospels, the sacred texts of Christianity, has favored such a reflection. Three of the Gospels (Mark, Matthew and Luke) are defined as "synoptic," from a Greek word meaning precisely "seen together," as they follow a similar, and sometimes identical,

22. Napolitano Valditara, *Sguardo*, 7 (translation mine).

23. Bergson, *Durée*, 9 (6).

24. Mitchell, *Language of Images*, 274.

25. Struik, *Source Book*, 138n4; cf. Aristotle, *Physics* 4.11, 220a4–20; Barnes, *Complete Works*, 1:71.

narrative structure, while giving different stress and focus to the same or similar episodes. Already in the first centuries of the Christian era, the "Ammonian sections" offered a visual opportunity to compare the three narratives; we know about this lost early prototype of synopsis thanks to a letter of Eusebius of Caesarea (ca. 260–340). Interestingly, it was the same Eusebius who wrote a famous *Chronicle* in which events of the Jewish-Christian sacred history were (visually) juxtaposed to those reported by pagan writers, so that, in the words of Rosenberg and Grafton, "by comparing individual histories to one another and the uniform progress of the years, the reader could see the hand of providence at work."[26]

Christian art successfully exploited the symbolic potential of visually juxtaposing events happening at different moments. Episodes from different biblical events were portrayed on a single painting or could decorate walls of the same church or chapel, thus allowing a similarly synchronic view of multiple events which had originally taken place at different times. By observing Giotto's frescoes at the Scrovegni Chapel in Padua, the faithful could admire the unfolding of the history of salvation and its purposeful progress toward the events of Christ's incarnation, passion, and resurrection. The individual events could be seen as distinct moments, depicted in the vivid and real colors of the daily lives of actual people; but, at the same time, they guided the focus to the point of arrival of that history and of those stories, i.e., the redemption realized by Jesus Christ. This and similar works of art helped the observer to see human history with almost divine eyes, with a comprehensive sight and insight which can be compared to God's eternal present.

Thus, in many depictions of biblical events, anachronisms were not seen as inconsistencies or faults, but rather as symbolically charged allusions to the providential view of human history: the cross represented in some Nativity scenes pointed to the teleology of Christ's incarnation, while the grouping of various Passion scenes within a single painting allowed the observer to see the different episodes as integral and integrated components of a unified narrative with a clear purpose.

Oresme: The First Graphs

Rosenberg and Grafton have masterfully narrated the development of the concept of "timeline," following in detail the evolution of Eusebius's model

26. Rosenberg and Grafton, *Cartographies*, 15.

during the Middle Ages, and its later adaptations. In their otherwise excellent book, however, the figure of Nicole Oresme (a fourteenth-century Protean genius who left fundamental works in a variety of disciplines including music and mathematics) is regrettably missing. Through his study of Euclidean geometry and physical phenomena, Oresme had the intuition to represent, by way of geometrical figures, the modifications undergone by objects in time. Oresme "employed a graphic representation in order to study not only the magnitude of the qualities in themselves, but also their variability in space and time."[27] In other words, "He represented, as one of the first to do so, such a variable value, and especially that of a velocity, for any point of a body or for any instant of time by a line segment plotted in a given direction, and thus drawing the first graph."[28] The impressive novelty of Oresme's thought is all the more relevant here by virtue of his own studies in the musical field; moreover, Oresme befriended Philippe de Vitry, one of the greatest composers and theorists of his time. As Della Seta puts it, "For Oresme, sound itself is a quality which can be measured according to extension and *intension*";[29] moreover,

> the aspects of sound described so accurately by Oresme are considered by him in their temporal extension; . . . all of the figures representing them have the line as their basis, representing their temporal extension; . . . their qualities are represented by the areas of the resulting figures. The temporal dimension of sound is thus *necessarily* implied in all of the preceding discussions on the various aspects of sound.[30]

In Oresme's representation and in its later evolutions (such as a Cartesian graph whose *x*-axis represents Time), it is also possible to "foresee" a future event if past events show a pattern of recurring regularity or a recognizable evolution. As Bergson writes,

> We cannot convert into space the time already elapsed without treating all of time the same way. The act by which we usher the past and present into space spreads out the future there without consulting us. To be sure, this future remains concealed from us by a screen; but now we have it there, all complete, given along with the rest. Indeed, what we called the passing of time was only the

27. Della Seta, "Idee musicali," 227.
28. Struik, *Source Book*, 134. See also Grant, *Source Book*, 306–11.
29. Della Seta, "Idee musicali," 230.
30. Della Seta, "Idee musicali," 239–40.

> steady sliding of the screen and the gradually obtained vision of what lay waiting, globally, in eternity.[31]

We will later see how this "foreseeability" can acquire a theological significance and be translated into a theological term.

Similar to Oresme, also Heinrich Glareanus left important writings in the field of music theory, and is also remembered for his contributions to the development of the concept of timeline. Glareanus, a sixteenth-century scholar, is in fact cited in the manuals of music history for his *Dodecachordon*, an important discussion of modal theory, but also notably adopted "a Eusebian coordinate system of dates against which readers could follow the events without becoming confused or lost."[32]

Priestley: The Timeline as a Musical Score

The fully developed linear representation of time as the horizontal axis in a system of coordinates framing historical events appears in a chart published in 1765 by the English scientist and theologian, Joseph Priestley. The lives of great figures of the past were represented by segments of lines starting at their birth year and ending at their death year, thus allowing an immediate visualization of synchronicity and contemporaneity. Priestley was aware of the innovative features of his graph: "If the reader carry his eye vertically, he will see the contemporary state of all the empires subsisting in the world, at any particular time," he maintained, adding: "In the charts, as in history, *the whole is before us*. We see men and things at their full length, as we may say; and we likewise generally see them through a medium which is less partial than that of experience."[33]

The theological import of his representation was not lost on his contemporaries; in the words of Rosenberg and Grafton, "For Priestley himself, the empty timeline . . . was not supposed to take God out of history. To the contrary, Priestley thought that, by revealing aggregate social phenomena

31. Bergson, *Durée*, 46 (61). It is very fascinating to compare this simile by Bergson with the actual research method employed by psychologists of music for studying the process of sight reading (i.e., precisely the use of a "moving-window technique" [Truitt et al., "Perceptual Span," 143–61]).

32. Rosenberg and Grafton, *Cartographies*, 52.

33. Priestley, "Description," 480–81 (emphasis mine).

consistent with the operation of Providence, it would beautifully illuminate God's plan."[34]

The immediacy of the visual medium for the representation of time was self-evident: those lines were understood as "suggest[ing] the ideas; and this they do immediately, without the intervention of words: and what words would do but very imperfectly, and in a long time, this method effects in the completest manner possible, and almost at a single glance."[35] Years later, when Priestley's idea had affirmed itself as a model for visualizing and for speaking about time, the experience of this simultaneous observation of history's unfolding was advertised as a pedagogical tool and as a means for intellectual enjoyment: "In truth we can hardly conceive of a more pleasant employment, than to seat oneself in the center of a room, around which the world from the beginning to this day is hung up, and its nations with their rise, and decline, and all the important events in their exact order, visible at one view, making an impression that cannot be effaced."[36] In that fashion, the graphical representation of time offered the feeling of "that unity which impresses itself on the attention, and presents the vicissitudes of centuries as a vast, continuous, harmonious whole."[37]

In the next chapter, I will discuss at greater length how musical and aesthetic/theological concepts of time may intertwine in a meaningful fashion. The notation of music, along with the graphs of physical phenomena (as represented in Cartesian coordinate systems, which in turn are a development of Oresme's intuition), and with the notation of dance movements, is one of the principal means by which human beings attempted to achieve a "bird's eye view" of temporal events. Cartesian graphs and musical/choreographic notations frequently involve a constant, regular, and/or proportional representation of time, in the form of a graduated axis, of regular bars and beats, of movements which depend on the cyclicity of the dances' musical rhythm.

34. Rosenberg and Grafton, *Cartographies*, 140.

35. Priestley, "Description," 467.

36. Review of Priestley's *Historical Chart*, *Philanthropist*, August 30, 1843, in Rosenberg and Grafton, *Cartographies*, 169.

37. Labberton, *Outlines*, 3–4, in Rosenberg and Grafton, *Cartographies*, 172.

2

Musical Scores and Temporality

We have seen, in the last lines of chapter 1, that musical scores, the notation of dance, and Cartesian graphs are three of the most efficacious visual representations of time. Among them, musical notation is probably the most ancient and the first to develop in a thorough and consistent fashion.[1] In Paddison's words, "While music, as a performing art, is necessarily a temporal art, in that it unfolds through time, it is not bound by its temporality, but, in the form of the score, is also characterized by spatialization, as the spatialization of the temporal."[2] Elsewhere, Paddison himself efficaciously summarized its role: "the score can be seen as the spatialization of what happens in the music, while the performed music is the interpretation of the score as a temporal unfolding of the structure it contains."[3] Temporality fundamentally characterizes the very essence of music and the typical experience of it, and therefore it should be impossible to imagine music outside time.[4] In spite of this, the notation of music succeeds in creating a visual representation of musical time, which, moreover, not just *describes* what happens when music is performed, but also determines it in a prescriptive fashion. Furthermore, as Illiano argues, the Western musicians'

1. Kramer, "Studies of Time."

2. Paddison, "Performance and the Silent Work." I wish to express my gratitude to Prof. Paddison for generously sharing his research with me.

3. Paddison, "Performance, Reification and the Score," 157. In the following pages I will suggest a possible further development of this thought.

4. This is what Arthur Schopenhauer maintained: "Music is perceived . . . in and through time alone, with absolute exclusion of space, even without the influence of the knowledge of causality, and thus of the understanding" (Schopenhauer, *World as Will*, 1:266).

acquaintance with the score as the means of writing, preserving, and dictating the performance of music determines the vocabulary of music itself, and the modes of its conceptualization:

> If the relationship amongst sound phenomena takes place in our minds, we should conclude that musical logic has an intrinsically spatial nature: our mind construes time according to spatial categories. The notions of "before" and "after," as well [as] sound pitches (high and low notes) are automatically turned into spatial concepts.[5]

"Before" and "after" also naturally characterize a written verbal text and its reading. However, with respect to their implied temporality, there is a fundamental difference between the writing and reading of a verbal text on the one hand, and the writing, reading, and performance of a musical score on the other. It is true that many written texts, especially in the past, were intended first and foremost for public reading, which pointed out their temporal quality in a fashion which today's texts, mostly read silently, cannot express as efficaciously. However, the reader of a written text can intervene in a much more flexible fashion on the temporality and pace of his or her reading. Furthermore, the possibility of browsing a text, of skipping some sections or re-reading others is much more common in verbal reading than in musical reading. In this respect, the temporal dimension of musical scores is far more pronounced than that of written texts.

The Beginnings of Western Music Notation

I will now briefly, summarily and sketchily recall some important stages in the evolution of musical notation in the Western tradition, since each of these stages provides us with a particular viewpoint on its function and purpose.

Unsurprisingly, the majority of early examples of a spatial conceptualization of sound originate in the philosophical schools of ancient Greece. As Gianluca Capuano points out,[6] if Plato could speak of "the colors of music,"[7] this implied an already-developed visual imagination of music. Thus, "when the necessity arose of speaking about sound, it was unavoidable

5. Illiano, "Musical Notation," xii. I am very grateful to Prof. Illiano for kindly sharing his research with me.

6. Capuano, *Segni della voce*, 123.

7. See Plato, *Republic*, 314 (601b).

to refer primarily to visual coordinates."[8] Moreover, then as today, sound does indeed translate into space through the practice of playing musical instruments, where the positions of the performer's fingers on a string, on a keyboard, on the holes of a wind instrument determine the pitch. By moving a finger on a string's length, a higher or lower sound can be produced; furthermore, the shorter or longer movement of a bow on a string determines the shorter or longer duration of a note, if the bowing speed is constant.[9]

Some of the earliest examples of musical notation in Western Christendom are the so-called *neumes*, i.e., a kind of stenographic reproduction of the "movement" of music; symbolically they recalled cheironomic practices (i.e., the hand gestures through which choirmasters indicated pitch and speed when conducting a choir). Pitches are not identified in absolute terms, and rhythm is not specified: the neumatic symbols served as an *aide-memoire* suggesting the "direction" of an already-known tune, whose unmeasured speed largely depended on the articulation of speech. (In turn, most of the sung texts had no metrical regularity, either in the disposition of accents or in the quantitative structure; in the absence of all regular pulse or beat, the element of cyclicity or repetition which is crucial for the "counting of time" was missing). For Petersen:

> Graphic representations of chant from around 900—new at the time—represent in pictures what could earlier only be retained in the memory. Performative acts were now represented in discernible shapes through neume notation. At least since St. Augustine, a theologically-reflected theory of time and history had been available, which in book eleven of his *Confessiones* was exemplified through the discussion of the performance of a *canticum*. This *canticum*, however, as well as any segment of time could only be measured in the mind—using the memory. The beginnings of visual representations of music in the Carolingian era, by contrast, may be constructed as a new departure: it became possible to visualize the intangible and ineffable.[10]

8. Capuano *Segni della voce*, 127 (translation mine).

9. Analyzing the implications of this phenomenon as observed on the monochord, Erwin Schadel underpinned the "relationality and time and space" from the viewpoint of musical harmony. Since space and time are the main components of our experience of the world, then music becomes a symbol of the world. Schadel, *Musik als Trinitätssymbol*, 163.

10. Petersen, "Carolingian Music," 27. Once more, I wish to thank Prof. Petersen for his kindness in sharing his research with me.

One of the greatest twentieth-century philosophers of music, Theodor W. Adorno, interpreted cheironomy and its symbolization through neumes in a Marxist perspective. While this viewpoint is different from the theological approach adopted here, one can see how the point of arrival of his argument is suggestively consonant with mine. For Adorno, "The musical symbol eternalizes that which is musically ephemeral, namely the mimic impulse; the notes on the page invoke the musically constant."[11] This process is explicitly connected with the "Christianization of music": "Intention is concerned with eternity: it kills music as a natural phenomenon in order to preserve it, broken, as spirit: music's survival in its duration depends on the termination of its here and now, while its survival in writing presupposes the spell of its mimic representation."[12] Music is naturally temporal; the process of notation expresses therefore a paradox. For Adorno, when we notate music we aim at mastering its temporality, while we are *de facto* renouncing it: "making available what has passed at once makes it irretrievable. Therein lies the desperate utopia of all musical reproduction: to retrieve the irretrievable through availability. All music-making is a *recherche du temps perdu*."[13] Adorno later hinted at the role of musical scores as a symbol for the eternal present: "Spatializing means being there: an absolute present would be timeless, and only what is entirely there can be controlled. Spatialization is by its nature controllability."[14] Even though Adorno's viewpoint is expressed in unequivocally critical terms, he explicitly acknowledges that, by spatializing (musical) time in a score, notation makes time "available" as an object to be observed and even, to a certain extent, manipulated.

Time, Tempo, and Rhythm

Adorno's discussion is applicable to all notated music, but it was prompted by his studies on the transition from cheironomy (hand gestures, thus a "temporal notation") to neumatic notation (a written, and thus, from a certain viewpoint, "atemporal" notation). Early neumatic notation was employed for monodic pieces (i.e., single unaccompanied melodies); yet, it did

11. Adorno, *Towards a Theory*, 185.

12. Adorno, *Towards a Theory*, 178.

13. Adorno, *Towards a Theory*, 53.

14. Adorno, *Towards a Theory*, 172–73. See also Zuckerkandl, *Sound and Symbol*, 1:336–48 (chapter 18, "Space as Place and Space as Force").

contain an element of synchronicity ("while" this word was pronounced, that melodic fragment was sung) which was visible at sight, in the superimposition of the neumes above the corresponding words. The words themselves, however, preserved their primacy both at the aural level (since the time of the spoken word frequently determined that of singing) and visually (the spacing on the page was largely dictated by the layout of the written text). At the same time, the indeterminacy of pitch as an absolute value pointed to the elements of continuity and fluency in the emission of the sung tunes, since a single symbol could represent several "notes" and thus highlighted their seamless movement in time. Moreover, as stated above, the function of neumatic notation was primarily mnemonic, describing the musical elements rather than prescribing them. It served to preserve the musical events, as an aid for the memory: it attempted to fix in time the perceived transiency of music itself. We have seen that St. Augustine discussed the reading of a verbal text and the recalling of a song within the framework of his treatment of the measurement of time (in spatial terms!) and of God's eternal present, and we noted there that the impossibility of notating musical durations was conspicuous by its absence. As Isidore of Seville put it in his *Etymologiae*, "The myth fabricated by the poets makes the Muses daughters of Jupiter and Memory. Indeed, unless sounds are held in the memory by someone, they die. Because sounds cannot be written down."[15] Early musical notations gradually evolved so as to respond to the challenge of temporality.

"Moving" Music

Guido of Arezzo, the eleventh-century Italian monk to whom several foundational theoretical works are ascribed, employed pioneering notational techniques in some of his treatises. For example, he placed the sung words in between two parallel lines of text where pitches were indicated through letters. This enabled a simple two-part polyphony to be viewed in the simultaneity of the two voices with each other and in their simultaneous intonation of the same text.[16] The notational form known as "Dasian," found in the anonymous treatise *Musica enchiriadis*,[17] attempts instead to

15. "A poetis Iovis et Memoriae filias Musas esse confictum est. Nisi enim ab homine memoria teneantur soni, pereunt, quia scribi non possunt" (Isidore of Seville, *Etymologiae* 3.15.2, in Isidore, *Isidori Hispalensis*, 1:148).

16. See Guido, *Micrologus*, 46.

17. See *Musica Hogeri*, fols. 28r–31v.

convey the idea of the voices' "movements" and of their coordination in pitch and rhythm by positioning the syllables of the sung text on a system of parallel lines. This idea easily evolved into an early form of musical "score," in which the reciprocal melodic "displacement" of the voices could be viewed simultaneously, the flowing of time was faithfully represented by the left-to-right movement of the eyes (and emphasized by the horizontal lines which channeled it), and the "movement" of the pitch was put into relief by the tiny lines connecting two successive syllables. Such notational habits deeply influenced the conceptualization of music and how it was imagined, as Capuano writes:

> Writing generates an odd effect: it is as if those who sing, when reading, would realize a sublimation of the graphical material they are beholding, and transform it into sound; at the same time, [this sound] would quickly be reconverted into an interior graph in the minds of the listeners, who know well the image behind the singer's pronunciation.[18]

This effect was further enhanced by the advent of diastemacy. The precise indication of melodic intervals implied a decidedly prescriptive function of notation (though conceived in very different terms from today's). Even on the musical page music acquired a new primacy with respect to the written words. The spacing on the page was determined by the quantity of musical events, and words could appear fragmented and almost dismembered when the ornamentation of a syllable was particularly abundant. Moreover, the graphic appearance allowed the observer to distinguish and individuate, at a glance, recurring musical structures or pitches, as well as particular musical features or salient moments of the piece and of its articulation. Interestingly, in many manuscripts of chant there is a smaller-sized note at the bottom-right corner of the page, indicating the first not to be sung on the next page.[19] The practical purpose of this habit is evident: the musicians were allowed to glimpse what they would be expected to sing after the page-turn, and thus prepare themselves for what followed. This sensible notation habit provides us with an important insight into an element which will be discussed later, i.e., the musician's capability to "navigate" time and to be ahead of it, anticipating, in a potential presence, an event which will take

18. Capuano, *Segni della voce*, 43 (translation mine).

19. This practice corresponds, of course, to that found in many books consisting entirely of verbal texts, and in which the first word of the following page is anticipated at the bottom of the previous page.

place in the future. "The same note" which will be written in normal size on the next page is already "present" as a foresight in the preceding page; the same event is doubled, in an anticipated presence which invades the otherwise constant flow of musical time, and in an actual presence which will happen in the future of music.

Polyphony: Coordination in Sounds

Some of the notational forms discussed above were elaborated as a response to the new challenges posed by early polyphonic forms, and this did not happen by chance. Indeed, the connection between time (in its musical articulations as rhythm and tempo), polyphony, and notation is one of the pivotal aspects of my argument.

In fact, when polyphony began to be written down, and consequently reached an increasingly high degree of complexity, it became necessary to develop strategies to express rhythm. It was crucial that each singer (or each section of the choir) knew the duration of one note in relation to others, and that all performers adopted the same regular pulse as a measure. Musical rhythm and tempo of the vocal repertoire developed discrete, regular, recurring, and hierarchically structured units enabling the realization of polyphonic singing in its complexity. And one of the many paradoxes of music lies precisely here: a clear underlying, discrete beat, precisely felt by the performers of polyphonic vocal music, produces a seamless, effortless and flowing audible result. In fact, by coordinating the vocal lines through an extremely accurate division of time, the individual melodies may become increasingly independent from each other in their acoustic profile, and the listener's impression is that of an almost prodigious coordination of "free" musical wills whose unexpected (and yet very much expected) intertwining and eventual meeting provides one of the greatest wonders of polyphonic music, as will be discussed at greater length in chapter 6.

The role of simultaneous perception in the enjoyment of music and in qualifying it as art proper was underpinned also by Leonardo da Vinci, who contrasted music with poetry and with painting. While, in his opinion, music ranked *below* visual art precisely as a consequence of its temporal nature,[20] the simultaneous presence of many voices in a polyphonic piece created something akin to the compresence of different layers of time. In fact, he argued that (read) poetry cannot be fully enjoyed, as it represents

20. See discussion below. See also Melzi, *Trattato della Pittura* 29, in Winternitz, "La musica," 86; Farago, *Leonardo da Vinci's*, 241–45.

beauty in a succession of descriptions[21] which cannot be grasped simultaneously and "at a glance," as happens in painting. This "linear" representation is likened by Leonardo to the spoiled experience of music by someone who, alone, would sing in succession the various parts of a polyphonic piece, thus missing the "grace of harmonic proportionality."[22] This seems to imply that the simultaneous singing of the polyphonic piece's parts would somehow create a multi-layered temporality, a non-linear (or at least a multilinear) flowing of time.

According to Oskar Söhngen, polyphony is the language enabling music ("the most ephemeral of all arts"[23]) to overcome time. Moreover, in his view, polyphony allows a translation of time into space, through the juxtaposition of different melodies and rhythms and the possibility of beholding this layering on a musical score.

Indeed, a polyphonic piece coordinates and superimposes different melodic lines; they are conceived in such a fashion that they can and should be sung simultaneously by different singers. The chronological time of the singers will be one and the same, while their experience of that same time will be different (both because of their different subjectivities and individualities, and because of the different notes they will have to sing). A four-part polyphonic piece creates therefore a single shared and collective time, in spite of the diversity in the subjective experience of the singers. A polyphonic score embodying this collective and shared time is therefore something akin to a multi-dimensional representation of time. The

21. Melzi, *Trattato della Pittura* 22, in Winternitz, "La musica," 80–81. English translation adapted from Farago, *Leonardo da Vinci's*, 219: "A poem . . . does not result in any grace other than what is heard as music if each tone were (to be) heard only by itself at various times, which would not compose any concept. It is as if we would want to show a face part by part, always covering up the part which was shown before. Oblivion does not allow any proportionality of harmony to be composed because the eye does not embrace a proportionality with its visual virtue at one and the same time in such demonstration."

22. Melzi, *Trattato della Pittura* 32, in Winternitz, "La musica," 93; DaVinci, *Thoughts*, 88: "The poet cannot express in words the true likeness of the limbs which compose a whole, as can the painter, who places it before you with the truth of nature. And the same thing befalls the poet as the musician, who sings by himself a song composed for four singers; and he sings the treble first, then the tenor, then the alto and then the bass, whence there results no grace of harmonious concord such as harmonious rhythms produce." It is fascinating to compare this metaphor devised by Leonardo with Bergson's image of the screen which progressively reveals a future which is already present in eternity (Bergson, *Durée*, 46 [61]). See footnote 30 in chapter 1 and compare with the experiments of psychologists of music described in Truitt, "Perceptual Span."

23. Söhngen, *Musik und Theologie*, 307.

experience suggested by Leonardo (i.e., that one and the same person sing, in succession, the four parts of an originally polyphonic piece) can thus be likened to the realization of the development of surface of an object, which can represent a three-dimensional object on a two-dimensional plane. Conversely, a score which demonstrates simultaneity through its vertical dimension—similar to an actual performance of sung polyphony—can transform "linear time" (that of a single individual's performance of the four voices in succession) into multi-dimensional, simultaneous time. Thus, the aural experience of parallel temporalities can become even more "evident," quite literally, in the case of written polyphony.[24]

Foreseeing Time through Space

Indeed, several of the earliest surviving manuscripts of polyphonic music are written in a fashion which might appear similar to the modern musical score. However, composers in the "golden age" of polyphony favored other methods. For example, frequently the individual melodic lines were either juxtaposed (but not superimposed) on facing pages of the same choirbook or written into partbooks. This lack of visual immediacy notwithstanding, the composer of polyphonic music had to develop a musical imagination that would enable him or her to coordinate the individual melodic "lines" (note the use of this common spatial metaphor) into a unified, harmonious whole.[25] The composer's creative insight required qualities proper to a "godlike" perspective: the ability to "foresee" the "direction" of each "line" (once more, the terms are all spatial), and to order and coordinate them in the seemingly spontaneous interaction of distinct musical characters. Indeed, the role of the composer of polyphony could be seen as an icon of God's coordination of the forces of nature, and particularly of the astronomic entities (which were believed by many to possess "harmonies" of their own, which were observed in their visible and coordinate movements but could also be thought as producing sounds—see also chapter 6).

It is therefore not by chance that both Oresme in the fourteenth century and Glarean in the sixteenth were, at the same time, experts in

24. Fascinatingly, Galia Hanoch-Roe has proposed to employ a notation derived from the scores of polyphony for designing and describing architectural elements (Hanoch-Roe, "Scoring the Path," 111–33).

25. This coordinated imagination was embodied in the *Tabulae compositoriae*, i.e., tablets used by the composers with precisely this purpose. See Owens, *Composers at Work*, 74–107.

polyphonic music *and* perceptive thinkers about the visualization of time. Even before the creation of musical scores proper, whereby the individual instrumental and vocal parts could be simultaneously visualized, the creative imagination of the composer had to be skilled in such a mental "view." Moreover, as we have seen, since its very inception musical notation provided some form of simultaneous visualization of time, whose degree of specification increased progressively. Starting from the description of the synchronicity of musical "movement" with speech in the neumatic notation, it later offered the possibility of "navigating" a notated page of plainchant at a glance, and arrived to the adoption of discrete rhythmic quantities which subdivided both the visual space of the page and the aural time of singing into countable and proportional units. When these began to be grouped into bars or measures visually, musical notation became the first (widespread) technique to allow a reader to view the constant progress of time in a synoptic fashion. Indeed, musical scores of the modern type had already been commonly used for centuries when Priestley published his synoptic chart. It is remarkable that the visual appearance and the layout of Priestley's innovative graph closely match that of musical scores: time is observed through a left-to-right interpretation of the page's space, while the lines representing each person's lifetime can be likened to the duration of sung or played notes in the individual parts of the musicians participating in a collective performance.

As briefly mentioned above, when "scores" proper were developed, musical notation was enabled to provide one of the most striking experiences of "eternal present" possible to human beings on earth. In a musical score, the individual vocal and/or instrumental lines are superimposed on individual staves; thus, the vertical dimension of the score specifies both the *temporal* aspect of simultaneity and succession, and also an exquisitely *spatial* dimension. In fact, when orchestral scores became standardized in the "place" they assign to the various instruments and instrumental groups on the page, every musical stave also began to represent a point in the space of the orchestra, a point from which the sound of a particular instrument originates: the musician's place corresponds to a point on the score's page. An experienced conductor will immediately associate a particular point of the page to a particular point in the orchestral body. Similarly, players of instruments such as keyboards will automatically translate a conglomeration of notes on the musical staves into hand positions in the two/three-dimensional space of the keyboard, mapping the position of notes on the score into the position of the keys one needs to touch in order to produce a sound (which will be spatialized in turn, as the sounding strings are ordered from left to right according to their pitch). This experience is a musical translation of the idea of simultaneity as Bergson defined it:

> Such a consciousness would grasp, in a single, instantaneous perception, multiple events lying at different points in space; simultaneity would be precisely the possibility of two or more events entering within a single, instantaneous perception.[26]

Playing with Time

If the superimposition represents *simultaneity*, the flowing of time is represented by the direction of reading, left to right. However, in the age of polyphony, and particularly (though not exclusively) in the case of the Franco-Flemish masters, some of the most refined and complex musical compositions actively played with spatial/temporal paradoxes. Canons *per augmentationem* and *per diminutionem* were based on the principle that two or more voices could begin the same melodic line at the same time (or at different times), but its duration could be markedly different depending on the mensuration[27] applied to it. The underlying principle of such a practice was that a tune's "time" could be lengthened or shortened at (the composer's) will, and yet remain "harmonious" with its original self in an almost prodigious fashion. Distinct temporalities, embodied by the different musicians performing the piece, could coexist and be simultaneously perceived. In the definition by Christoph Wolff, "The canon addresses the phenomenon of progressive and regressive time in that it can be performed forward and backward."[28]

In fact, and even more paradoxically, time could also be reversed: in its *cancrizans* form, the melodic tune of a canon could be read from left to right or from right to left, and the two could be performed together. The composer's skill, once more, was to create a melody which could bear this extremely complex treatment, and still produce a satisfactory aural result. The possibility of reading the melody backwards, however, was an extraordinary attempt to reverse time; as Adorno put it, "musical retrogrades are

26. Bergson, *Durée*, 36 (45).

27. I.e., the system of proportional durations.

28. Wolff, *Johann Sebastian Bach*, 337.

anti-temporal, they organize music as if it were intrinsic simultaneity. . . . They contain an element of indifference towards succession, something like a disposition toward musical saturation of space."[29] Though it is doubtful that normal listeners could actually perceive that a melody was being performed at the same time as its retrograde form, this was clearly observable in written music;[30] frequently, this aspect featured prominently in notation itself. These canons were seldom explicated in full; often, the possibility of performing them in the two directions was hinted to by conventional signs. As Trippett puts it, palindromic structures in music "embody a logic of undoing, or more specifically, a mechanism that can imply either spatial inversion or temporal reversal, depending on whether music is treated as an abstract or narrative form."[31] Indeed, in my opinion, mirror structures in musical notation are not only able but do in fact embody *both* spatial and temporal inversion.

In a still clearer fashion, circle canons (which could be prolonged infinitely by starting them time and again) could be written in a round form,[32] which immediately suggested a circular (and therefore non-linear) representation of time. The circle's perfection as a geometrical figure symbolized God, and the fact that circles have no "beginning, middle or end"[33] seemed to allude to God's eternity. Frequently, circular canons were indicated through mottos such as *Ma fin est mon commencement*, "my end is my beginning"; the implied model is a justly famous *rondel* by Guillaume de Machaut (1300–1377) whose very lyrics play with temporality in an explicit fashion:

> My end is my beginning / And my beginning my end. / This truly my tenor. / My end is my beginning. / My third line three times only / Goes back on itself and so finishes. / My end is my beginning / And my beginning my end.[34]

29. Adorno, *Gesammelte Schriften*, 341–42; Lee, "Deinen Wuchs," 185.

30. This is maintained, for example, by Pierre Boulez, who stated that retrogradation is a compositional technique which can be immediately appreciated by the eye, but very hardly perceived by the ear (Boulez, *Pays fertile*, 98).

31. Trippett, "Composing Time," 523.

32. Forms of musical notation in which circular (or spiral-like) staves are employed can be also found (though not exclusively) in several twentieth-century compositions.

33. See Elders, *Composers*, 70–71.

34. "Ma fin est mon commencement / Et mon commencement ma fin / Et teneüre vraiment. / Ma fin est mon commencement. / Mes tiers chans, iij fois seulement / se retrograde et einsi fin. / Ma fin est mon commencement / Et mon commencement ma fin" (Machaut, *Poésies Lyriques*, 2:575).

In this case the lyrics help listeners to grasp the circularity of the canon; on a purely musical plane, the capability of hearing a circular canon as a "circular" composition, and, *a fortiori*, the capability of hearing a retrograde canon as a work defying the unidirectionality of time far exceeds the capabilities of most listeners. If, therefore, these musical/temporal paradoxes are mostly conceived for the enjoyment of the eye and of the intellect, the aural reality and temporality of music work through processes and constructs of their own, many of which fall into the domain of psychoacoustics. The capability to understand the musical "direction" of a piece of music, to give musical meaning to it, depends on the listener's familiarity with a certain language. And many of these listening processes are culturally and historically determined constructs.

In fact, on the purely aural plane, the musical language of early polyphony was grounded on structures employing modes for the organization of pitch. Hearing these works from the vantage point of our current musical tradition is not ideal, in fact culturally flawed, as we are likely to project tonal constructs onto a repertoire conceived on the basis of different assumptions. However, I deem it safe to assert that both in our ears, and in those of the first creators and listeners of this repertoire, the enjoyability and (musical) intelligibility of these modal polyphonic works depends on the interplay of the melodic lines. It is possible for the listener to form expectations about their evolution, on the plane of both their individual shapes and their overall interaction; and the eventual encounter of the various melodic lines on a point of stasis and of consonance—at least at the end of a piece, but more frequently on the occasion of important structural nodes—is one expectation which is almost invariably fulfilled. While contemporaneous listeners may have formulated sets of expectations different from those of today's hearers, the anticipation of the final consonance unites both classes of listeners in a similar perspective.

Bach and Circular Time

This orientation toward a final resolution of the musical tensions becomes more important in parallel with the rising focus on tonal features, and with the growth of a harmonic awareness.[35] As Richard Taruskin put it,

35. The metaphysical writings of Erwin Schadel see the main chord of tonal harmony, i.e., the triad, as the foundation of a Trinitarian understanding of Being. Schadel proposes the concept of *in-ek-con*sistency as a philosophical interpretation of the triad, and

> Thanks to this newly psychologized deployment of harmonic functions—in which harmonic goals are at once identified and postponed, and in which harmonic motion is at once directed and delayed—"abstract" musical structures could achieve both vaster dimensions and a vastly more compelling emotional force than any previously envisioned.[36]

According to Karol Berger, this process caused a major shift in perspective during the so-called Classical era (interestingly, in the very same years in which Priestley was creating and publishing his charts). In Berger's words,

> In the later eighteenth-century European art music began to take seriously the flow of time from past to future. Until then music was simply "in time," it "took time"—events had somehow to be arranged successively, but the distinction between past and future, "earlier" and "later," mattered little to the way the music was experienced and understood. From that point on music added the experience of linear time, of time's arrow, to its essential subject matter. Music could no longer be experienced with understanding unless one recognized the temporal ordering of events.[37]

For Berger, this process embodied in music a trend which was observable in the philosophical, aesthetic and religious tendencies of the Western world as a whole: "just as their experience and image of historical time shifted from cyclical to linear, composers dropped the predominantly cyclical model of time in favour of a predominantly linear one."[38]

Berger advances a thought-provoking view through his analysis of some of the most iconic masterpieces of early- and late-eighteenth century European music. On the plane of musical technique, Bach is commonly regarded as the composer who succeeded in balancing an extremely sophisticated mastery of the harmonic language with an equally impressive skill in the creation and combination of melodies in their polyphonic interaction.[39] In his fugues, Bach demonstrates the ability to immediately realize the

---

as a possibility of overcoming the spatio-temporal conditions of music and contingency. See Schadel, *Musik als Trinitätssymbol*, 75–76.

36. Berger, *Bach's Cycle*, 11.

37. Berger, *Bach's Cycle*, 9.

38. Berger, *Bach's Cycle*, 9.

39. This was already maintained by Bach's sons, and articulated by Forkel in his 1802 biography of Bach; cf. Berger, *Bach's Cycle*, 126.

combinatory potential of a subject, as his second son Carl Philipp Emanuel wrote: "he needed only to have heard any them to be aware—it seemed in the same instant—of almost every intricacy that artistry could produce in the treatment of it."[40] Following in Dreyfus's footsteps,[41] therefore, Berger believes that Bach's compositional interest lay primarily in the *inventio* and exploitation of a theme's full potential, and only secondarily in the actual presentation of the temporal order embodied in the final score and in its performance.

> The "invention" of a piece . . . was the sum total of the material and its transformations. Since all transformations could not be presented at once in sounding music, they had somehow to be ordered in time. But this temporal "disposition" was a matter of relative indifference: Bach found a suitable order in full awareness that other arrangements might do equally well.[42]

A similar attitude can be observed even in the concerto form, which is seemingly less dependent on strict polyphonic rules than a fugue:

> The specific individual transformations of the ritornello, like the specific individual contrapuntal devices of the fugue, need to be disposed in a temporal sequence: they cannot be presented all at once. . . . The ritornello transformations are an essentially unordered set, articulating the timeless contemplation of various aspects of a single thought.[43]

Berger argues that in this fashion Bach could create telescoped temporalities, in which the choice to present two or more combined melodies simultaneously or successively could embody the same process we have already encountered in Leonardo da Vinci's thought experiment,[44] i.e., in the possibility of superimposing several temporalities sounding together in polyphony, or of juxtaposing them in a linear sequence. In Berger's view, this compositional perspective could have important theological implications: in his convincing analysis of the opening chorus of the *St. Matthew Passion*, he argues that

40. David et al., *New Bach Reader*, 305.

41. Dreyfus, *Bach and the Patterns*.

42. Berger, *Bach's Cycle*, 99.

43. Berger, *Bach's Cycle*, 99.

44. See footnote 21 in chapter 2.

> The chorus is based on a *da capo* aria text, and its shape makes sense only against the background of the generic conventions that govern Bach's da capo arias. Heard against the background of these conventions, the chorus can for the first time be seen to possess an extraordinary conceit, namely, an ending that conflates into a single phrase what normally is presented in successive ones. It makes simultaneous what should be successive—abolishing the succession of past, present, and future in favour of the simultaneity of the present and thus neutralising the flow of time in favour of the eternal Now.[45]

Moreover, for my purposes, I am persuaded by Berger's suggestion that Bach's successful organization of the musical material in this Chorus is grounded on some iconic moments of the piece, and, in particular, on Bach's musical treatment of the word "*sehet*," "see," with the purpose of conveying theological meanings by superimposing musical events which were elsewhere presented sequentially:

> Picander and Bach help to attenuate the distance between Jesus's time and the time of the faithful by emphasising "seeing" over "hearing" the story. "*Sehet*" (see), Zion repeatedly urges, and Bach makes this "*sehet*" the pivotal moment of his setting. . . . Bach's insistence on seeing rather than hearing is, again, reminiscent of the Titian and Caravaggio paintings in which representatives of two distinct worlds exchange glances and, in "seeing" one another, are linked across the ontological divide. It is this sort of a glance, this pivotal "*sehet*" in m. 72 at the very moment when normal musical time flow is transfigured into eternity, that opens our understanding of the contemplators' role in the Passion: the "*sehet*" that converts time into eternity is the "*sehet*" of hermeneutics.[46]

Mozart and the Tales of Sounds

In Berger's opinion, this contrasts with many works by Mozart and by later composers, which display an alternative concept of time and temporality. "At some point between early and late eighteenth century, between Bach and Mozart, musical form became primarily temporal, and . . . the center of attention for musicians—composers, performers, and listeners alike—shifted

45. Berger, *Bach's Cycle*, 13; cf. 59.

46. Berger, *Bach's Cycle*, 109–10.

toward the temporal disposition of events."[47] In Mozart's concertos, the order of presentation of the melodic ideas is not an ancillary element of the piece's composition, but rather one of its main *raisons d'être*; underlying their musical "plot" there is an eminently narrative concept which may or may not be told in words (as happens in Mozart's operas), but whose intelligibility and enjoyability directly derives from its consequential planning.

Berger's argument is not flawed by the fact that many works of the Classical era seem to retrace their steps very often. In his view,

> In [Mozart's] concerto allegros the main focus of interest is the order in which melodic ideas are presented within each of the three tellings of the story . . . making each of the tellings progressively more complete and logical. The point is to tell an amusing, moving, and coherent story, a story with a beginning, middle and end, and to tell it not once but three times, with each successive version clarifying and closing the gaps in the preceding one.[48]

Different from many other forms of art, in fact, music does not consider repetition as a fault; indeed, the art of sounds enjoys it both on the small- and large-scale. A repeat sign in a movement of a symphony indicates that a portion of a piece should be started afresh after its first hearing; performers frequently have to turn back the pages of their scores in order to play a portion of a piece again, or, at least, to direct their glance back to a passage they had already performed. Even in performance, then (and not only in a silent reading), a musical score can embody time not just in a linear fashion:[49] but this is and remains music's utopian attempt to escape the inexorable flowing of time. In fact, even in the most perfect of the repetitions, even if "the same" portion of a work is played twice and consecutively in exactly the same way, the two repetitions will occupy two different portions of chronological time. They will be similar, but there will not be identity between them, as—in the experience of created beings—time cannot be reversed or repeated.

Thus, for Berger, Bach's temporality is "circular," while Mozart's is more teleological and goal-oriented. However, in Mozart's oeuvre Berger sets apart a particular case, embodied by the iconic figure of Don Giovanni. In the episodes lived by this character, the sequence of the events in the plot creates an experience of time which is paradoxically opposed to that of

47. Berger, *Bach's Cycle*, 14.

48. Berger, *Bach's Cycle*, 14

49. See below for Pierre Boulez's views on this topic.

the "eternal present": in Berger's words, "Kierkegaard brilliantly recognized that Don Giovanni lives only in the present; his existence as he experiences and understands it is a series of Nows—not a story but a catalogue or list."[50] Bach's "telescoping" of human time through the use of multidimensional superimposition of temporalities contrasts with the more pronounced directionality of a musical narrative as experienced in the Classical style; however, the "catalogue" of Don Giovanni's conquests embodies an utterly different view of time. In Bach's "simultaneous" working out of the subject's contrapuntal possibilities we may glimpse, by analogy, a mental construct akin to the "eternal present"; in the tonal musical narratives we may observe a purposeful and teleological order, which may embody (as we will later see) a "history of salvation"; Don Giovanni, instead, symbolizes the disconnected reality of modernity (and even of post-modernity), in which "lists" and "catalogues" replace stories and tales, thus contributing to the lack of meaning which many of our contemporaries experience in their lives. And this is what differentiates history from chronology, as pointed out by White, since history not only must

> deal in real, rather than merely imaginary, events; and it is not enough that [it represent] events in its order of discourse according to the chronological framework in which they originally occurred. The events must be . . . revealed as possessing a structure, an order of meaning, that they do not possess as mere sequence.[51]

Similar to tales, musical structures possess an "order of meaning": we can therefore make use of musical metaphors and analogies for discussing time, understanding the role of musical events in time in a symbolic fashion. Such a process largely depends on our perception and interpretation of the articulation of the language of music. Though I am inclined to think that such an experience may transcend many cultural and historical boundaries, and contribute to the enjoyment of music by people from a variety of backgrounds, it is particular clear in the case of tonal music and in its use of harmonic functions, as I will now proceed to demonstrate.

50. Berger, *Bach's Cycle*, 253.

51. White, *Content of the Form*, 4–5.

3

Music as a Syntax of Time

It is a common experience of all human beings that "clock time," the absolute articulation of time units of equal duration, only very rarely coincides with psychological time, i.e., the experience we have of the passing of time. We experience extremely short hours, and other hours which seem to last unendingly; the time separating Christmas on two consecutive years seems to be dramatically longer to a child than to an adult.

Even those functions of our body which, in a healthy person, proceed regularly and "almost" clocklike are frequently altered by our mental or physical states, as our pulse increases with emotion, stress, fatigue, or physical activity, and our breathing becomes quicker or slower. These dynamics are known and exploited by music, which constructs an "artificial" psychological time and imposes it onto the listener's perception of time.[1] The experience of musical listening, when successful, manages to replace the articulation of the listener's psychological time with that created by the articulation of music.[2]

1. In Stuckenschmidt's words: "Music is capable of lengthening or shortening the duration of a minute in our perception" (Stuckenschmidt, "Short Operas," 204). Susanne Langer differentiated between time in music ("virtual time") and objective time ("the sequence of actual happenings"). See Langer, *Feeling and Form*, 104–19.

2. A similar view is found in an article by Louis Laloy: "Of course, the reading of a poem is successive, and we cannot contemplate a painting or a statue without covering it thoroughly through the eyes as a book. But there is this difference: music is never complete but in performance, and this performance does not depend only on the duration we will like to choose, but on a particular duration, whose form and movement are determined" (Laloy, "Henri Bergson," 3). Thus, for him, it is thanks to this feature that music can absorb our souls into "its soul" while we listen to it.

Elliott Carter saw time as a "screen" on which music is "projected": the "measurable time of practical life" (the "screen") receives the colors and lights of music, which "may be incorporating another kind of time," even though it "needs measurable time for its presentation."[3] With a structure made (normally) of regular beats, musical time "mimics" chronological time in being discrete, rhythmical, and—therefore—predictable.

However, both the composer and the performer of music can (and normally do) play with this predictability, by subtly anticipating or postponing an event expected by the listener. Interpreters, for example, employ "rubato" (i.e., the slight anticipation or retardation of a beat with respect to its metronomic position) in order to convey an expressive meaning, thus reproducing the acceleration or retardation of our physiological functions when an external impression strikes us; composers may delay the resolution of a tonal or dynamic tension in order to increase it precisely by virtue of its procrastinated appearance. As Goldman writes:

> Starting in Paris during the fourteenth century, and coming to full realization during the fifteenth, Western musicians found means to create tonal expectations so compelling that the hearer's perception of the flow of musical time is guided by a sense of the musical future. Tonality—the system in which the horizontal unfolding of melody in time integrates with vertical consonance—has the unique capacity to generate a sense of the future. Once musicians discovered how to link musical rhythm to the resolution of dissonance into consonance, Western music acquired a teleology.[4]

Thus, the regular beats of music may seem to mirror the unvarying regularity of clock time, but the (very frequent) alterations of this regular pattern rule the listeners' perception of their own psychological time.

Expectations and Surprises

Through the syntactical structures of music, listeners are led to formulate a set of expectations about the future development of the musical piece, and to give meaning, in retrospect, to the musical events they have just heard within the framework of the events' "story," of their role in the piece, of

3. Carter, "Music and the Time Screen," 63.

4. Goldman, "Sacred Music." Compare this view with Johnson, *Out of Time*, 118–20, where the musical meaning of tonality is interestingly related to the development of (printed) musical scores and with the mapping of geographical landscapes.

the listeners' knowledge of the musical language and of its history. Thus, the piece's tonal structure, its motivic organization, its macro- and microform, and even its timbral choices (for example, the symbolic associations of certain instrumental sounds with particular affections, situations or feelings) are interpreted and continuously reinterpreted in the process of listening, and they are put into dialogue with the repertoire stored in the listeners' memories and with their listening history. By virtue of musical sensitivity, literacy, knowledge, and perceptiveness, listeners enjoy music in the interplay between the fulfilment and the surprising (and therefore equally enjoyable) non-fulfilment of their expectations, of their forward projections as to how the music will develop. This faithfully mirrors Husserl's understanding of our experience of time as a two-dimensional "now," which encompasses the *retention* of the past and the *protention* toward the future; this view interprets "the now" not as "a line of division between past and soon," but rather as "a centre of tension."[5]

Seen this way, the fruition of music can become a particularly "in-tense" experience of the now. In Adlington's words,

> What makes us believe in the existence of past and future in tonal music, other than an uncritical confidence that it constitutes an objective fact about the form of experience? It is the fact, first, that the present is made partly dependent for its meaning upon what is not present, and, second, that that dependent relationship takes the form of a connection that is not only aurally recognizable but also readily encoded in memory, thus encouraging the music's concretization as a fixed sequence, extending back into the past and (a listener presumes) forward into the future.[6]

The skilled composer will delicately balance the surprising and foreseeable elements, so that an excess of surprise will not make music impossible to follow and unintelligible, and an excess of predictability will not make it trivial and boring.[7] In a manner not unlike that already suggested in the case of modal music, there is one expectation which is nearly always fulfilled

5. Husserl, *Ideas*, 140–43. See Bjerstedt et al., "Musical Present," 18.

6. Adlington, "Musical Temporality," 46.

7. Arnold Schönberg purposefully challenged these dynamics (thus implicitly acknowledging their validity) when he abandoned the tonal system: "A melodic line, a voice part, or even a melody derives from horizontal projections of tonal relations. A chord results similarly from projections in the vertical direction. Dissonant tones in the melody, that is, tones of a more remote relationship to the occasional centre, cause difficulties of comprehension" (Schönberg, *Style and Idea*, 87).

in tonal music, and it is the eventual resolution of all the preceding tensions into the final chord or unison.

This is a very "theological" dimension of music itself. By acknowledging the musically meaningful syntactic elements of a composition and their role (even implicitly, or without possessing the technical lexicon for expressing it), and by enjoying the eventual resolution of the musical tensions created during the piece, music listeners are led to live and to recognize a "story" in what they hear. To be sure, such a "story" can only occasionally be articulated in words (as happens in program music or symphonic poems); it consists however of the perceived intelligibility of the musical discourse, in which every element has its place, and all concur in the creation and resolution of a dynamic tension.

Significantly employing a metaphor drawn from architecture (the art of rhythm in space, just as music plays with rhythm in time), Werner Oehlmann suggested that our enjoyment of music is linked to an experience of time perceived as full of meaning and significance. In his words, "The minutes and hours that are filled with experienced music have been wrested from the scurrying nothingness; they are as full of reality as the space bounded by a stone cathedral. The victory of order over chaotic superiority, of abundance over nothingness, is the deepest reason for the joy that music gives to people."[8]

Instead of the casual juxtaposition of capricious and haphazard sounds, music possesses a logic of its own, a teleology; there is a "providence" (here identified as the composer's creative organization of the musical material) regulating what happens in the piece. I introduce here the term "providence." It will be one of the pillars of my subsequent argument, since it embodies, literally, the "foresight" ("*pro-video*," "fore-see") deployed by the composer in the organization of musical events happening in time, and the visual component of this process. Thus, the teleology of music renders it theological: music is perceived as a meaningful "tale of sounds," as a logical (albeit surprising) narrative, as a coherent whole, in much the same way as a person's history or that of humankind are perceived, by a believer, as the providential unfolding of purposeful events rather than as a meaningless juxtaposition of casual absurdities. We will see in the following chapters how this parallels the role (the "mission") of the narrator, and how this theology of providence may be articulated in musical terms and similes.

8. Oehlmann, "Musik in Zeit und Ewigkeit."

According to Goldman, it is here that the "sacredness" of music can be found. By exploiting the underlying conflict of "durational and tonal rhythm, that is, between metronome time and the pace of tonal motion," composers of music create the preconditions for a musical experience of the sacred, which necessarily involves "a transformation in our perception of time." "Because we are mortal, and because all religion responds to mortality, our intimations of the sacred arise from our experience of the tension between the mortal existence of humankind and the eternal life of God."[9] Also for Kramer, who discusses music and time in a philosophical and analytical (rather than theological) fashion, "musical time . . . is like sacred time: repeatable, reversible, accelerating and decelerating, possibly stopping. The special time sense evoked by music recalls music's origins in ritual." This does not simply allude to music's attempts to "reverse" time (see chapter 2, e.g., in the case of retrograde canons), but rather to the capability of music to evoke multiple layers of time in our consciousness and imagination.

Thus, the interplay between memory and expectation which rules and determines our listening patterns and our enjoyment of music acquires a radically theological significance. In purely acoustic and psychoacoustic terms, therefore, listening to music is a powerful symbolic experience which helps the sensitive listener to understand the unfolding of events in time as a story, as "Providence in action," so that, beyond the immediate enjoyment of an aural pleasure, the power of music to console, comfort and touch can also be found in its capacity to give order and meaning to the flowing of time.

"Vertical Time" and the Eternal Present

While, as stated above, music can be experienced as a syntax of time in a variety of historical, cultural and social contexts (and it is by no means found uniquely in tonal music), undoubtedly Western culture has deeply problematized this aspect when it rejected tonality. According to György Ligeti's perceptive description of this phenomenon, we can observe a "pseudo-morphosis" of music to painting in the twentieth century, consisting in the "seeming conversion of temporal relations into spatial ones."[10] In Ligeti's opinion, in contemporary music

9. Goldman, "Sacred Music."

10. Ligeti, "Metamorphoses," 15–16. Reportedly, Edward Lowinsky defined time as

> the course of the form is no longer experienced as a "process of congestion and relaxation," but as a juxtaposition of colors and surfaces, just as in a picture. The succession of events is a mere exposition of something that in its nature is simultaneous; in this way, in fact, one's glance wanders over the canvas of a painting. As opposed to this, the individual moments of hierarchic-tonal music were not restricted to maintaining their mere "presence," they also included the "just past" and at the same time pointed forward to the immediate "future." That they were able to do this was a consequence of the—historically conditioned—"cadential" successive ordering of the harmonies. The music was, thanks to this faculty for embracing the immediate future, able to negotiate points, as it were, and even fork off into several parallel lines of events, but the formal course of the music was limited to a single direction of movement in time. The onward flow of the music was further protected by the generally even pulse of the music's metre. If unexpected events did occur—as for instance interrupted cadences or sudden modulations—they would immediately be confronted in the hurrying imagination of the listener with the hoped for and expected, not experienced as any hesitation in the flow of time, but rather as a diversion or branching off, always of course in the same direction as the general current. This sort of successivity gave an aura of logic to the tonal forms, hence their "similarity to language."[11]

It is not by chance, therefore, that twentieth-century music (particularly in its avant-garde forms) tended to emphasize such aspects as temporality, rhythm and alternative ways of organizing pitch, either rebelling against the teleology of tonal structures, or embodying traditional values in novel languages. Several great composers of the twentieth century wrote extensively about time and its aesthetic implications,[12] in particular by exploring the possibility of replacing the teleology of tonal music with a

---

"the canvas on which you consider music to be presented, just as the spatial canvas of a painting furnishes the surface on which a painting is presented" (Lowinsky in Carter, "Music and the Time Screen," 63). I would like to emphasize that Ligeti's use of visual and spatial imagery in his argument is different from that I am arguing for in this book: as I understand him, he uses painting and colors to symbolize musical events which do not concur in the creation of a narrative. This however does not undermine the substantial consonance of his viewpoint with what I have just stated.

11. Ligeti, "Metamorphoses," 15–6.

12. See, among others, Babbitt, "Synthesis"; Ferneyhough, "Taktilität"; Stockhausen, "Structure."

"suspended" time whose sensory fruition symbolizes stasis. Kramer defines the "non-linear" (i.e., non "goal-oriented," non-narrative) reception of music as "vertical time":

> In one kind of music, however, there are *no* proportions, because time does seem to be suspended. This most radical species of musical time is vertical time . . . the static, unchanging, frozen eternity of certain contemporary music. Is listening to this music really a timeless experience?[13]

This concept of "frozen eternity" is subtly different from the "eternal present" we are discussing. In theological terms, the entire history of humankind, the history of salvation, our personal stories are embraced, contained, and (at the same time) displayed in God's eternal present; thus, that infinite moment represents the maximum of dynamicity and "life." The stasis, the "frozen eternity" sought by many contemporary composers is, instead, something akin to the suspension of time, the suspension of life. In Jeremy Begbie's words, "Talk of stasis can only be shorthand for various degrees of *approximation* to the cessation of change and motion—in the music and/or in our perception of it."[14]

In fact, the word stasis implies the absence of movement within a given time. Movement is measured in space (the variation in an object's position in time). In a primarily temporal art, such as music, the "movement" can be thought of as:

1) the physical movement of the performers, who produce vibrations;

2) the audible "movement" between two different pitches;

3) the continuum of sounds in time.[15]

The experience which represents musical stasis more closely is perhaps that of an invariable note or sound, prolonged for some time. For Thomas Mann, this idea was paradoxical: intriguingly, he compared it to an attempt to narrate "Time" itself, rather than events happening in time:

> Can one tell—that is to say, narrate—time, time itself, as such, for its own sake? That would surely be an absurd undertaking. A story which read: "Time passed, it ran on, the time flowed onward" and so forth—no one in his senses could consider that a narrative. It

13. Kramer, *Time of Music*, 7.

14. Begbie, *Theology*, 139.

15. See Clifton, *Music as Heard*, 97.

> would be as though one held a single note or chord for a whole hour, and called it music.[16]

However, what was a paradox in Mann's eyes has been attempted by contemporary composers. For example, *ASLSP* and *Organ2/ASLSP* by John Cage require the performer to play "as slow as possible," as the titles themselves indicate. While in the piano version (*ASLSP*) the physical limits represented by sound decay on the piano determine the maximum acceptable length of the piece, the later organ version "is being" realized in a performance planned to last for 639 years.[17] The duration of the individual sounds and chords has been directly derived from the observation of Cage's score, where lines of various lengths follow each note, representing duration through timelines (in a fashion entirely similar to that of Priestley's chart).[18] It could thus be argued that the case of *Organ2/ASLSP* and of its centuries-long performance is the perfect embodiment of the view suggested here: that a few pages of a musical score may represent and determine, and make observable at a glance, an extremely long time (at least by human standards). On the one hand, this is in fact the case, and these examples are striking embodiments of the thesis of this book. On the other, one should be very careful not to confuse "a very long time" with eternity, or the impression of timelessness with the eternal present: there may be analogies, but there are also crucial differences. For example, another iconic contemporary work deliberately plays with stasis, and has been interpreted as an embodiment of eternity—but of a rather different kind than the eternity of theology: Karlheinz Stockhausen's *Stimmung* consists of a single chord, to be played for more than one hour. The resulting immutable aural shape is likened by Reiner to "a feeling of timelessness—an experience in which the awareness of past, present and future is replaced by a seemingly all-pervasive simultaneity."[19] This kind of timeless experience is defined by

16. Mann, *Magic Mountain*, 570. See also Reiner, "Chameleon."

17. See www.aslsp.org.

18. Rob Haskins describes the score as follows: "The precise length of a sound is indicated by extending a straight line from the notehead; the performer reads his score as a succession of proportionate time points," quoting Cage, who added: "just as maps give proportional distances" (Haskins, "Cage's Organ Music"). The analogy between topography and musical scores is one we have frequently noted and on which we will often return.

19. Reiner, "Chameleon," 19.

Kramer as "a temporal continuum of the unchanging, in which there are no separate events and in which everything seems part of an eternal present."[20]

Adopting Kramer's definition of "linear time" (as opposed to "vertical time") as "the temporal continuum created by a succession [of] events in which earlier events imply later ones and later ones are consequences of earlier ones,"[21] one might see that the "line" of narrative/teleological time, or rather the *lines* of the polyphony of history and story are embraced by God's eternal present.[22] By way of contrast,

> A vertically conceived piece, then, does not exhibit large-scale closure. It does not begin but merely starts. It does not build to a climax, does not purposefully set up internal expectations, does not seek to fulfill any expectations that might arise accidentally, does not build or release tension, and does not end but simply ceases. . . . No event depends on any other event. Or, to put it another way, an entire composition is just one large event.[23]

Again, this view differs from that outlined in this chapter, whereby the musical events of music and their relationship are symbolically understood as an icon for the narrative and understandable succession of events constituting our story and our history. In the final chapter of *The Time of Music*, Kramer boldly speaks of the "schizophrenia" of modernity, which tends to conflate past, present, and future in a fashion not dissimilar to what happens to those affected by some forms of mental illness. This lack of historical perspective, or rather the incapability to "narrate" our story *as a story* is faithfully mirrored by the non-linear (non-teleological) quality of a substantial component of the contemporary musical output. In a theological view, instead, the teleology of music and of time itself is made visible in one instant.

Messiaen's Butterflies

An artist who could be numbered among the most profound innovators of musical style, but whose aesthetical and religious stance was deeply

20. Kramer, *Time of Music*, 454.

21. Kramer, *Time of Music*, 20.

22. Jeremy Begbie rightfully suggests that several contemporary composers pursue a musical embodiment of eternity which is "construed largely in terms of the *negation of time*" (Begbie, *Theology*, 145).

23. Kramer, *Time of Music*, 55.

Christian was Olivier Messiaen[24] (1908–1992). In his oeuvre, he made extensive use of palindromic rhythms, which he called "non retrogradable." They are symmetrical rhythms which can be read both left-to-right and right-to-left. For Messiaen, such rhythms possessed a "great power, a kind of explosive force . . . a magical strength,"[25] because they were grounded around a "free central value, which joins the two outer groups of the non-retrogradable rhythm as analogous to the present, which, in life, links the past and future."[26]

Messiaen observed the presence of symmetries similar to those of the non-retrogradable rhythms in several examples, some of which were the product of human creativity (e.g., architecture) and some were found in nature:

> When butterflies are enclosed in their chrysalis, their wings are folded and stuck one against the other; the pattern on one is thus reproduced in the opposite direction on the other. Later, when the wings unfold, there will be a pattern with colors on the right wing which mirror those on the left, and the body of the butterfly, the thorax and the antennae placed between the two wings constitute the central value. These are marvelous living non-retrogradable rhythms.[27]

This particular example is particularly relevant to the object of our present discussion. The butterfly is a creature whose development is marked by distinctly observable stages, and thus embodies Time's action in a literal fashion. Moreover, if we analyze Messiaen's simile, we come to realize that the symmetrical pattern of an open-winged butterfly is taken by the composer to represent the unfolding in time of a non-retrogradable rhythm: the butterfly's body is the axis of the symmetry of its wings, similar to the central value of the palindromic rhythm in Messiaen's theory. If the simile

24. Messiaen was also famous for the phenomena of synesthesia he experienced, in which sounds (in particular chords) were allegedly perceived by the musician also as colors. Indeed, synesthesia is still another aspect through which the relationships between sight and hearing could be discussed (see, for example, Arcimboldo's theories on the greyscale, Isaac Newton's association of the seven colors to the seven notes, Louis-Bertrand Castel's "*clavecin pour les yeux*" and works such as Scriabin's *Prometheus*), though it is distinct from the topic of this book; however, it is worth mentioning here because it may have influenced Messiaen's interest in the visual "translations" of musical time.

25. Rössler, *Contributions*, 42.

26. Wu, "Mystical Symbols," 98.

27. Samuel, *Conversations*, 44.

is further developed, the "folded and stuck" wings of the chrysalis can be seen as the "eternal present," in which both the "past" (the insect's "left wing," or the note-values preceding the axis of symmetry, the central note in the non-retrogradable rhythm) and the "future" (the "right wing," or the notes following the central note-value) are coincident. When the butterfly unfolds its wings, what used to be wrapped around its body is unraveled; its "past" and its "future" (i.e., its two wings) become distinct from its "present" (its body) and from each other; in the animal's former stage, however, "past," "present," and "future" were all concentrated in a fuse-like form, all wrapped around its "present," all enfolded around its body.

Though Messiaen did not develop his own metaphor so explicitly, it seems to me that his use of this particular visual image to represent the temporal meaning of his palindromic rhythms fully permits such a reading. In fact, in the following lines, Messiaen himself affirmed that non-retrogradable rhythms became, for him, a symbol for life and eternity: "A final symbol: this moment which I live, this thought which crosses my mind, this movement which I accomplish, this time which I beat: before it and after it lies eternity: it's a non-retrogradable rhythm."[28]

Messiaen used the non-retrogradable rhythms in a theological perspective: in his opinion, they allowed human beings to transcend the temporal boundaries of human life. In his words,

> The musician possesses a mysterious power: by means of his rhythms, he can chop up Time here and there, and can even put it together again in the reverse order, a little as though he were going for a walk through different points of time, or as though he were amassing the future by turning to the past, in the process of which, his memory of the past becomes transformed into a memory of the future. The "symmetrical permutations" and the "non-retrogradable rhythms" utilize this power, nevertheless working against it.[29]

And, for the purpose of the present discussion, it is worth mentioning that Messiaen resorted to visual imagery in order to explain the inspiration he derived from the palindromic rhythms. In his own words, "It's as if in traversing a landscape, beginning from two opposite points, you were to meet

28. Messiaen, *Music and Color*, 77.

29. Rössler, *Contributions*, 41.

the same things at the same times in the same positions and in the same order."[30]

Mapping Music

These statements by Messiaen demonstrate that, for musicians, time is *imagined* as space on a score; in particular, it is also represented through the articulation of the score into highly visible units (framed by two vertical lines), called "bars" or "measures." The temporal duration of two bars of the same piece is, in most compositions before the twentieth century, largely homogeneous (with some notable exceptions I will discuss later). For the moment, suffice it to say that it can be assumed that two consecutive bars of the same piece will have roughly the same chronometric duration. They work, therefore, in a fashion similar to a graduated axis in which time is represented. At least on an *analogical* plane, it could thus be said that the visual notation of a monodic tune can be defined as the linear representation of a point-like universe of sound. In other words, the "horizontal" dimension of music can be seen as the variance in time of the quality of pitch possessed by a sounding body. When, however, simultaneous musical events are described in a score, such as in a piano score, it could be said that at least three dimensions are represented by musical notation: simultaneity, pitch and duration; when different instruments interact, such as in an orchestral score, the fourth dimension of timbre is added, which is, in turn, connected to the three-dimensional space of the orchestra as a collection of various and spatialized sources of sound.[31] The fact that a musical score can thus embody both space and time in a multidimensional fashion, misleadingly concealed by its seeming two-dimensional structure, is strikingly similar to the graphical representation of the theological concept of God's

30. Samuel, *Conversations*, 43; see also: "It's extraordinary to think that the Hindus were the first to point out and use—rhythmically and musically—this principle of non-retrogradation which has long been applied to architecture: thus in ancient art, gothic and Romanesque cathedrals and even in modern art, the decorative figures ornamenting the pediments of the portals are nearly always two symmetrically inverse figures framing a neutral central motif" (Messiaen, *Music and Color*, 76).

31. On this topic, see Zuckerkandl, *Sound and Symbol*, 1:39 ("The pre-polyphonic state of music is represented by Gregorian Chant: one single tonal line, complete and whole in itself; a one-dimensional process. The step from this to polyphony can be compared to the step in geometry from the line to the plane").

eternal present in William Craig's[32] analogical interpretation of the Stump-Kretzmann theory.[33]

Accordingly, even in the simplest forms of musical notation, the left-to-right direction of music reading can be seen as embodying the *x* axis of a graph of time. A major divergence between such a graph and a score, however, is that the *visual* appearance of two chronometrically equivalent bars may be dramatically different (while in an *x* axis, by definition, analogous durations will be represented by analogous units of space).[34] In a score, the visual width of a bar and the impression it conveys largely depend on its density (of lack thereof) in terms of the musical events it contains. For example, one can have very "crowded" or very "empty"' bars (in fact, some may consist entirely of silence); a single measure may occupy a whole page or a tiny portion of it. When the layout permits, for example in a piece written on few staves, and not particularly long, it is possible to receive a very complex visual and conceptual impression of Time by observing a musical piece. Supposing the entire piece is contained on one page or on two facing pages (this may happen, for example, with short piano works), the musically literate observer can visualize, at a glance:

1) musical events which happen contemporaneously with others (as, for example, in piano chords, or in what is played by the two hands, or in what is played by two or more instruments);
2) musical events which (will) happen before or after others, but are in meaningful and sometimes causal relationships with the others.

The attempt to condense the notational indications of an entire work into a one-page graphic score conveying information for the performance, to give an impression of the piece simultaneously and at a glance, led composer Ramón Barce to realize a series of works called *Síntesis de Siala*, 1965. The collection is based on a piece of music written by the same musician in traditional notation (*Siala* for clarinet and piano, 1964); the process from

32. Craig, "Eternal Present," see in particular Figure 2.

33. Stump and Kretzmann, "Eternity," 429–58.

34. This applies, of course, only to traditional notation. Writing about the use of tape in "experimental music," John Cage affirmed: "Since so many inches of tape equal so many seconds of time, it has become more and more usual that notation is in space rather than in symbols of quarter, half, and sixteenth notes and so on. Thus where on a page a note appears will correspond to when in a time it is to occur" (Cage, *Silence*, 11).

Siala to its *Síntesis*, described in *Grafización*,[35] also leads from a "musical" work (whose aural shape is symbolized graphically) to a "graphic" work in which the signs on the page become increasingly independent of the original aural phenomenon, and of its symbolic representation. Moreover, it can be argued that *Síntesis* is a work of art not only or solely in its *final* appearance, but also as the very process leading to it—a process which Barce thoroughly describes as a complex set of successive stages. His starting point was that *Siala* originally had thirteen pages, and he "had to reduce it to just one page," because "the current score must have a material extension," and "a traditionally-notated work must perforce occupy a space proportional to its duration,"[36] while "a graph does not mirror the relationship between space and duration: a single page may produce—if this is so established [by the composer]—even infinitely long versions."[37] He proceeded at first by reducing the quantity of musical events (i.e., operating cuts on the musical material), and later transforming the symbols of musical notation into simple graphical pretexts which he elaborated on a purely visual plane. It is significant for this book that a particular artistic need (or wish) to compress the notational description/prescription of a musical piece so it can be viewed instantaneously, has provoked a temporal, multi-stage process leading from the visual symbolization of a succession of musical events in time to a purely visual work which can be digested at a glance.

Graphic Scores and Open Works

This brief discussion of Barce's *Grafización* leads us to the further topic of graphic scores and open works. In fact, though this book focuses mainly on "traditional scores" of the Western musical tradition, I have to mention the numerous variants to the traditional concept of score which were developed and implemented in the twentieth and twenty-first centuries. A few examples pertinent to our discussion will suffice, although many others could be equally stimulating and worth mentioning.

One significant challenge to traditional notation was in fact represented by so-called "open works," in which a more-or-less conventional indication of pitches and durations on musical staves was presented in a non-sequential layout on the page; the performer(s) could choose the order

35. Barce, "Grafización."

36. Of course, this statement cannot be endorsed without qualifications.

37. See Barce, *Fronteras*, 73, in Villa-Rojo, *Notación*, 318–20.

in which the musical events represented should be played. As a creator of such open works, André Boucourechliev, stated:

> We live in a time where things are not certain or definite, where hierarchies are not *de facto* legitimate. Beethoven was the first to contest this order; he introduced doubt. . . . This putting into question became the essence of life and art. . . . Indeterminacy rather than certainty then became prominent within the forms themselves.[38]

Indeed, the philosophical import of this approach should not be downplayed as it is particularly relevant to the argument I am demonstrating in this book. Galia Hanoch-Roe put it like this:

> The conventions underlying the intelligibility of a traditional musical work as casual [sic] logic, linearity, continuity and predictability no longer endure, since in open compositions each unit is predominantly important in itself, and the initial order of these units has become less significant.[39]

In other words,

1) if—as I will discuss in greater detail in the pages to come—"classical" music used to embody a narrative teleology;
2) if this teleology acknowledged the meaningful ordering of musical events in time;
3) if this ordering used to parallel the meaningful (and providential) ordering of events in history;
4) if "traditional" notation symbolized this ordering and teleology;
5) and if this notation allowed its simultaneous conceptualization through spatial representation;

it follows that musical compositions such as some contemporary open works aptly embodied the denial of this order (both compositional and "providential").

The temporality of the performed work, with its (mainly) one-way development in time, was in fact challenged by these works:

38. Roy, "Entretiens avec Boucourechliev," in Poirier, *Boucourechliev*, 191; Bell, "Avant-gardes," 61.

39. Hanoch-Roe, *Scoring the Path*, 90. I assume "casual" to be a misprint for "causal."

> In such constructions, the function of the musical scores changes from an object to be read by the performer into a process to be constructed. The choice of movement ruptures the linearity of the score inherent in the performance of a musical composition up to that time, and resembles a silent reading of a score in which the reader may stop, turn back, and return. The process of performance becomes similar to that of a movement within a structural space, where the observer chooses his way about it.[40]

It must be pointed out, however, that there is only a *likeness* between the process of silently reading a score (or conceptualizing it in one's mind, or recalling it in memory) and the actual performance of open works. Though they normally do not impose a fixed order for the performance of the sounds they depict, these sounds are normally not given in isolation; rather, they constitute short (or longer) musical units or groupings, which, in turn, have a duration in time. Thus, the work in its globality may be non-"linear," but its constituting elements are mostly just miniaturized musical scores. An example of this approach is found in *From Here* (1963), by Earle Brown.[41]

Another case is that of so-called "graphic scores," in which, frequently, neither pitch nor duration (and often not even the instrument or timbre) are specified in detail. Graphic scores normally renounce the use of staves, clefs and the usual symbols of Western notation; they frequently lack a direct, causal correlation between a visual symbol or sign and a determined aural result.[42] It should be noted, however, that while they do not employ "traditional" musical notation, they nonetheless *exploit* it and the musicians' acquaintance with it. In other words, they suppose that the performing musician will be somehow "inspired" by the visual elements they display, and this "inspiration" will perforce consist in the (more or less conscious) interpretation of these signs in their similarity to traditional notation itself. Put more simply, a performing musician will be able to read a graphic score *as a musical notation* only insofar as he or she is familiar with traditional notation and with its conventions. Performers will normally tend to interpret the vertical dimension of signs as an indication of pitch, and the horizontal duration as a suggestion about duration.

40. Hanoch-Roe, *Scoring the Path*, 90–91.

41. See http://earle-brown.org/images/work/full.30.jpg.

42. For a very interesting survey of various types of graphical scores and of how they connect the visual/spatial to the musical/aural, see Bolpagni, "Musica visiva."

I would now suggest to compare graphic scores such as those of John Cage's *Imaginary Landscape No. 5*[43] (1952) or of Earle Brown's *4 Systems*[44] (1954) with Priestley's chart. The similarity in the visual impression given by both the musical scores and Priestley's graphical representation of the timeline is striking. Furthermore, the analogy between scores of musical "open works" and visual art has been poignantly highlighted by Hanoch-Roe, who writes that when studying such scores,

> the performer . . . takes the role of the observer. . . . Here, the process . . . is similar to an exploration of a spatial work of art. Observing a work of spatial art calls for movement, and movement in turn requires the use of time. A two-dimensional work of art requires movement of the eye, and a three-dimensional work requires the actual movement around or within the work. The actual movements of the eye or the observer around a work are in themselves limited, as are the musical sections of an open score, but their combinations create an infinite range of variation. The architect cannot predetermine all movements and thus must leave the observation of the building to chance, as does the composer of an open score. The movement of the observer, in turn, is also subject to chance, as his attention may drift to many different angles and views, focusing for long on one area, skipping another, et cetera.[45]

The fact that the observation of a work of visual art, or of a musical score, is an activity requiring time, does not constitute a fatal flaw in our argument. It is the conceptualization of music through the symbols of notation which can be likened by analogy to the simultaneous "presence" of various moments in time. Indeed, both the musical "open works" and the graphic scores (frequently also by virtue of the synthesis they achieve in the description of aural events) can be seen as embodiments of our idea of musical scores as symbols for the eternal present, inasmuch as they often portray considerable stretches of time in an immediate and concise fashion.

43. See http://exhibitions.nypl.org/johncage/taxonomy/term/79.

44. See http://earle-brown.org/images/work/full.12.jpg.

45. Hanoch-Roe, *Scoring the Path*, 92–3.

Xenakis: Music and/as Architecture

I would like to give one further and iconic example of relationship between the spatiality of visual notation and the temporality of music. The composer and visual artist Iannis Xenakis (1922–2001) had studied to become a civil engineer, while his musical education lacked formal training in performance. This background is fundamental to understand his predominantly *visual* approach to musical composition, because the graphical aspects of notation had a more determining impact than is the case of most other composers.[46] While Xenakis was cooperating with the studio of legendary architect Le Corbusier, he designed the justly famous *Philips Pavilion* (1958) for the Universal Exposition of Brussels. It is a fascinating structure whose curved surfaces are generated by continuous movements of straight lines. The germinating idea for this architectural masterpiece was intertwined with the concept underlying a musical composition by the same artist, *Metastaseis* (1954: note the name with is spatial implications). The preparatory drawing, the musical score and the building all clearly share common features. *Metastaseis* attempts to translate into sound a visual intuition, and it does so by assuming that the musical "glissando" (i.e., the successive execution of all pitches constituting the continuum within a given interval) represents the aural equivalent of a straight line. This assumption, though acceptable as a creative artistic stance, is actually physically incorrect (frequencies increase exponentially, not linearly) and it is debatable, at the very least, that a non-musically-literate listener would perceive these "glissandos" as musical straight lines;[47] nevertheless, *Metastaseis* builds upon the phenomenon cited at the very beginning of this book, whereby the use of spatial metaphors for speaking about music was linked to the actual and causal correlation between spatial movements and the sound they produce. Whereas most Western music was conceived *primarily* as sound, and *then* preserved through the notational medium, Xenakis's idea was evidently primarily visual, and only later came to be embodied in actual pitches. Xenakis himself admitted as much: "My first compositions were born from visual experiences";[48] instead of being first

46. On this topic, see also Solomos, "Complexity," 323–37.

47. On string instruments as those for which *Metasteis* is written, however, a *glissando* is realized by sliding a finger of the left hand on the straight line of the instrument's string. Thus, in this sense, a *glissando* can be seen as a "line" in musical terms.

48. "Le mie prime composizioni [sono] nate da esperienze visive" (Xenakis in Restagno, *Xenakis*, 39 [my translation]).

and foremost grounded on the physical reality of sound, his works were inspired by its graphical representation.[49]

The same process of translation from visual to aural encouraged Xenakis to create and implement a pioneering computer software, the UPIC, enabling the composer to create electronically generated sound waves by drawing them on a graphic tablet. As Xenakis recalled it: "Already at the time when I made my drawings for *Metastaseis*, I wondered why one could not have a machine capable of immediately translating drawings into sound. . . . It was . . . the inadequacy of traditional musical graphics which pushed me in this direction."[50] Here music is composed entirely by drawing all of its elements, which the software digitally transforms into sound. It could be virtually possible, therefore, for composers to visualize the whole of their musical work, and behold it as the simultaneous visual imagination of its graphical and notated shape, even before a single sound of it is actually performed, or even imagined in its temporal duration.[51] In works conceived this way, time is represented as one of the variables in a Cartesian chart, but the predominance of the visual/spatial aspect underplays its crucial role in the experience of music. At the same time, it is intriguing for the purpose of the present discussion to contemplate the possibility of a visually conceived, simultaneous and present musical work which only unfolds in time *after* having been entirely and virtually described in all (or some) of its parameters.

In Xenakis's case the connection between music and architecture is, quite literally, tangible; it is as if his work, along with other similar creative efforts, embodies the insight propounded by the philosopher Schelling, according to whom "Architecture is music in space, as if it were frozen

49. Cf. however another statement by Xenakis: "When you use tools like paper while writing and conceiving musical forms, you can think in terms of spatial qualities, but that is less important during composition itself. Music develops in time. . . . It is the interior of time that counts, not its absolute duration" (Xenakis in Harley, "Musique, espace," 13).

50. Xenakis in Restagno, *Xenakis*, 57 (my translation).

51. This view can be contrasted with the process of composition as described and experienced by Jean Sibelius, the Finnish composer, who noted in his journal on April 10, 1915: "In the evening [I worked] on the symphony. Arrangement of the themes. This important task, which fascinates me in a mysterious way. It's as if God the Father had thrown down the tiles of a mosaic from heaven's floor and asked me to determine what kind of picture it was. Maybe [this is] a good definition of 'composing.' Maybe not. How would I know!" (Sibelius in Hepokoski, *Sibelius*, 32). Implicit in this statement is the idea of "composition" as the aural reconstruction of an organic and "inspired" creative "vision," which will in turn be translated into visual notation.

music."[52] "Freezing" music, as beautifully summarized by Schelling's iconic expression, means to arrest its flow, to stabilize its movement, but also to become able to view it at a glance—as happens, in fact, in a musical score.

Kandinsky: Lines and Points

Within this framework, I want to mention—again briefly—the contributions of three great modern artists, the painters Vasilij Kandinsky (1866–1944) and Paul Klee (1879–1940), and the composer Pierre Boulez (1925–2016), who commented insightfully on Paul Klee's works. Both painters were intensely interested in music and in aural phenomena, and both wrote with astute perceptiveness about music and its relationships with painting. Their creations, like some of those by Piet Mondrian and Henri Matisse (such as *Jazz*), explore the possibility envisaged by Walter Pater, who affirmed that "all art aspires to the condition of music."[53] Among the writings of Kandinsky, Klee and Boulez, and among their many works inspired by music, I will succinctly discuss only those which relate most closely to the topic under discussion.

One of Kandinsky's more intriguing arguments relates to how graphic-spatial elements such as points and lines can find their aural equivalent in music. Interestingly, the commonly-found equation (inspired by the conventions of Western musical notation) between notes and dots, or between tunes and lines is not the only one explored by Kandinsky. For example, he writes:

> Most musical instruments are of a linear character. The pitch of the various instruments corresponds to the width of the line: a very fine line represents the sound produced by the violin, flute, piccolo; a somewhat thicker line represents the tone of the viola,

52. "Da sie [die Architektur] aber die Musik im Raume, gleichsame die erstarrte Musik ist" (Schelling, *Philosophie der Kunst*, 576; cf. Goethe, *Goethe's Literary Essays*, 267: "I have found a paper of mine among some others, in which I call architecture 'petrified music.' Really there is something in this; the tone of mind produced by architecture approaches the effect of music"). Jacques Handschin employed the word "architectonic" for defining a particular type of sonata allegro, but Alfred Dürr cautions against over-simplifications: whereas, for example, a da-capo aria can structurally resemble a building with two lateral wings, the temporal nature of music leads us to "enter via the wings (as if the listener were a servant)" (Dürr, *Johann Sebastian Bach's*, 125–26).

53. Pater, "School of Giorgione," 106. On the other hand, Susan Langer maintained that music "makes time audible" (Langer, *Feeling and Form*, 110).

> clarinet; and the lines become more broad via the deep-toned instruments, finally culminating in the broadest line representing the deepest tones produced by the bass-viol or the tuba. . . . The organ is quite as typical a "linear" instrument as the piano is a "point" instrument.[54]

In this passage, Kandinsky builds parallels between musical timbre and graphical elements, in a rather uncommon and therefore captivating fashion; contrasting the organ's "linearity" against the piano, seen as "point-like," is a very imaginative perspective indeed. However, his visual "translation" of elements excerpted from Beethoven's *Fifth Symphony* into visual representations[55] is a somewhat naïve visual reinterpretation of the musical score.[56] More interestingly, on a later occasion, Kandinsky suggested a further parallelism between musical and graphical lines by comparing the physical and gestural means of production of the two forms of art.

> The degrees of intensity from pianissimo to fortissimo can be expressed in an increasing or decreasing sharpness of the line, that is, in its degree of brilliance. The pressure of the hand on the bow corresponds exactly to the pressure of the hand on the pencil.[57]

This resonates with Adorno's discussion of the birth of cheironomy from gestures which he interpreted not as weightless dances of the hands in the air, but rather in their physical mass and energy.[58] Immediately afterwards, Kandinsky discusses the graphical aspect of musical notation proper, arguing that it is "nothing other than various combinations of point

54. Kandinsky, *Punkt und Linie*, 92 (98). I believe that Kandinsky's "Baßgeige" should be translated as double-bass in this context.

55. Kandinsky, *Punkt und Linie*, 37–39 (43–45). See also http://bit.ly/kandinsky-beethoven.

56. However, it is fascinating to observe that, in Figure 11 (Kandinsky, *Punkt und Linie*, 37 [43]) of his work, a musical "trattenuto" (slowing down) is represented: the three dots standing for the F-F-F-D of Beethoven's theme are more distant from another than the first three (G-G-G-E flat). Also interesting is the contrast between the curved line representing the legato theme and the points which symbolize the rhythmical energy of the opening motif (Kandinsky, *Punkt und Linie*, 39 [45]).

57. Kandinsky, *Punkt und Linie*, 93 [99]. As discussed above (see footnote 47 in chapter 3), this gestural/physical component (which is all too often overlooked) is also the only ground on which Xenakis's equation of a musical *glissando* with a line can be fully justified.

58. Cf. Adorno, *Towards a Theory*, 174–75.

and line,"[59] and that "time is recognizable therein only by means of the color of the point . . . and the number of pennant stripes (lines)."[60] Through these sentences, he constructed a very personal reinterpretation of the symbols of musical notation by de-structuring them into graphical elements. He observes that pitch is similarly indicated through a system of lines, and then comments:

> The unqualified brevity and the simplicity of the means of translation, which in clear language convey the most complex sound phenomena to the experienced eye (indirectly to the ear) are instructive. Both of these characteristics are very alluring for the other forms of art and it is understandable that painting or the dance should be in search of its own "notes." There is, however, only one way to arrive finally at their own graphic expression—analytic separation into fundamental elements.[61]

Thus, for Kandinsky, the spatial representation of music provided a conceptual/visual *synthesis* which was however the result of an *analysis* of its constituting elements. As we will see later, it can be argued that notation, and the conceptual tools it provides for looking at a piece in its articulation, stratification, and musical meaning, is what permits a true "reflection" (even in merely musical terms) on a musical work, a consideration of its ontology, and a perception of its fundamental unity.

Klee and Boulez: "Visual Polyphonies"

Similar to Kandinsky, who played the cello, Paul Klee received professional training as a violinist and was deeply acquainted with the conventions and particular features of musical notation.[62] This background enabled music and its visual representation to inspire many of his paintings and drawings. He even famously "translated" a polyphonic work by Bach into visual art (1922), proceeding in a fashion which is clearly influenced by the symbolism of musical scores and which can interestingly be compared with Kandinsky's interpretation of Beethoven's *Fifth Symphony* discussed above.

59. Kandinsky, *Punkt und Linie*, 93 (99).
60. Kandinsky, *Punkt und Linie*, 93 (99).
61. Kandinsky, *Punkt und Linie*, 93 (99).
62. See Boulez, *Pays fertile*, 92–93.

In several of his works, Klee studied the role of rhythm and of its organization and representation in music and in its notation. For Klee, the beat and its organization in measures constituted the conceptual grid through which music became intelligible:

> I am going to reach out into the field of music. Here the basic structure lies in the beat. The ear hears the beat more or less subconsciously; but it is felt through the sound as a structural framework over which the quantities and qualities of the musical ideas move.[63]

By engaging with Klee's theory of art (particularly as expressed in his lessons at the *Bauhaus*) and with his paintings, Pierre Boulez developed a complex and refined analysis of the relationships between musical time and space, notation and simultaneity, memory and rhythm: I will briefly recapitulate some of the main points of his argument, focusing in particular on those which pertain to aspects of the eternal present.

For Boulez, the sight of a musical score, with the black dots dislocated in space representing pitch and duration, can suggest an immediate translation of melodic lines into visible lines or traits. At the same time, Boulez is acutely aware that the aesthetic criteria by which melodic and visual lines are evaluated cannot be simplistically transferred from one art to the other.[64] The combination of several simultaneously sounding melodic lines produces polyphony; and Klee repeatedly tried to create "visual polyphonies" in his art, designing works inspired by the musical genre of the fugue or by the chessboard.

Subsequently, Boulez frequently discriminates between music and visual art by pointing out that the paintings offer themselves to an instantaneous and simultaneous perception, while music does not. For Boulez, the effect of spatiality in a painting is because of the possibility of perceiving its entire construction, its totality, instantaneously. A painting, in other words, is *first* viewed globally, and only later will the eye navigate its surface in order to appreciate its details. Boulez saw the process inverted in music: only the details can be heard, while the global perception is given only retrospectively and virtually, at the end of the piece. Thus, for him, the musical work is perceived as a whole only in imagination and memory, while its actual perception is always partial.[65]

63. Klee, *Bildnerische Denken*, 145–46; *Paul Klee Notebooks*, 1:271.

64. Boulez, *Pays fertile*, 52–53.

65. See Boulez, *Pays fertile*, 85–87. We may recall St. Augustine's discussion of music,

Though Boulez's statements are certainly consonant with many of the arguments discussed in this chapter, it must be pointed out that—within the framework of a discussion of space and time in music, as solicited by the study of a visual artist who took inspiration from musical notation—it is rather singular that Boulez seems not to see a musical score as the *actual* (and not just *potential*) presence of the whole of the musical work; a presence which translates the work's temporality into simultaneity.

Boulez's opinion on the simultaneous perception of visual art in comparison with the temporality of music is found in the writings of many musicians and philosophers of music, as it articulates a common experience. A contemporary Italian composer, Salvatore Sciarrino, expressed a very similar view:

> When we observe a picture, our eyes catch the whole image, they identify the individual forms and effortlessly organize them in a framework of relations. We all carry out such operations automatically. Unlike the eye shifting within the visual context, can our ear shift up and down along time? Absolutely not: music slides forward and never comes back, because music is rooted in time.[66]

Boulez, in turn, was explicit in stating that "the eye can read from right to left, the ear cannot listen against time."[67] Returning once more to the idea that visual art is passible of a simultaneous visualization, Boulez is careful to point out that visual art possesses a temporality of its own: after the first simultaneous and immediate perception of the entire painting, the observer can analyze it according to his or her own order and criteria, continuously alternating the appreciation of a detail with its contextualization within the frame of the whole work.[68] Thus, for Boulez, there is a temporality in the fruition of visual art, but it is a temporality that is imposed by the person viewing it.

Indeed, Klee himself had expressed this very view in a rather paradoxical fashion, precisely while proposing a comparison between music and visual art: "More and more parallels between music and graphic art force

---

memory and time in chapter 1, and we will further develop these relationships in chapter 5, particularly while examining the writings by Jacques de Liège.

66. Sciarrino, *Figure della musica*, 59; Illiano, "Musical Notation," xii.

67. Boulez, *Pays fertile*, 98 (translation mine). "L'œil peut lire de droite à gauche, l'oreille ne peut écouter contre le temps."

68. See Boulez, *Pays fertile*, 102. See also Laloy, "Henri Bergson," 3, cited in footnote 2 in chapter 3.

themselves upon my consciousness. Yet no analysis is successful. Certainly both arts are temporal; this could be proved easily."[69] A similar view was held by Vasilij Kandinsky, who was also highly perplexed by the simplistic assertion that space is to painting what time is to music. This "apparently clear and justifiable division," he argues, "has upon closer, though yet hasty, examination suddenly become doubtful and, as far as I know, this first became apparent to the painters."[70] He strongly supported the view that visual art (and particularly abstract art) possesses a unique temporality of its own.[71] For Boulez, on the other hand, the temporality of music renders it unidirectional; it channels the mode of its own perception and binds it to one-way rails. The only "simultaneous" perception which is possible with reference to music is its "virtual," *a posteriori* reconstruction in the listener's memory. The idea that this temporality may be reduced to a minimum, to the shortest possible quantity of time in which the totality of a work can be conceptually and visually grasped, is only briefly and cursorily mentioned by Boulez: in stating once more that a musical work can only be perceived in full after its ending, and that the listener has no choice but to follow its development in a chronological order, Boulez adds, as an afterthought, that this applies to concert performance.[72]

As we have previously seen, *even* in the case of a concert, the temporality of music *can* be altered (or it can create the illusion of an alteration in the sequential order of linear time), as happens as a result of repeat signs or the repetition of shorter or longer musical fragments. In the case of a score, it is possible to perceive it (or at least to *recognize* it) at a glance, and to navigate freely within its temporality by while being, at the same time, acutely aware of it.

69. Klee, *Tagebücher*, 3:215; *Diaries*, 177.

70. Kandinsky, *Punkt und Linie*, 28–29 (34–35).

71. Kandinsky, *Punkt und Linie*, 28–29 (34–35).

72. See Boulez, *Pays fertile*, 107.

4

Observing the Score

Artists such as Klee and Kandinsky engaged creatively with the visual appearance of music scores, by reinterpreting musical works and the traditional symbols of Western musical notation in their paintings. In Higgins's words, "Although designed primarily for preserving musical works and facilitating coordination among performers, the score is sometimes also visually attractive."[1] Beyond the aesthetic elegance of certain scores, their visual appearance has also a deep symbolic fashion: the numerous musical scores represented in visual artworks frequently symbolize temporality, both in its perishable dimension and as an anticipation of eternity.

Painted Scores

In the fifteenth century, Leonardo da Vinci depicted a *cartellino* of musical notation in the right hand of the protagonist of his *Portrait of a Man* (Pinacoteca Ambrosiana, Milan). Art critics have interpreted this *cartellino* as a symbol for the mortality of the sitter, "the finite, irrevocable unfolding of his life."[2] As briefly mentioned above, Leonardo himself had argued for the primacy of painting over music precisely because he believed that painting produced artworks which could last, whereas music could not: for him, painting "excels and rules over music, because it does not immediately die

1. Higgins, "Visual Music," 480.

2. Fugelso, "Music," 27. I am indebted to Fugelso's article for drawing my attention to Leonardo's views on the temporality of music.

after its creation the way unfortunate music does";[3] thus, "Music, which is consumed as it is born, is worth less than painting."[4] He also understood that painting can eternalize what is doomed to decay: a painter "makes beauty permanent for many, many years, and it is of such excellence that the harmony of its proportionate members is kept alive, which nature with all her powers could not conserve. How many paintings have preserved the simulacrum of a divine beauty where time or death . . . has destroyed nature's model!"[5] At the same time, he also acknowledged that the power of musical notation preserves the most temporal of all arts, stating that "music lasts forever by being written down."[6] Thus, his choice to use music notation in the *Portrait of a Man* to symbolize both the transitory nature of life and eternal life would be entirely consistent with his written theory of the arts.

In fact, musical symbols such as instruments were to become popular, not least in the *vanitas* and still-life paintings of the seventeenth century,[7] as a symbol for the transiency of life. The temporal nature of music, elusively bound to the constant flowing of time, was a powerful and poignant symbol for the fleetingness of life, at least as powerful as the two most common symbols of fruits or hourglasses. At the same time, to represent a sheet or a book of music within this context was subtly different from employing any other musical symbol: notation was the (successful) attempt to fix music in time and space, to eternalize it in a viewable form, to make music present, forever, or at least as long as the painting would survive. This paradox of the *vanitas* paintings could also be applied to the other decaying elements represented in this genre: a flower whose nature would allow only a very

3. Melzi, *Trattato* 29, in Winternitz, "La musica," 86; Farago, *Leonardo da Vinci's*, 241–42.

4. Melzi, *Trattato* 31b, in Winternitz, "La musica," 90; Farago, *Leonardo da Vinci's*, 245.

5. Melzi, *Trattato* 30, in Winternitz, "La musica," 88; Farago, *Leonardo da Vinci's*, 243.

6. "La musica s'eterna con lo scriverla." Melzi, *Trattato* 31b, in Winternitz, "La musica," 91; Farago, *Leonardo da Vinci's*, 247.

7. Among the most notable examples of the genre are Vincent van der Vinne, *Vanitas with a Royal Crown* (ca. 1650, Louvre); Evaristo Baschenis, *Still Life with Musical Instruments, Books and Sculpture* (ca. 1650, Museum Boijmans van Beuningen; the musical notation is a tablature); Andries Benedetti, *Still Life* (1646, Cesare Lampronty Gallery); Giuseppe Recco, *Still Life with the Five Senses* (1676); Pierfrancesco Cittadini, *Vanitas. Still Life with Violin, Score, Flower Vase and Skull* (1681); Pierre Subleyras, *Attributes of the Arts* (1700, Musée des Augustins); Anne Vallayer-Coster, *Attributes of Music* (1770, Louvre), but this listing aims merely at exemplifying the genre and by no means at exhaustiveness.

brief blossoming[8] could be frozen by a painting whose aim was precisely to underpin the caducity of created life. On other occasions, musical scores were depicted as allegorical representations of the *Three Ages* of human beings: for example, in the *Concerto* by a Venetian painter (presently at the Royal Collections of Hampton Court), the eldest character portrayed, embodying senility, does not read any more from a musical score, but simply holds the book closed in his hands, showing the approaching end of his mortal time.[9] Similarly, in the *Concerto* by Lionello Spada (1576–1622), presently in Rome, Galleria Borghese, the eldest musician does not play or sing, but only distributes the notes to the younger characters, as a symbol for his "acquired wisdom."[10]

A musical book is also depicted in Edwaert Collier's *Vanitas*, juxtaposed to another *cartellino* displaying the biblical quote from Ecclesiastes which in fact gave its name to the *vanitas* genre.[11] Here, the readable musical score reproduces an instrumental arrangement, by Jacob van Eyck (in *Der Fluyten Lust-Hof*, "The Flute of the Garden of Pleasure"), after a secular madrigal by Gian Giacomo Gastoldi (1593), *Questa dolce Sirena*.[12] This painting poignantly symbolizes the human desire to savor the instants of pleasure: its title mentions a "garden of pleasure" where one would willingly linger; it alludes to the Siren, who "binds" (i.e., arrests) those listening to her singing, freezing time for them while simultaneously wasting it forever in an inescapable enchantment. An analogous experience of how music can stop the flow of time and create a (symbolic or analogic) "eternity outside time" is described by Dante in his *Purgatorio*, when Casella's singing enraptures, conquers and arrests the souls going to their penance.[13] Paradoxically, then, the most transient of all arts has the power of expanding

8. This is a topic frequently found also in the Bible. See 2 Kgs 19:26; Ps 37:2; 90:5; 102:11; 103:15; 129:6; Isa 37:27; 40:7–8; 51:12; Matt 6:30; Luke 12:28; 1 Pet 1:24; Jas 1:11.

9. See Terribile, "Musica nella cultura," 89.

10. See Economopoulos, "Lionello Spada," 68.

11. Edwaert Collier, *Vanitas Still Life* (1662, Metropolitan Museum of Art, New York).

12. "Questa dolce Sirena, / col canto acqueta il mar, / un suo leggiadro riso / po l'aria serenar. // Chi mira 'l suo bel viso / resta prigion d'Amor, / ch'i suoi bei lumi vede / sente legars'il cor [This sweet Siren / calms the sea by her singing; / a graceful laughter of hers / can clear up the air. // He who sees her beautiful face / becomes a prisoner of love; / he who sees her beautiful eyes / feels his heart being bound]" (my translation).

13. *Purgatorio* 2:76–133. On this topic, see Schurr, *Dante e la musica*, 49; Bertoglio, *Through Music to Truth*, 20. The "femmina balba" of Dante's dream in *Purgatorio* 19:7–33 is another embodiment of this idea.

the perception of an instant by forcing and imposing its own time over our perception of time.

A book of music is represented among many other symbols that relate to caducity (most notably a series of skulls, one of which anamorphic) in the justly famous double portrait *The Ambassadors* (1533) by Hans Holbein the Younger (National Gallery, London). As John North demonstrates,[14] the numerous instruments, in combination with the half-hidden crucifix, point to the date of Good Friday 1533, the 1500th anniversary, according to church tradition, of Christ's death. As I have argued elsewhere,[15] however, the book of music is, in my opinion, not *only* a symbol for temporality, but also, in conjunction with the lute with a broken string, a symbol for the failing harmony in the *corpus christianum* at the time of the Reformations, and for the necessity of preserving it. While the unplayable lute can be interpreted as standing for the interrupted communion of the Christians, the hymnbook may temper that otherwise pessimistic view with something more hopeful.

The book shows two religious hymns, very clearly depicted on *facing* pages, *both* of which are readable at the same time. While Holbein painstakingly reproduces an actual book, he deliberately alters the pagination here so as to combine these two hymns. To the left, we recognize a Lutheran hymn inspired by the Sequence for Pentecost—*Kom heiliger Geyst*, after the Latin *Veni Sancte Spiritus*—and to the right, we see a song on the Ten Commandments. Thus, by showing both "Law" (the Commandments) and "Grace" (which is poured by the Holy Spirit) as two facing pages of the same book, which can be read at the same time, Holbein might have aimed at transmitting the message that Law and Grace are not in competition or opposition; rather, they are in *harmony* with each other, and this harmony is symbolized by music itself and by its embodiment in notation.[16]

A similar simultaneity is found in two much later paintings by William Michael Harnett, although on this occasion the inexorable passing of time is evoked. In *The Old Violin* (1886, Washington, National Gallery of Art), the splendidly reproduced music notation depicts two songs (while, significantly, omitting their lyrics, as the pieces are transcribed for the violin). Whilst "Hélas, quelle douleur" is a religious canticle by Edmond Servel

14. North, *Ambassadors' Secret.*

15. Bertoglio, *Reforming Music*, 570–71.

16. See Bertoglio, *Reforming Music*, 569–72.

focusing on the non-recoverability of time past,[17] the aria from Bellini's *La Sonnambula*, "Vi ravviso, o luoghi ameni"[18] embodies the decay of temporal realities through spatial elements, through the "pleasant places" mentioned in the lyrics. Though a person can find again the *space* of joyful memories, the *time* of their happening has vanished forever.[19] Here again, to spatialize music through notation and to eternalize music in a *painting* depicting a sheet of music is to insist in a poignant fashion on the paradoxical dialectics of time and space embodied by a musical score.

In summary, music notation has been employed, in countless examples in the history of art, as a symbol for temporality, for eternity, and also for simultaneity: by representing an art which lasts only in memory, it stood for transience; by fixing it forever, it stood for something which could overcome death (frequently within a religious framework); by allowing the multiple representation and simultaneous visualization of different moments of time and/or of different, and sometimes contrasting, pieces of music, it stood for simultaneity, and, therefore, for the eternal present.[20]

A Score at a Glance

Just as a musical score depicted in a work of visual art instantly conveys a symbolic meaning pertaining to temporality, the capability of reading it

17. This canticle is reproduced also in the other of the two paintings by Harnett mentioned above, i.e., in *My Gems* (1888, Washington, National Gallery of Art).

18. "Vi ravviso, o luoghi ameni / in cui lieti, in cui sereni / sì tranquillo i dì passai / della prima gioventù! / Cari luoghi, io vi trovai, / ma quei dì non trovo più [I recognize you, o pleasant places, in which I tranquilly spent the joyful and serene days of my first youth! Dear places, I found you, but I can find those days no more]" (Lyrics by Felice Romani [my translation]).

19. Commenting on Løgstrup's philosophy, Nils Holger Petersen fascinatingly affirmed: "When a melody can be retained in our consciousness, either through retention or reproduction, this is an expression of man's philosophically speaking necessary rebellion against annihilation (through memory) which retains what has physically disappeared, in a form that is defined by what happened, what has become past, but which is retained as remembered in its unchanged spatiality" (Petersen, "Time and Space," 304).

20. Another painting is worth mentioning here, though there is no visible musical score. It is *St. Cecilia and the vision of St. John* (Naples, Museo di Capodimonte) by Jan Soens (1547–1611?). Cecilia, the patron saint of music, is portrayed playing the organ, while St. John, to the left, is seeing the Time to come, or rather Time outside Time—in the Revelation of eschatology. The female saint's music, the ephemeral art of time, is thus absorbed into the angels' eternal praise of God, whose glory is both in time and outside it.

as a piece of music may transmit an aural content. Thanks to the graphical strategies developed in musical notation, and to an acquired expertise in musical reading, any skilled musician will be able to quickly identify syntactically meaningful structures of the piece: for example, idiosyncratic melodic movements (such as scales), known harmonies (such as common chords, grasped by the musician as a whole rather than note by note), particular rhythms, as well as notable dynamic phenomena (such as indications of *crescendo, ff*), structural highpoints (such as a repeat sign or a fermata), and timbral idiosyncrasies (such as the sudden "Tutti" following a solo on an orchestral score), and so on.

It is interesting that the French composer Jean-Philippe Rameau argued against the proposal of a new system of musical notation by philosopher Jean-Jacques Rousseau precisely on these grounds. In a typically rationalist fashion, Rousseau had devised a *Project Concerning New Signs for Music*, using numbers instead of notes on staves, and submitting it in 1742 to the French Academy of Sciences. While the Academicians expressed some perplexities about his plan, the only criticism Rousseau acted upon was that by Rameau:

> The only solid objection to my system was made by Rameau. I had scarcely explained it to him before he discovered its weak part. "Your signs," said he, "are very good inasmuch as they clearly and simply determine the length of notes, exactly represent intervals, and show the simple in the double note, which the common notation does not do; but they are objectionable on account of their requiring an operation of the mind, which cannot always accompany the rapidity of execution. The position of our notes," continued he, "is described to the eye without the concurrence of this operation. If two notes, one very high and the other very low, be joined by a series of intermediate ones, I see at the first glance the progress from one to the other by conjoined degrees; but in your system, to perceive this series, I must necessarily run over your ciphers one after the other; the glance of the eye is here useless." The objection appeared to me insurmountable, and I instantly assented to it. Although it be simple and striking, nothing can suggest it but great knowledge and practice of the art, and it is by no means astonishing that not one of the academicians should have thought of it.[21]

21. Rousseau, *Confessions*, 231–32.

Even when sight-reading a piece, accomplished musicians are able to scrutinize the score for such "landmarks," which will suggest them the "direction" of music, and thus enable them to give a relatively convincing interpretation of entirely unfamiliar works. Sight-reading implies that experienced musicians will, at the same time, *play* a new piece in a continuous, proportionate, and uninterrupted fashion, and *read* in advance what they will need to play later.[22] This not only allows them to prepare physically for what will follow and to adjust accordingly the coordination of bodily parts to produce the sound, but also to "interpret" the piece by conforming their performance to the "direction" of the work, to its climaxes, to its points of tension and relaxation, and so on. In this way a kind of structural/functional analysis of the score is realized, by taking in elements of music "to come" while, at the same time, following the ordered succession of the musical events which are actually played. The sight of an expert musician will thus be able to navigate a score, searching for a meaningful *Gestalt* and rapidly finding it.

This process is considerably easier when musicians observe the score of a known, and sometimes memorized, work. In this case, they will be able to identify and read almost at a glance the entire score—an activity which will be, for them, more similar to the recognition of a familiar landscape than to the "reading" of a text—and to immediately find the point of the score where particular information is stored. Alfred Lorenz described this experience:

> If you have completely mastered a major work in all its details, you sometimes experience moments in which your consciousness of time suddenly disappears and the entire work seems to be what one might call "spatial," that is, with everything present simultaneously in the mind with precision.[23]

Silent Readings

This can also happen when a musician silently reads a musical score. According to Adorno, reading a score is the "genuinely conceptual element of musical interpretation"; and it is precisely by being able to behold a score's

22. This phenomenon is also discussed by Kramer, who defines the multi-temporal consciousness of the sight-reader as a kind of "specious present" (Kramer, *Time of Music*, 372).

23. Lorenz, *Geheimnis der Form*, 1:292; Adorno, *Towards a Theory*, 266–67.

musical significance at a glance that performers can be said to have an *idea* of it, in the full meaning of the term. For Adorno, "the 'image' of the score always refers to the whole, and its revelation occurs through a glance at the page, not at a particular bar or individual voice." However, this comprehensive contemplation must be integrated into a deep understanding of the details: "For the musical totality, as a temporal one, necessarily goes beyond immediacy through recollection and expectation. Understanding a musical form means first of all attaining a synthesis between each musical moment and the epitome of all the temporal relations it inhabits."[24] Though Adorno was careful to avoid all references to religious concepts such as the "eternal present," I think that his mention of the "epitome of all the temporal relations" conveys a very similar concept, albeit in philosophical terms.

In Paddison's words, commenting on Adorno's theories,

> The performed work is the mediation of performer and score, of subject and object (in the relative and dialectical senses in which these terms need to be understood in Adorno), the spatiality of the score temporalized in performance, the pastness of the work as reified text made present through the warming subjectivity of the performer. . . . The accomplished reader of the score traces and retraces the shape of the work through an act of focused imagination, drawing on the accumulated experience of harmonic, timbral and rhythmic relationships and correspondences which makes such an activity possible at all, and of course within a cultural and historical tradition of music that is score based. Whether such an accomplished reader actually exists—or still exists—or whether it is to be regarded simply as an ideal-type or historical category belonging to an earlier age, is open to debate. . . . The score, as the bringing together of separate parts viewable simultaneously on the page, provides an indispensable point of convergence for the work—the endpoint for the compositional process and the commencement point for the performance process.[25]

Conversely, the listened work can become a visual imagination, as Robert Schumann maintained: "A perfect musician must be able, on the first hearing of a complicated orchestral work, to see it as in bodily score before him. That is the highest that can be conceived of."[26]

24. Adorno, *Towards a Theory*, 184.

25. Paddison, "Performance and the Silent Work."

26. Schumann, "Rules," 35 (rule LXVII). Contrast with Bergson's views, as expressed in Bergson, *Durée*, 35, 38 (44, 49).

For the silent readers of music, particularly if the score merely refreshes their memory of a known piece, written music makes the whole piece simultaneously present. They will possess a mental mapping of the work, based on structural units of musical meaning, whose articulation frequently coincides with graphic elements which are visually prominent in the page's layout. The mental topography of a memorized or well-known piece is grounded on an almost "tree-like" structure, by which musicians represent to themselves the work's form, its main thematic elements, its overall harmonic itinerary, and eventually the actual details. As mentioned above, this is something which can be referred to by the term of *Gestalt*, or simply as a shape, as Rink suggested:

> Referring to this as "performer's analysis" (that is, "considered study of the score with particular attention to contextual functions and [the] means of projecting them"), I noted the importance of musical "shape," rather than structure, in the performer's conceptualization of music—an elusive but elucidatory notion more temporally conceived than that of structure. Music's temporality is indeed critical in this regard, a factor either ignored or downplayed in at least some "rigorous analysis," to invidious effect when the results thereof are directly harnessed to performance.[27]

This mental map of the piece of music works precisely like symbolic cartography, since it excerpts significant "landmarks" from the set of all the notes of the piece, and builds from them a system of references. These landmarks may be, and normally are, also visually recognizable on the score, particularly when the piece is short and can be encompassed in a single glance, i.e., where no page turns are needed, as we have seen on a precedent occasion. Through the visual representation of music, its aural shape can also be conceptualized as a unity, and as a whole. As Capuano wrote: "Sight is essentially characterized as the sense which, better than any other, manages to recognize a whole in a [series of] discrete elements."[28] The perception of the piece's overall form, of its organic shape (which, according to Boulez, can only be achieved in memory after the end of its actual performance) is also possible in the musicians' mind and/or in their observation of a score, in which they can behold the piece in its entirety. And if, as Rink maintains, "rigorous analysis" can fragment the piece's unity into a series of nearly a-temporal compositional bricks, other forms of analysis (such

27. Rink, "Analysis," 36.

28. Capuano, *Segni della voce*, 18 (translation mine).

as Schenker's[29]) employ modified forms of traditional notation in order to point out precisely those landmarks and those pillars on which the work rests.[30]

Navigating (Musical) Time During Performance

Musicians derive from their relationship with the score a perception of the flow of time, which is in turn both regular or continuous *and* quantified by rhythmical units. They derive a perception of the possibility of embracing it simultaneously, and of the possibility of moving forwards and backwards, in fast or slow motion, with respect to the fixed time of performance. During performance, musicians recall this mental cartography and the performative analysis it embodies. On the one hand, they will follow the constant time required by the execution of the prescribed notes and by the (normal) chronometric equivalence of the bars. On the other, the mental representation which flows during the performance will contradict this constant time. This phenomenon has been studied and discussed at length by Stachó:

> The performer's mental representation of the musical process which unfolds in time, together with their attentional process and strategy related to the expression of musical meaning, define performance features—especially related (but not limited) to timing—and determine the expressive quality of a performance.[31]

In Stachó's view, this allows the simultaneous, paradoxical, and yet real compresence of past, present and future:

> In the act of performance, moments of deep attentional immersion, which are connected to the imagery process and in which the musician generates quick and transient, very brief shifts of consciousness, embody the three time perspectives—the past, the present and the future—and have multiple functions related to psychology and music theory.[32]

29. Among others, see Schenker, *Der Tonwille*.

30. A similar process is observed in Alfred Lorenz's analyses of Wagner's operas (Lorenz, *Geheimnis der Form*).

31. Stachó, "Mental virtuosity," 545.

32. Stachó, "Mental virtuosity," 546.

And all this is an integral, common and characteristic experience of music reading and music making, rather than being an exceptional accomplishment:

> [The] "navigating" mental imagery, which includes directing the attention forward (anticipating), backward (retrospecting), and to the present moment at well-definable points of the musical process, not only significantly contributes to the perceived expressivity, intelligibility and individuality of performance, but also helps the musician to feel security and ease during performance. Furthermore, performers' navigating imagery significantly contributes to technical security through an enhanced cognitive control of fine motor movements.[33]

If this is recognized by studies in the psychology of music and of its performance, it is also known and experienced by the philosophers of music. According to Teixeira and Ferraz, "Even the idea of an irreversible time seems to have something reversible for the performer who . . . is anticipating the next movement while producing a sound that related to the previous one."[34]

In their opinion, therefore, this produces a particular experience which, once more, is represented as analogous to the "eternal present":

> Musical performance thus demands another sense of time, an *extended present* where the whole being is applied in the actualization of a musical action between movement and sound and, at the same time, connects these movements and sounds to those just produced, already anticipating and planning the next technical step, listening internally to the next time or the next attack. But of course, even that description is out-of-time. All these movements happen simultaneously, like an energy that rationalization cannot contain. It is indeed a dilation of the present that promotes the synthesis of past and future in the performative act.[35]

As we have seen, this "navigation" of time can happen both visually and mentally, and can take place during an actual performance with or without a score, and during the mental recalling of a piece or its silent reading on a score. Indeed, if simultaneity must be defined primarily in terms of its *perception* by human beings, as theorized by Bergson, it could be argued

33. Stachó, "Mental virtuosity," 546.

34. Teixeira and Ferraz, "Performance of Time," 497.

35. Teixeira and Ferraz, "Performance of Time," 500.

that, in the performing musician's mind, different temporal sequences can actually be simultaneous: "I call two instantaneous perceptions 'simultaneous' that are apprehended in one and the same mental act, the attention here again being able to make one or two out of them at will."[36]

It is worth mentioning briefly here that a number of studies have also investigated the eye movement of musicians who play from a score, and these substantially confirm the common experience of practical musicians.[37] The process of reading a score consists of a continuous alternation of "saccades" and "fixations," the former being rapid eye movements which scan the surface of the text and the latter being longer moments in which the greatest part of the information contained in the score is actually processed. Studies by Goolsby[38] and by Smith[39] demonstrate that the time of a musician reading a score is composed by a 10 percent of saccades and a 90 percent of fixations. This helps us to clarify a point: by "simultaneous" observation of a score I do not mean to imply that the entire information contained in a score is actually processed "simultaneously," nor that the musician's eyes can actually, as it were, "photograph" the score and digest it in a single instant. Eye movements should be taken into account, and they involve both space and time, even though that time might be in the order of milliseconds. (As we have just seen, the same can be said of the fruition of visual art). What I mean is that the *mental depiction* of a known piece, as *supported and elicited* by the observation of a known score, is—in my opinion—as similar to the "eternal present" as human, temporal reality can experience.

This view is supported by the practical experience and the scientific studies analyzing how musicians read and play music, particularly as concerns their coordination of sight and action. Sloboda has researched on the "eye-hand span," that is on the difference between the position of the eyes of performing musicians who are reading a score and that of their hands as they play, i.e., between what is being read and what is being played. He noticed that this span tended to coincide with musical phrasing, i.e., with meaningful musical structures.[40] As I have argued above, this enables the musician to "interpret" the work even when sight-reading; the capability

36. Bergson, *Durée*, 40 (51).

37. See "Music and Eye Tracking."

38. Goolsby, "Parameters."

39. Smith, *Investigation.*

40. Sloboda, "Eye-Hand Span," 4–10.

of recognizing the musically meaningful units depends on the musician's acquired familiarity with the musical language. (This is reminiscent of the smaller-sized notes found in the liturgical books of plainchant, which similarly aimed at providing an advance insight into the progress of the musical discourse[41]). As László Stachó observed, this skill can be defined as "mental dexterity," and "includes the ability to quickly position oneself into different temporal perspectives in real time during performance."[42]

In summary, we have seen that, in different forms and degrees, many aspects of musical notation and of its reading and performance concur in providing to the human beings involved an understanding of the possible and "actual" synchronicity of different moments in time, which are distinctly and yet simultaneously experienced and thought of by the musicians themselves. In fact, in Bergson's discussion of the compresence of different "flows" of movement which can be simultaneously perceived by the human mind and therefore grasped in both their independency and their relatedness, he added:

> We can interiorize the whole, dealing with a single perception that carries along the three flows, mingled, in its course; or we can leave the first two outside and then divide our attention between the inner and the outer; or, better yet, we can do both at one and the same time, our attention uniting and yet differentiating the three flows, thanks to its singular privilege of being one and several. Such is our primary idea of simultaneity.[43]

The unity and multiplicity of human consciousness discussed by Bergson happens in a very actual and perceivable fashion in the process of listening to polyphonic music. This compresence can also be recognized in the activity of reading music (both during performance and in the silent visualization of a score). With reference to silent reading, one might wonder if it is equivalent to, "better" or "worse" than the performed reading. The answer depends largely upon aesthetic judgment. Adorno writes, "Whereas any musical performance is fallible, the truly precise idea gained from reading

41. As discussed above, compare Leonardo da Vinci's (footenote 21 in chapter 2) and Bergson's (footnote 30 in chapter 1) similes with the findings of music psychologists (Truitt et al., "Perceptual Span").

42. Stachó, "Mental virtuosity," 539. I am particularly grateful to Dr Stachó for sharing his research with me.

43. Bergson, *Durée*, 40 (52).

can serve as the ideal for performance that cannot be attained as such. The musical work is thus cleansed of the fortuity of its realization."[44]

With all due respect for Adorno, I believe that to deprive music of its sounding, humanly mediated and temporal dimension is not the ideal condition of its existence.[45] Leaving these aesthetical judgments apart, however, we can be sure that the silent and the performed readings differ substantially in how they relate to the score's spaces of indeterminacy.

Discrete Temporal Units and the Continuous Flow of Musical Time

Numerous thinkers, including composers, performers, philosophers, and musicologists have argued that neither musical scores, nor any form of musical notation have been able to specify all details of a performance. This implies that notation is "unsatisfactory" as a means of *describing* music, while it is open to debate whether this lack of determinacy is a positive or negative feature of its *prescriptive* character.[46] Some composers, such as Igor Stravinsky,[47] have not concealed their longing for more precise and unequivocal forms of notation, which could convey more clearly and bindingly their idea of the work, while others[48] have vehemently supported the idea that these "spaces of indeterminacy" are among the most fascinating elements of music performance. As maintained by Roman Ingarden, "because of the imperfection of musical notation, the score is an incomplete,

44. Adorno, *Towards a Theory*, 162.

45. Kierkegaard maintained a more extreme opinion on the matter: for him, music did not exist in actuality unless it was performed: "Music does not exist except in the moment it is performed, for even if a person can read notes ever so well and has an ever so vivid imagination, he still cannot deny that only in a figurative sense does music exist when it is being read. It actually exists only when it is being performed" (Kierkegaard, *Either/Or*, 68). As I argued in the preceding pages, it is my opinion that a musical score is something more than the mere "potency" of music, and that it does embody the actuality of the work, though in a different fashion with respect to an actual performance. At the same time, I also maintain that the fullness of music is expressed in its audible performance.

46. Cf. Davies, "Notations," 75–76.

47. See Stravinsky, *Poetics*, 119–35, esp. 123 (and the entire sixth lesson, "Performance of Music").

48. See, for example, Ingarden, *Untersuchungen*, 115–36.

schematic prescription for performance,"[49] and it is always, and constitutively, "riddled with places of indeterminacy."[50]

A score, by its very nature, describes the musical events in a *discrete* fashion. In fact, each note is indicated as a punctiform element, but some of the most interesting musical phenomena happen *while* a note's sound lasts (e.g., vibrato, *messa di voce* etc.), particularly in the human voice and in instruments such as winds or bowed strings, and they are mostly impossible to notate. Other constitutive elements of a good performance (such as rubato, dynamic and agogic details) similarly resist all attempts to notate them precisely.

Visually, the layout and width of a bar of music depends on the density of the musical events it comprises, but temporally, and unless specific agogic indications are written by the composer, the chronometric duration of two consecutive bars on the written score is supposed to be the same. The translation of this "chronometric" time into the "musical time" which attempts to replace or conquer the listeners' "psychological time" depends on the performer's skill and sensitivity, and it includes the acceptable and accepted violation of this regularity.

Thus, from the written score, which leaves many of these details unspecified, to the actual performance, where choices have to be made univocally and unequivocally (though not always explicitly or consciously, particularly by the less experienced musicians), the spaces of indeterminacy are filled. It may happen that the composer had in mind a particular way to "fill" a particular space with an ideal rubato or vibrato; if the performer happens to realize that particular ideal, this coincidence will be "speculative and contingent," in the brilliant definition by Taruskin,[51] and will not by itself determine the success of an interpretation.

What is most relevant here is that the score, by virtue of its spaces of indeterminacy, is to be considered a *discrete* description (or prescription) of sound events, a scheme, a "map" sampled from the actuality of performance, which is instead a *continuum* of sound events in time—including pauses among the sound events. This distinction mirrors the famous differentiation between *temps-durée* and *temps-espace* proposed by Bergson in his *Time and Free Will*. As Paddison summarizes it,

49. Ingarden, *Work of Music*, 116.

50. Ingarden, *Ontology*, 90.

51. Taruskin, *Text and Act*, 94.

> For Bergson, *temps-durée*—duration—is the flux of experience, fleeting, elusive, not measurable, and identified with intuition, and *temps-espace*—as its designation clearly indicates—identifies measured time, clock time, with space, and with intellect, reason and rationality. The former is characterized by continuity, the latter by discontinuity.[52]

This has led Fubini to compare performance and score to these two concepts: "Musical time is experiential time [duration], while that of the score is space-time."[53] Koechlin spoke of "auditory time" (the internal perception of time in music) as "the kind [of time] which comes closest to pure duration." In spite of this, however, musical time is also made of discrete units, which seem to allude to a spatial dimension: thus, for him, "The divisions embodied in musical note values (whole notes, half-notes etc.) lead to a spatialization of time very different from that (based on vision) which Bergson talks about."[54] This divergence between continuity and discreteness is one of the elements which makes Time virtually impossible to represent spatially in a non-symbolic fashion (though the concept of "eternal present" as expressed by Eleonore Stump and Norman Kretzmann in 1981[55] is a powerful analogical medium for conceptualizing it). In the words of Barry Mazur,

> One might yearn for a representation of time—if even only on a metaphorical level—that expresses our felt experience of the smooth continuity of time. No matter whether Time corresponds to anything real or not, its legato is viscerally experienced: one feels the continuity of a tennis stroke, one sees the continuity of an eagle swoop, one hears the continuity of a sustained musical note.[56]

In this difference, the analogy between the observation of a musical score and the reality of the eternal present in the divine reality breaks down. For human beings, scores are telescopic mappings of musical events sampled from a continuum: these events may be simultaneously conceived precisely because the scores represent a "shorthand" summary of more complex

52. Paddison, "Performance, Reification and the Score," 159.

53. Fubini, "Temporalité," 22; Paddison, "Performance, Reification and the Score," 159. See also Fubini, "Sufficienza," 27–37.

54. Koechlin, "Temps," in Carter, "Music and the Time Screen," 65.

55. Stump and Kretzmann, *Eternity*.

56. Mazur, "On Time."

musical elements. Instead, the divine eternal present is, and transcends, the concrete actuality of a temporal continuum.

It is significant, therefore, that Bergson adopted a musical image when depicting the idea of *time perceived in its continuity*. However, he stressed the fact that this perception, if its very essence is to be preserved, should *not* be translated into a visualization of the score (as in Schumann's example) or into a neuromotor activity reproducing the physical acts whereby similar sounds could be produced:

> A melody to which we listen with our eyes closed, heeding it alone, comes close to coinciding with this time which is the very fluidity of our inner life; but it still has too many qualities, too much definition, and we must first efface the difference among the sounds, then do away with the distinctive features of sound itself, retaining of it only the continuation of what precedes into what follows and the uninterrupted transition, multiplicity without divisibility and succession without separation, in order finally to rediscover basic time.[57]

Elsewhere, he further expanded his discussion of this topic:

> But we cannot superimpose successive durations to test whether they are equal or unequal; by hypothesis, the one no longer exists when the other appears; the idea of verifiable equality loses all meaning here. Moreover, if real duration becomes divisible, as we shall see, by means of the community that is established between it and the line symbolising it, it consists in itself of an indivisible and total progress. Listen to a melody with your eyes closed, thinking of it alone, no longer juxtaposing on paper or an imaginary keyboard notes which you thus preserved one for the other, which then agreed to become simultaneous and renounced their fluid continuity in time to congeal in space; you will rediscover, undivided and indivisible, the melody or portion of the melody that you will have replaced within pure duration. Now, our inner duration, considered from the first to the last moment of our conscious life, is something like this melody. Our attention may turn away from it and, consequently, from its indivisibility; but when we try to cut it, it is as if we suddenly passed a blade through a flame—we divide only the space it occupied.[58]

57. Bergson, *Durée*, 35 (44).

58. Bergson, *Durée*, 38 (49).

Actually, it is Bergson's opinion that the very idea of *instant*, as the shortest possible duration in temporal terms, is due to our mental habit of imagining time as space, as a line: just as a point is the "atomic," indivisible constituent of a line, similarly an instant is the indivisible constituent of time.[59] However, whereas the "dots" representing notes on a musical score can be seen as the musical equivalent of points, they also signify duration, and what happens, musically, within that duration: thus, they stress the continuity of musical time while also dividing it into perceivable units.

We have already seen that Iannis Xenakis imagined this continuity of musical time in the visual form of lines (as in *Metastaseis*). On other occasions, however, he held that, by conceiving musical notes as *points*, one could "view" music as something akin to Brownian motions:

> It is not difficult to interpret in this way the music of the past: let us take, for example, a melody by Bach. In this case you have not points, but rather sustained lines corresponding to the notes: one here, one there, etc. Of course, the notes have been excerpted from a scale or mode defined by tradition, but this is not particularly relevant. Let us try and generalize; let us imagine shortening these notes until they are reduced to points. In that case, you would have a movement of points which practically looks like a Brownian motion. Now, imagine that you inject symmetries within this chaotic motion: you will then obtain the repetition of certain parts of the movement; something much more consistent, then, both for the eye and the ear, which becomes a musical theme.[60]

It is unclear how Xenakis understood the relationship between lines and points. As we have just discussed, pitches are visually represented in a point-like fashion through notation (the notes) but (momentarily disregarding vibrato or the possibility of changing intonation), pitch is sustained in

59. Bergson, *Durée*, 41. "Real time has no instants. But we naturally form the idea of instant, as well as of simultaneous instants, as soon as we acquire the habit of converting time into space. For, if a duration has no instants, a line terminates in points" (Bergson, *Duration*, 52–53). Fascinatingly, this perspective had already been developed by Leonardo da Vinci, who wrote: "A point should be equated to an instant in time, while a line is similar to the length of quantity of time. And as points are the beginning and end of the above-mentioned line, so instants are the end and beginning of any given space of a time. And if a line is divisible infinitely, the space of a time is not alien to such a division; and if the divided parts of a line can be proportioned to each other, so will the parts of time be proportionable to among themselves" (DaVinci, "Codex Arundel 263, 1736," British Museum, in Winternitz, "La musica," 98 [my translation]).

60. Xenakis in Restagno, *Xenakis*, 50–51 (my translation).

time, making its representation through lines more accurate than through points. We may therefore wonder whether Xenakis imagined musical notes of infinitesimal duration, or constantly varying pitches. The impossibility to find an unequivocal answer should make us alert to the risks caused by an excessive reliance on the visual (rather than acoustic) dimension of music. As Adlington rightfully points out:

> The tonal classical tradition has typically fostered an emphasis upon its linear, sequential aspects, a view of music emboldened by the centrality of notation to this tradition. . . . Too seldom do we question the degree to which the score, and forms of discussion focused on the score, constrain the sorts of organization we attribute to heard musical experience. . . . Music as *sound* is in fact uncommonly well-paced to alert us to other possible forms of organization, ones less obviously spatio-linear in inclination. . . . The fact that this is not generally recognized as such partly reflects upon our reluctance to think (or incomprehension of the possibility) that music, and other forms of experience, might be organized "non spatially."[61]

While the potential of music to move in time in a more flexible fashion than that symbolically represented by the orderly unfolding of sound events on the score should be acknowledged, however, it is also to the "linear" dimension of the temporality of music that we can ascribe the teleology (and therefore a crucial aspect of the "theology") of its unfolding.

61. Adlington, "Musical Temporality," 25.

Cadenza

In literature, in philosophy, in musicology, in psychology and in various other fields of human knowledge touched upon in Part One of this book, the struggle of human beings who attempt to give meaning to Time emerges as one of the greatest challenges of our createdness. And yet, the inexpressible and touching mystery of music seems to convey a "glimpse" of a reality beyond Time and beyond the boundaries it sets for our lives and horizons. Through the time of music, we seem to transcend Time; the comprehensive, all-encompassing reality of musical thought gives us a foretaste of deeper, limitless forms of knowledge.

I began by presenting the writings of theologians who understood the concept of eternity as the presence, in a God who transcends Time, of all Time of history; and this God is the same who has chosen Time as the *locus* for his self-revelation in the "history of salvation," in the narrative of his love for his people.

I next showed how human beings have conceptualized and visualized Time as space, particularly when attempting to view simultaneously events taking place at different times. In mathematics and geometry, the idea of representing uniform quantities of time through uniform quantities of space emerged slowly; the possibility of representing graphically the past evolution of a quantity also implied and entailed, for mathematicians and scientists, the possibility of "foreseeing" its future evolution. Interestingly, this possibility was developed by thinkers who had also a direct experience of music. Conversely, it seems to me that the emergence of the "timeline" as a way of representing history, as embodied in Priestley's chart, was indebted to the conventions of representation of polyphonic music in notation.

Next, I turned to the history of musical notation, tracking the main stages of its development and how it tried to express time and synchronicity. While the first neumatic forms of notation were intended mainly as mnemonic aids, and showed their dependence on the underlying text, diastemacy affirmed the primacy of musical "events" on the written page, and allowed the immediate recognition of musical "landmarks" and repetitions by the skilled reader.

Polyphony imposed the need for a precise representation of time units. When counterpoint was notated as in modern scores, the possibility emerged of viewing simultaneously a series of distinct, parallel and intertwining temporalities, whose time was precisely organized and prescribed by the articulation of the musical events taking place in them. Musical genres which actively exploited the temporality of music, such as retrograde or circular canons, not only represented an attempt to reverse time or to eternalize it in repetition, but were also often pictured on paper so as to suggest this same idea. This concept was also employed in modern times, e.g., by Olivier Messiaen, whereas the possibility of combining musical events in a non-fixed order has been explored in musical "open works" and graphic scores. In the case of Iannis Xenakis, the germinating idea for many of his musical works was the possibility of translating space into time, rather than vice-versa.

Music scores not only allow, but actually encourage and demand the conceptualization of multiple temporalities; the imagination and mental representation of music by the performer requires the capability of identifying meaningful structures in music, of reading "ahead" of time, and of playing a musical structure while, at the same time, reading or recalling another, or several others. Bars are the (normally) homogeneous unit of musical chronological time, and yet their visual appearance depends on the thinness or thickness of musical events taking place in them; this suggests a *qualitative* dimension of time which musical notation embodies along with quantitative aspects.

The possibility of seeing music, of embracing its temporal development at a glance and of viewing a temporal succession simultaneously has been understood also by visual artists, who have frequently exploited this possibility in still-life and *vanitas* paintings; while music itself was often a symbol for the decaying and the ephemeral, musical scores could embody also the concepts of synchronicity and, occasionally, of eternity—also in an exquisitely Christian framework. In more recent times, the art of Vasilij Kandinsky, as well as that of Paul Klee and its interpretation by Pierre Boulez, offered further occasions for reflecting on the "temporality" of both painting and music and on their possibility of transcending it.

The processes of musical reading and performance, in fact, suggest on the one hand that no simultaneity or instantaneity can truly happen in "no time," as all processes of human knowledge and conceptualization do take place in time; on the other, however, they come as close as possible to the experience of a simultaneous presence of evolving temporalities, thus representing a powerful human and creatural analogy to the theological concept of "eternal present."

In fact, we have hitherto discussed what is meant by the expression and concept of "eternal present," as distinct from our experience of temporality; we have seen how humankind tended to think of time through concepts drawn from the visual and spatial sphere, and how the development of musical notation dovetailed with this process of abstraction and representation. We have also discussed how music, in its temporal dimension, can be considered as a "syntax of time," in which the order of the sounds mirrors the intelligibility, causality and providentiality of history, and how music can also defy our normal experience of time, both by superimposing its own time onto our chronometric time, and by suggesting the possibility of navigating time backwards through canons, repetitions etc. We have then discussed how musical scores are seen, represented and imagined in their temporal and a-temporal reality, by practicing musicians, philosophers and visual artists, and how traditional forms of notation have been transformed in the experiments of the twentieth-century avant-garde.

Thus, I hope to have demonstrated the following points:

1. That most Western music is understood and experienced as the (musically) meaningful succession of aural events in time;
2. That its notation represents, visually and spatially, an aural and temporal phenomenon;
3. That by doing so it allows musicians to experience, recollect and imagine an exquisitely temporal phenomenon in an (almost) simultaneous fashion and mental imagination;
4. That this process may be considered as a human analogue to the (utterly supernatural) reality of the "Eternal Present," in which Time and History are contained, embraced and transcended;
5. That this capacity of beholding the unfolding of a temporal phenomenon in an immediate fashion has a "providential" dimension, since

the musician can "see" or imagine the musical "narrative" of a piece (i.e., the role and functions of its musical components) at a glance.

In Part 2 I will illustrate through literature and theology how music has been deemed capable to symbolize God's eternal present, the condition of those creatures whose knowledge comes from the contemplation of Him, and the providential unfolding of both the history of humankind and of individual narratives in a consistent fashion.

Intermezzo

The interdisciplinary itinerary of Part One has shown how musical scores may be understood as human analogues for the Eternal Present. They are one of the most important forms by which human beings have translated a temporal phenomenon into observable shapes; their history intertwines with that of the conceptualization of Time by philosophers and theologians, and with the development of the musical language. The evolution of musical notation responded to the challenges of the contemporaneous musical styles; yet, the different shapes they took jointly contribute to our musical thought, to our experience of music, and also to our experience of time.

Stimuli coming from very different fields, such as the psychology of music, the philosophy of music, but also literature, the visual arts, and physics compose, together, an overall and harmonious picture; their interaction allows the powerful symbolic meaning of musical scores to emerge.

If the unfolding of Time is wrapped in the atemporal reality of God's Eternal Present, similar to a music whose temporality is observable in a score, then the gift of the contemplation of God allows created beings to behold temporality in a single instant.

In Part Two, I will explore how this analogy can be developed by proposing a theological reading of the Book of Genesis inspired by Tolkien's *The Silmarillion*. Tolkien's work is a literary rereading of God's creation of the angels; of his self-revelation to them; of how this self-revelation implies a *kenosis* on God's part, but also the gift of life for his creatures; of how this gift also represents the disclosure of the ultimate truth about *their* own being and their ultimate vocation. We will see that the acceptance of this gift and of this revelation represents the fullness of a creature's freedom, in the truest sense of the word, and also the possibility of an essentially harmonious coexistence with other created beings; thus, those who adhere to God's will and accept His calling are both "performing" the music He composed for them, *and* being perfectly free to improvise following their heart's innermost and freest inclinations. Christian theology and Tolkien's narrative emphatically proclaim that this coordination of wills "for the good" and "for the beautiful" is *not* a mortification of an individual's freedom or creativity; rather, by responding to God's calling, all express themselves, all fulfil their talents, and all contribute to the symphony of the universe.

We will also see that this calling and this freedom are not accepted by all, and that rebellion (called "sin" in the Christian tradition) is a possibility for all intelligent and free beings. However, the consequences of such a choice are dire: discord, suffering, disharmony and pain. The Fall of Lucifer is narrated in musical terms by Tolkien, and can therefore be likened to a leading musician abandoning his "part" and disrupting the balanced and harmonious performance of this symphony. The "score" of God's will is not obeyed, not followed anymore; the temporal unfolding of this score in the music of History bears the marks of this disruption.

However, History itself is believed by Christians to be redeemed and saved by God's Providence: God's capability of bringing even the harshest dissonances to a harmonious resolution is contemplated, outside Time, by those who already behold the fullness of human history in the mystery of God's love.

Moreover, this perspective lies behind the human calling to creativity, which is also one of the characterizing traits of the biblical account of Genesis. The creation of stories by authors, or of musical works by composers, is a forceful statement that there is a logic in Time and in the events happening in it. Our belief that there is a sense in our time is encouraged and strengthened by listening to these pieces, or by reading a novel. By recalling a musical piece (as seen in a score, or as preserved in memory) we perceive that the individual aural events it comprised were ordered to a purpose, were intelligible as a teleology; thus, we intuit that the sense of life is akin to the unfolding of a music, which we cannot fully comprehend until it has reached its final chord, but whose meaning does exist. And those who can see the score can already perceive where the music is leading us.

PART TWO

5

Beholding God

At the still point of the turning world. Neither flesh nor fleshless;
Neither from nor towards; at the still point, there the dance is,
But neither arrest nor movement. And do not call it fixity,
Where past and future are gathered. Neither movement from nor towards,
Neither ascent nor decline. Except for the point, the still point,
There would be no dance, and there is only the dance.
(Thomas Stearns Eliot, *Four Quartets*, "Burnt Norton," II)

Introduction

If the "eternal present" is God's mode of being in relationship to temporality, then, as we have seen, his knowledge and providence cause, encompass and transcend all created reality. The Christian God, however, is constantly in dialogue with the created world. Indeed, this dialogue is rooted into and caused by the intra-trinitarian relationships which are an everlasting exchange of love, a continuous intercommunication and indwelling, and a reciprocal gift. The Father's begetting of the Son, and their spiration of the Spirit are acts of self-revelation, self-giving and of supreme love; arguably, the image of a beautifully sounding polyphony is not entirely out of place when discussing trinitarian life. The three Persons of the Trinity jointly create the world; they create Time (which is not the only mode of being of the created beings—it is *ours*, and *now*); they create those creatures who are not bound by its constraints. The angels, in Christian theology, are pure spirits who exist in God's eternity and who, partaking in one of his qualities, are endowed with the possibility of intervening and acting within the created world and in time. God's Providence is one way by which we define his capability and willingness to sustain the world which lives in time, both ordinarily (since Christians believe that "everything is Grace," all we have and are is a gift of God) and extraordinarily. The most significant event of God's extraordinary Providence is, of course, the Son's incarnation, his passion, death and resurrection.

Christ's incarnation is a *kenosis*, a self-emptying, by which the divine Logos took human flesh and accepted to undergo the laws by which material and created beings live, including the capability to suffer and to die. However, there is a kenotic dimension also in God's process of self-revelation, which takes place both in time (and is understood by Christians to include first and foremost the privileged revelation to Israel, partially embodied in the Scriptures, but also what is known as "natural theology," i.e., those truths which are accessible to human reason, philosophy, intuition etc.) and outside time, in the contemplation of God enjoyed forever by the angels. The communication of God's Being to creatures is a gift. It is a life-creating, and life-sustaining gift for us created beings, but also another form of God's kenosis: it takes place whenever he, as it were, "bends" himself and his utter unknowability to what is comprehensible by us creatures. God's supreme humiliation is found in his acceptance of our flesh and mortality in Christ's incarnation, which is understood also as the gate by which Eternity (God's eternal present) enters Time: not only as its cause (as in the creation of the world) but also as an experience (Christ's life).

This theological framework developed in Christian thought, drawing from earlier traditions that germinated both from the Old Testament and from the encounter with Greek philosophy. It involved also relatively peripheral aspects of faith and culture, such as the idea of the "harmony of the spheres." This pervasive image and belief in the Greek tradition was subsumed by Christian thinkers, forming part of the Church's cosmology and of her theology proper, in the intertwining of physical phenomena (the organization of the heavenly bodies), theological concepts (the angels' perennial contemplation of God and their unceasing praise of him) and aesthetic/spiritual ideas (the beauty of music as a symbol for the perfect "harmony" of a heavenly society).

It is not my aim, in this second part of the book, to trace all declinations of these topics in Western culture and in Christianity in a consistent and thorough fashion; rather, I will take as my primary focus two fragments from two cornerstones of the Western literature (i.e., J. R. R.

Tolkien's *The Silmarillion* and Dante Alighieri's *Commedia*) and discuss how they enter into relationship with the tradition preceding (and even occasionally following) them, as concerns the eternal present and its musical symbolization.

As we will see, both Tolkien and Dante, in common with countless other authors and theologians, discuss the blessed spirits' contemplation of God in musical terms.[1] For both writers, God's eternally present life encompasses a process of self-revelation to the created world; and though this process may happen outside Time, it comprises a dimension of graduality and increase. The Judeo-Christian tradition suggests that, just as the angels and blessed may progress in their knowledge of God (even if this happens outside time), their thanksgiving to God may similarly take the form of a "song," notwithstanding the paradox that music is an exquisitely temporal art.

We will also see that both Dante and Tolkien understand the heavenly court's praise to God in terms of *polyphonic* music, and this is perfectly consistent with traditional Christian theology. In fact, those who contemplate God in his radiant perfection are perfectly free, just as a beautiful polyphonic work gives the impression that all voices enjoy a total freedom. Being entirely in God's will, whose purpose is the fullness of life and perfect happiness for all of his creatures, their freedom will never conflict with that of the others. In other words, the blessed spirits contemplate, in God, how every individual's happiness is increased and perfected by the happiness of others. Being joined in their communal desire to fulfil God's will, they all cooperate in a harmonious fashion to the establishment of an utterly "harmonious" society. Since God wills the happiness of all, the inhabitants of the "City of God" are perfectly free, perfectly fulfilled in their individual talents, wishes and aspirations, and in perfect harmony with God and with each other.

Thus, it may be argued that, in a symbolic fashion, the contemplation of God is similar to the "musical score" in which every member of the heavenly choir may "read" his or her part. Of course, both the aural and the visual symbolism should not be interpreted literally: in the reality of the resurrected bodies there will certainly be a physical and sensorial element, but the knowledge of God is primarily a matter of intellectual intuition and spiritual union through absolute love. As Goethe wrote, when describing an

1. In Dante's case, the heavenly court he depicts in the *Paradiso* is composed both of angels and of the souls of the blessed men, women and children.

intuitive experience, "It is as if the eternal harmony were conversing within itself, as it may have done in the bosom of God just before the creation of the world.[2] So likewise did it move in my inmost soul, and it seemed as if I neither possessed nor needed ears, nor any other sense—least of all eyes."[3]

The blessed spirits' "reading" of the heavenly musical score is therefore a process which may be likened to the "performance" of a work in which all singers obey the composer's prescriptions as embodied in the score, but, *at the same time*, it can be compared to a collective improvisation. This is paradoxical in our eyes, since the created reality of our earthly experience of music is that *either* we obey a composer, *or* we are the composers of our own music, possibly in the spontaneous fashion of an improvisation. In an otherworldly society, however, these two realities may coexist, since all creatures spontaneously will what is best for them, coinciding both with God's will and with what is best for all other members of the choir. It is therefore an experience utterly different from that portrayed in Dostoevsky's *Notes from the Underground*, where the protagonist rebels against being reduced to a "piano-key," and it is argued that "the whole work of man really seems to consist in nothing but proving to himself every minute that he is a man and not a piano-key!"[4] While piano keys have no choice but to let themselves be depressed by the pianist's touch, the song of creation is the coincidence of the creatures' free will with God's will.

In the following discussion I will take the opening pages of Tolkien's *Ainulindalë* and the episode of Cacciaguida in Dante's *Commedia* as "pretexts" for discussing this fecund symbolic image. I will selectively discuss examples of other literary works which—quite literally—"resonate" with this perspective, in a theological fashion. I will also discuss some related ideas, most notably that connecting the origins of evil with a "discord" in the heavenly choir and the role of the artists (writers and musicians) as

2. There is more than an echo of Plato here (*Timaeus* 37a), but especially of Ficino's interpretation of the World-Soul and of its harmony: "When Plato represents the Maker of the world as one who speaks both by reasoning with himself and by commanding everything else, he considers the utterance itself, like the highly musical hymn of Apollo, to be the origin both of the world-soul and of the body" (Ficino, *All Things Natural*, 53). The Italian Baroque poet Giovanni B. Marino quoted Ficino and commented: "When God converses with Himself, somehow taking counsel in Himself, He forms a musical song and a music for singing, whence the entire universal concert of the world originates" (Marino, *Dicerie sacre*, 181).

3. Goethe in Bodley, *Goethe and Zelter*, 383.

4. Dostoevsky, *Notes*, 23.

"sub-creators," as well as the interpretation of Christ's incarnation seen in musical terms by other authors.

Framing the *Ainulindalë*

The so-called *Ainulindalë* (meaning "The Music of the Ainur" in the Elvish language called *Quenya*, created by Tolkien himself) is found at the beginning of *The Silmarillion*, a collection of tales compiled and published posthumously by Tolkien's son, Christopher. The first few pages are not only an epic narrative, with a solemn and compelling tone, but also a superb reinterpretation of the Judeo-Christian understanding of Creation, as found in the Book of Genesis, and as interpreted by spiritual and theological authors throughout the history of Judaism and Christendom. As is well known, Tolkien was profoundly inspired by his Christian faith, and yet (or precisely for this reason) he eschewed an explicit presence of Christian figures and beliefs in his *legendarium*: therefore, while his literary work is deeply rooted into the Christian values and worldview, it omits all evident references to that tradition. *The Silmarillion* is presented as the Elves' mythology.[5] It is, therefore, a religious interpretation of the real, as expressed by a particular race of created beings (similar to humans, but not subject to natural mortality and with many superior qualities, including a special gift for music and a penchant for nostalgia).

Being a mythology does not imply, for Tolkien, that the *Ainulindalë* is simply "fiction." As we will see, Tolkien believed that myths are not just fictional tales, but embody a seminal truth. We may therefore assume that, in his creative and theological worldview, the *Ainulindalë* is the form chosen by the Godhead for revealing some truths about his mode of being and the origins of the world to the Elves. Just as the Judeo-Christian revelation is understood by believers as being the way in which God "tells" us about himself in such a way that we may comprehend, or at least intuit something important and true about him, similarly the *Ainulindalë* represents "the same content" as intuited by the race of Elves. Since the Elves are both called to, and tempted by, the vocation to be the preservers of beauty,[6] it is particularly fitting that a *musical* myth should be the form in which the Elves express their deepest beliefs about the origin and meaning of the world (given that music lives in the present, is a syntax of time, and

5. Tolkien, *Letters*, 147; cf. Flieger, *Interrupted Music*, 51.

6. Milbank, "In a Dark Wood," 7.

yet eludes all attempts to be frozen and fixed). As we have been discussing, in a reality outside time, such as that of the divine mind, all moments are simultaneously present in an eternal instant. Therefore, the unfolding and revelation of the divine thought in the comprehension of created beings is a translation from the atemporal to the temporal, symbolized by the most temporal of all arts, music.

The *Ainulindalë* opens with the presentation of the Godhead: "There was Eru, the One, who in Arda is called Ilúvatar."[7] This is immediately followed by the introduction of the Ainur: "and he made first the Ainur, the Holy Ones." The Ainur are creatures similar to the Christian angels, in their being "with him before aught else was made," in their spiritual nature and in their exceptional gifts. Ilúvatar then speaks to them, declaring a musical theme: "And he spoke to them, propounding to them themes of music." On later occasions Tolkien is very careful to avoid all singing-related terms when referring to Ilúvatar, who is constantly said to speak: "[Ilúvatar] declared to them a mighty theme," "the theme I have declared to you."[8] How are we to understand this "declaration" of a "theme of music"? I will argue later that this singular choice may signify the transmission to the Ainur of a form of *knowledge*, rather than an immediately *poietic* (or musical) activity by Ilúvatar.

The themes he "propounds" to the Ainur are given to them. The Ainur first sing individually, "for each comprehended only that part of the mind of Ilúvatar from which he came, and in the understanding of their brethren they grew but slowly." And then "they came to deeper understanding, and increased in unison and harmony."[9] Ilúvatar then asks the Ainur to "adorn" this theme, and the Ainur's singing progressively unfolds in "endless interchanging melodies woven in harmony."[10] The Ainur's music is later "shown" to them by Ilúvatar, and it becomes matter and history in "Arda." As Tolkien narrates so beautifully,

7. Tolkien, *Silmarillion*, 15. On the musical aspect of the *Ainulindalë*, see also Caldecott, "New Light"; Carswell, *Tolkien's Overture*; Eden, "Music of the Spheres"; Flieger, *Interrupted Music*; Halsall, *Creation and Beauty*; "Critical Assessment"; Houghton, "Augustine and the Ainulindalë"; Jensen, "Dissonance"; McIntosh, "Ainulindalë"; Meyer, "From the Music"; Naveh, "Tonality"; Whobrey, "From *Ainulindalë* to Valhalla."

8. Tolkien, *Silmarillion*, 15; cf. *Book of Lost Tales*, 1:52, where just one initial reference is made to Ilúvatar "singing [the Ainur] into being."

9. Tolkien, *Silmarillion*, 15.

10. Tolkien, *Silmarillion*, 15.

> When they were come into the Void, Ilúvatar said to them: "Behold your Music!" And he showed to them a vision, giving to them sight where before was only hearing; and they saw a new World made visible before them . . . And as they looked and wondered this World began to unfold its history, and it seemed to them that it lived and grew. And when the Ainur had gazed for a while and were silent, Ilúvatar said again: "Behold your Music! This is your minstrelsy; and each of you shall find contained herein, amid the design that I set before you, all those things which it may seem that he himself devised or added." . . . And they perceived that they themselves in the labour of their music had been busy with the preparation of this dwelling, and yet knew not that it had any purpose beyond its own beauty.[11]

The Holy Ones' Knowledge of God

At the very beginning of *The Silmarillion*, Ilúvatar "speaks" his theme of music to the Ainur. This is a primeval and original form of self-revelation of the Godhead to the firstborn of his creation. Reading the biblical account of Genesis through the lens of the Prologue to St. John's Gospel, Christian theology has interpreted God's "utterances," by which the world was created, as a manifestation of the divine Logos, the second Person of the Holy Trinity. It has also been argued that the Father's eternal generation of the Son within the Holy Trinity, as well as the creation of the world by the Father through the Son in the Spirit, are two aspects of a kenotic process which will culminate in Christ's incarnation and in his passion. In other words, the Father "gives himself" eternally and wholly to the Son, gives life to the created world through the Son, and gives His divine life to humankind through the Incarnation and the ultimate Gift of Christ's Cross.

Since God's self-revelation to the angels does not take place in a temporality such as we are acquainted with, it is possible to say, in an equally acceptable fashion, that it is akin *both* to a simultaneous, visual contemplation, *and* to a speech or music happening in time. It is similar both to the observation of a musical score and to the listening of the music it represents. The mystery of the knowledge of God as experienced by the angels is discussed by many authors in the history of the Christian culture, and occasionally outside it.

11. Tolkien, *Silmarillion*, 17–18.

In *The Literal Meaning of Genesis*, Augustine understands the alternation of "evening" and "morning" in the biblical account of creation as a process in two stages, whereby the angels at first receive knowledge from God, and then praise him:

> If the light originally created is not material but spiritual, then this light [namely, the company of angels] was made after the darkness in the sense that it turned from its unformed state to its Creator and was thus formed. Consequently, after evening, morning is made, when after its knowledge of its own nature as something distinct from God, this light directs itself to praise the Light that is God, in the contemplation of which it is formed. . . . Evening of the first day, therefore, is the knowledge spiritual beings have of themselves, inasmuch as they know they are not God. . . . The morning which begins the second day is the conversion of spiritual beings, by which they direct to the praise of their Creator the gift of their creation, and receive from the Word of God a knowledge of the creature next made, namely, the firmament.[12]

This process is faithfully echoed in Tolkien's description of the Ainur's acceptance of Ilúvatar's theme, and in their consequent adornment of his music in their praise. As Houghton correctly points out,[13] the "five-part internal structure" of the divine creation as seen by Augustine in his *Literal Meaning of Genesis* (6.14.25–6.18.29) is the simultaneous happening of "God's eternal intention to create," creation "in the minds of the angels of a knowledge of what is to be made," creation proper (in reality or causal reason), the angels' beholding of creation, and "God's eternal support of the Creation through the Holy Spirit." Similarly, in his *City of God*,[14] Augustine discusses how the citizens of heaven (human beings and angels) will know God and will know each other in the contemplation of God: as I will discuss later, this knowledge is indispensable for a harmonious musical understanding. Thus, Augustine depicts the eschatological reality as a harmonious concert of diverse voices, whose possibility lies in the mutual knowledge given to the blessed by their contemplation of God; that same knowledge "in God" was present in the creative act, when some comprehension of God's deliberation and action were transmitted to the angels. Augustine's model is discernible also behind the description of creation

12. Augustine, *De Genesi ad litteram libri duodecim* 4.22; *Literal Meaning*, 1:130.

13. Houghton, "Augustine and the Ainulindalë," 5–7.

14. Augustine, *De Civitate Dei* 22.29.6; *City of God*, 2:373–74.

provided by Hugh of St. Victor:[15] for both of them, and even though what we perceive as a sequence of events did actually happen simultaneously, a series of stages can be observed in God's creative process, consisting of the divine will to create, the transmission to the angels of some kind of knowledge of this divine will and what we would call "creation proper."

This theological view is beautifully summarized by Edith Stein in her works. In *Potency and Act*, she affirms that, "unlike us, angels do not gradually acquire additional knowledge; in them there is no 'discursive' knowing." The angels' knowledge encompasses "general forms and with a single look they take in all the things that correspond to the actualized form," and, of course, "God encompasses all real and possible individual things with his simple essence."[16] In *Finite and Eternal Being*, she added: "The perfection of knowledge consists in this case in an inward affirmation, in a yea-saying [*Jasagen*] to God, to all created things and beings, and therewith also to this spirit's own being. This harmonious accord and concord is love, joy, and willingness to serve."[17] This passage points out the relational quality of knowledge, understood as the acceptance of the divine self-revelation, and the creatures' response depicted in musical terms ("harmonious accord and concord," translating the German "*Einklang*"). While all angels contemplate God and receive knowledge from him, it is also possible that this knowledge comes to their intellect through the mediation of other angels: "'enlightenment' takes place when the higher angel shares its knowledge with the lower and the lower intuits it in the 'higher.'" This sharing of knowledge, she argues, "occurs when one [angel] 'opens, discloses itself' to the other," since "no angel by itself can see inside another since this cannot occur unless the angel that is to be known wills it." Thus,

> The knowledge that angels have in God, their intuition of creatures in the Word (called "morning knowledge" after St. Augustine), differs from the knowledge they have by nature through their essence and their impressed forms. There seems to be an essential difference between their intuition in God and their intuition in a higher angel (and so between their being enlightened by God and by a higher angel).[18]

15. Taylor, *Didascalicon*, 156.
16. Stein, *Potency and Act*, 137.
17. Stein, *Finite and Eternal Being*, 403.
18. Stein, *Potency and Act*, 137.

This view expresses in a theological fashion the parallel process whereby Tolkien's Ainur listen to (the revelation of) each other.

Along with Augustinian influences, Thomist perspectives are clearly distinguishable in Tolkien's vision. St. Thomas Aquinas discusses in *Summa*[19] how the angels may know God, and the ultimate unknowability of God's essence: his account of this heavenly epistemology seems to provide a model for Tolkien's description of the Ainur's knowledge of the mind of Ilúvatar and of their brethren.[20]

Jacques de Liège: Angelic Choirs

In roughly the same years as Aquinas, Jacques de Liège[21] (Iacobus Leodiensis, ca. 1260–ca. 1330) treated several theoretical, technical and theological aspects of music in his *Speculum musicae.* While discussing the musicality of the blessed souls (1.5), he affirms that they contemplate the Trinity's harmony in an intuitive vision, and, in turn, address to God eternal and everlasting praise. In 1.12, he states that "in that celestial Church . . . there will be a place for music by which God may be praised incessantly by those citizens" of heaven. This song, in his view, exceeds all other songs just as the blessed spirits' condition exceeds that of the mortal beings. These "citizens of heaven . . . have this music in perfection, they who no longer contemplate God in a glass darkly through any exterior representation, but behold him directly, face to face."[22] Jacques defines the condition of the blessed as the "hearing" of the divine mysteries, the ("visual") contemplation of the Trinity, and an unceasing song of praise: the blessed spirits "are seized up and hear what is not lawful for a man to utter," and "they see what cannot be fully spoken of, namely the concord and inseparable fellowship of the Divine Persons and their perfect union in one utterly simple essence, replete with every perfection." Moreover, "they contemplate in that voluntary and eternal mirror, in that Book of Life, things which cannot be told us." Thus, for Jacques, the heavenly citizens' beholding of the Godhead is not unlike "reading" from the Book of Life, in which the history of salvation is written and recounted. Those excellent singers, who "have . . . music in perfection,"

19. *ST* I, q. 58.

20. See also Halsall, "Critical Assessment," 42.

21. I adopt here the traditional identification, but (following Bent, *Magister Jacobus*) he should be more appropriately be indicated as James of Spain.

22. Cf. 1 Cor 13:12.

are therefore portrayed as gazing into a Book in which a history can both unfold and be seen at a glance.

Jacques's image is further detailed in the following paragraphs: the blessed spirits "see there the specific nature of everything else: their order, connection and concord among themselves and with God." Fascinatingly,

> in these, . . . just as they find the most excellent harmonic modulation, so they also find the most perfect music. Therefore the best musicians are those who in their contemplation [*intuitive*] observe that eternal book. For in it there lies open and shines forth every proportion, every concord, every consonance, every melody; and whatever things are needed for music are written down there.[23]

In Book 6 Jacques then discusses the origins of musical notation. Pitches were indicated through the same letters which are also employed for transmitting a verbal thought; thus, using the letters, "the meaning and the words are introduced through the eyes, not through the ears," in order to "fix the concepts in memory." Since Christ defined himself as the Alpha and Omega (Rev 1:3; 21:6; 22:1), Jacques maintains that everything is encompassed by God, just as the entire alphabet, and the words it makes, are encompassed by Christ (6.7). And so when one employs letters in order to transmit and preserve music, the "sweet song" can last "in memory and posterity."

In summary, Jacques de Liège affirms that music, the most temporal of all arts, exists in God's eternity, as one of the most perfect forms in which he is praised forever by the immortal beings. Music is one of the forms through which their love for him is expressed. The knowledge which is necessary for making music, and for making music together—a knowledge embodied by musical scores in our present and mortal experience—is replaced by the knowledge which the blessed spirits receive from their contemplation of God, in whom everything is simultaneously present and who is the source of all knowledge. By contemplating God, the blessed spirits also contemplate and know each other. This knowledge, springing from the vision of God, is what enables them to make music in harmony and beauty, and therefore glorify God in love and perfection.

A very similar perspective is found in a work by the Italian Baroque poet Giovan Battista Marino (1569–1625). Marino[24] affirms that the skill of God, the "Archmusician," is demonstrated by his works (1.18), and that

23. Godwin, *Harmony of the Spheres*, 134.

24. Marino, *Dicerie sacre*.

the harmony of the universe is ultimately caused by the inherent concord of the Trinity (1.19), whereby the Spirit "enlivens the limbs of this immense body [of the world] and binds them together with a harmonious knot, thus making consonant the instrument of the world" (1.20). He subsequently continues by equating "those celestial spirits, who are called Intelligences by our theologians" (i.e., the Angels) with the Platonic Sirens. He then affirms that "the happiness of the blessed who participate in the Vision of God is nothing but music," adding that it is possible that the angels speak to each other with "a corporeal" voice (1.21). Regardless of the actual audibility of these angelic communications, which may well be purely intellectual, Marino maintains that the angels employ whatever form of expression they have both for praising God and for "speaking" with each other (1.25). Thus "those spiritual substances do not only make an intellectual harmony, but frequently allow us to hear them with a sound of music. . . . Taking part in the Paradise's beatitude and mirroring themselves in God's glorious face, they never cease their eternal singing" (1.26). The concert of the angels and of all the created world is conducted by the supreme musician: "the divine mind gathers the variety of the world in a single and well-ordered concert by its eternal and infallible supervision."[25] We find in Marino many of the fundamental concepts proposed in the argument of this book and in Tolkien's *Ainulindalë*, that is, the idea of God as a musician who "composes" and "conducts" the concert of the created world and the angels' music as a form of knowledge, of communication, and of praise.

The Ainur's Song

The angels (in Christian terms) and the Ainur (in Tolkien's *legendarium*) enjoy an eternal contemplation of the Godhead, who reveals himself to them through a "Word" (the Christian divine *Logos*, or Ilúvatar's "themes" in *The Silmarillion*), which is a Gift establishing a relationship. The self-revelation of God establishes the Other. In this radically asymmetrical relationship between Creator and creature, between Him who gives life and those who depend on him for their being and their permanence in being, God's utterance establishes the Other as worthy of his friendship. Moreover, creatures know themselves within the framework of this relationship: by learning to know God, the creatures also learn to know themselves, particularly in their deepest vocation, which coincides with the ultimate truth about their

25. Marino, *Dicerie sacre*, 181–90; 1.36.

being. Furthermore, all other relationships among creatures depend on that fundamental and primeval relationship between Creator and creature. In God we learn the truth about Him, about ourselves, and about the others, and thus are made capable of establishing meaningful relationships both on the horizontal and on the vertical plane.

Rehearsing once more what has been said above, we may recall that Tolkien describes this in the *Ainulindalë*, when Ilúvatar commits his themes to the Ainur, entrusting these angelic creatures with the task of "adorning" them. At first, the Ainur sing one at a time, since, as we have seen, each has been imparted knowledge only of the "part of the mind of Ilúvatar" whence he or she originates.[26] By the act of listening to each other, the Ainur slowly learn to know their brethren, and "as they listened they came to deeper understanding, and increased in unison and harmony." The self-revelation of each Ainu to their brethren consists in his or her "interpretation" of Ilúvatar's theme; thus, the relationship among the Ainur is deeply rooted within the Godhead's revelation of himself. No knowledge is possible, except knowledge of the truth; no truth exists outside God; nothing regarding God can be learnt outside a relationship with him. And therefore the knowledge of one's self and of the others needs also to be understood within this relationship. The song of each Ainu causally and inseparably derives from Ilúvatar's theme, just as their being is caused by his Being. Their innermost self is revealed by their individual song, since, in Tolkien's words, they derive that self from the Godhead's "thought."[27]

Each adorns the theme according to his or her own gifts, talents, inclinations and character, thus actively contributing to the beauty of the song: Tolkien's theology does not display a unilateral and deterministic view of the relationship between Creator and creature, which would consist only of the creatures' dependence on God without involving their active and creative participation. Therefore, by creatively intervening on Ilúvatar's theme, each Ainu *reveals* and *fulfils* his or her own self. The theme of Ilúvatar (i.e., God's creative thought) is such that all of his creatures can realize their full potential, and in this way reach perfect happiness and fulfilment, without clashing with the freedom and realization of the others. When the Ainur learn to know each other in Ilúvatar, they discover that the melody which

26. In their spiritual essence, the Ainur are neither male nor female, but they can take visible form as gendered individuals. Moreover, the reader gathers the impression that, for Tolkien, these Ainur did not simply "appear" as males or females, but actually *were* male or female.

27. Tolkien, *Silmarillion*, 15.

expresses each one's innermost nature intertwines beautifully with all others. Moreover, they learn that the resulting polyphony far exceeds in beauty the sum total of all the individual melodic lines. By singing together, in the freedom which results from their loving acceptance of the relationship with the Godhead and of the call to Being and to music it entails, they make a concert which actually empowers them all, by making them participate in a beauty exceeding the capabilities of each individual singer. When they later "behold" their music, they discover in it a mysterious dimension: "And so it was that as this vision of the World was played before them, the Ainur saw that it contained things which they had not thought."[28]

The use of musical imagery is particularly apt; as David Cunningham perceptively summarizes,

> In a concert hall, we often hear many notes played simultaneously, and are the richer for doing so. In fact, we often hear more than one melody played simultaneously; thus, we hear not only multiple tones (as in a chord), but also entirely different sequences overlapping one another. Music theory has a technical term for this—*polyphony*. We can apply the same term to other contexts: any time we understand two or more different (even, possibly, "opposing") ideas being performed or enacted simultaneously, we have located an example of polyphony. . . . In music, multiple themes are not necessarily contrastive; music is not a zero-sum game. The addition of a new contrapuntal theme does not obliterate (or even necessarily diminish) the significance of the theme(s) already in place; nor does a symphony's brilliant cello part, for example, eliminate the need for trombones. . . . Christianity proclaims a polyphonic understanding of God—one in which *difference* provides an alternative to a monolithic homogeneity, yet without becoming a source of exclusion. . . . Moreover, we can come to understand the created order as marked by the polyphonic character of its Maker.[29]

This view of polyphony as a symbol for love, or at least for a society ruled by charity, is similar to the example used by Edmund Husserl to describe the parallelism of (multiple) "intentionalities." His simile of a mother who can at the same time love all of her children in an individual and specifically deliberate fashion is in fact yet another embodiment of this

28. Tolkien, *Silmarillion*, 18.

29. Cunningham, *These Three are One*, 128–29.

multi-dimensional concept.[30] I find it both touching and significant that such a view of a "polyphony of love" is symbolized, in Husserl's view, by the kind of human love which is possibly the most perfect on earth—i.e., the self-giving love of a parent. Leijonhufvud applies Husserl's example to the complexity of musical experience, evoking ideas such as the possibility of mentally "navigating" time during a performance of music, discussed in chapter 4.[31]

Within a Christian framework, the possibility for each and every creature with their unique voice to participate in the great polyphony of creation is rooted within the "polyphony" of the Triune God. Tolkien's Ilúvatar is not an explicitly trinitarian figure (although some argue, with reason, that trinitarian traits are found in Tolkien's description of the Godhead). Certainly, though, the author's *forma mentis* as a Christian believer shaped his understanding of the polyphony of the created world.

The Ainur's singing is depicted by Tolkien as an instrumental concert, rather than as a choir:

> The voices of the Ainur, like unto harps and lutes, and pipes and trumpets, and viols and organs, and like unto countless choirs singing with words, began to fashion the theme of Ilúvatar to a great music; and a sound arose of endless interchanging melodies woven in harmony that passed beyond hearing into the depths and into the heights, and the places of the dwelling of Ilúvatar were filled to overflowing, and the music and the echo of the music went out into the Void, and it was not void.[32]

Though I cannot claim that Tolkien was familiar with Ferruccio Busoni's writings, I find it interesting that the Italian composer, pianist and philosopher held a similar view to Tolkien's, and expressed his vision of "The Realm of Music" in analogous fashion, rehearsing, albeit in modern terms, the ancient topic of the harmony of the spheres:

> You still hear nothing because everything sounds. Now already you begin to differentiate. Listen, every star has its rhythm and every world its measure. And on each of the stars and each of the worlds, the heart of every separate living being is beating in its own individual way. And all the beats agree and are separate and yet are a whole. Your inner ear becomes sharper. Do you hear the

30. Husserl, *Ideas*, 248 (see also pp. 259–60).

31. See Leijonhufvud, "Sångupplevelse," 60–61.

32. Tolkien, *Silmarillion*, 15.

> depths and the heights? They are as immeasurable as space and endless as numbers. Unthought of scales extend like bands from one world to another, stationary and yet eternally in motion. Every tone is the centre of immeasurable circles. And now Sound is revealed to you! Innumerable are its voices; compared with them the murmuring of the harp is a din; the blare of a thousand trombones a chirrup. All, all melodies heard before or never heard, resound completely and simultaneously, carry you, hang over you, or skim lightly past you—of love and passion, of spring and of winter, of melancholy and of hilarity, they are themselves the souls of millions of beings in millions of epochs. If you focus your attention on one of them you perceive how it is connected with all the others, how it is combined with all the rhythms, colored by all kinds of sounds, accompanied by all harmonies, down to unfathomable depths and up to the vaulted roof of heaven.[33]

Like Tolkien, Busoni chooses imagery that has spatial dimensions (both speak of "depths" and of "heights"), timbral features (both mention harps and trombones), and in Busoni's idea that "all melodies . . . resound completely and simultaneously" we can observe a parallel to the notion of the eternal present, embodied in Tolkien's narrative by the Ainur's Vision of their Music.

Even before they are granted this Vision, and thanks to the knowledge imparted to them by the Godhead, the Ainur's music is akin both to a polyphonic improvisation and to their "reading" of a polyphonic score. I will therefore briefly discuss how the birth of polyphony and improvisational practices intertwine in our musical culture, and how they may contribute to our understanding of Tolkien's *Ainulindalë* and of the theological concepts it embodies.

33. Busoni, *Essence of Music*, 188–89.

6

Polyphonic Improvisations

Polyphony, in the historical development of Western musical language, arose from a variety of practices, mostly involving improvisation. These practices were historically and geographically diverse, and their evolution took different paths; however, polyphonic improvisation as such embodies the utopia of free, creative and yet coordinated improvisation.

It is therefore fitting that Tolkien employed this particular image to signify the harmonious liberty of the heavenly society: the theological content of his work suggestively dovetails with the actual shapes took by Western polyphony in its earliest forms.

Tolkien was certainly familiar with at least some stages of this development: as a scholar specializing in medieval English, he encountered some technical terms of the polyphonic language. In particular, in his *Middle English Vocabulary*,[1] Tolkien elucidated the meaning of *deschaunt*, i.e., the English discant. This style, and its Continental homologues, was grounded on the liturgical plainchant, used as a *cantus firmus*, to which one or more voices were added. These were "composed not simultaneously in relation to each other, but either independently or each one in relation to the tenor alone,"[2] so that the *cantus firmus* determined the overall structure of early polyphonic works. In consequence, "each of the added lines agre[ed] with this melody but not necessarily with each other,"[3] and the result was rather similar to improvised polyphony.

1. Tolkien, *Middle English*.
2. Flotzinger, "Discant" 1.4.
3. Horsley, "Improvisation" 2.2.1.

This could be observed in a particularly clear fashion in the case of the *faburden*, a polyphonic form typical for medieval England, and which may be loosely defined as a kind of improvisation with strict rules, or performance without a written score. The governing principles of *faburden*, as of other semi-improvised forms, were: (a) the knowledge of the *cantus firmus* (which could be read from a choirbook or known by memory); (b) a rigid set of rules; (c) a system of mental transpositions called "sights." In consequence, the pitches sung by each musician were not defined beforehand, so that the result was different from what we would call "performance of a written score";[4] however, the range of possible choices was so limited that a consonant aural result was expected. As Horsley puts it, "while at first the improvising singer may have relied on his memory of the chant to which he was adding a counter-melody, the improvisers eventually saw this chant in some sort of visual notation so that they could anticipate its notes."[5]

When successful, polyphonic improvisation was not only aurally pleasing: it also symbolized a mysterious concord in the musicians' wills. Giraldus Cambrensis, writing in the 1190s, described the improvised practices of Welsh musicians as follows:

> When they make music together, they sing their tunes not in unison, as is done elsewhere, but in parts with many simultaneous modes and phrases. Therefore, in a group of singers (which one very often meets within Wales) you will hear as many melodies as there are people, and a distinct variety of parts; yet they all accord in one consonant and properly constituted composition.[6]

The fact that all musicians could sing their own tunes, and yet be consonant with all others was perceived as an almost mystical embodiment of a communion of souls.

Cantus Firmus and Polyphony

Summarizing, the majority of early polyphony repertoire was grounded on the *cantus firmus*, to which an improvised/composed second voice could be added, note against note (discant), or which could be framed by the

4. Erasmus defined the English *faburden* as a kind of music "in which many sing together, but none of the singers produces those sounds which the notes on the page indicate" (Miller, "Erasmus on Music," 341).

5. Horsley, "Improvisation" 2.2.1.

6. Sternfeld, *History of Western Music*, 1:264.

lower and upper melodies extemporaneously created by faburden singers, or which could be sung in long values, upon which more elaborated melodies created lighter musical garlands (*organum melismaticum*). Since most *cantus firmus* in early polyphony were taken from the liturgical plainchant repertoire, the role of *cantus firmus* in determining the most important features of the polyphonic composition corresponded to the religious sacredness of the plainchant repertoire. The *cantus firmus* was not only the root of the eventual composition, but its germinating force; since all parts had to relate themselves with it, the *cantus firmus* could be seen as embodying the entire range of musical possibilities, as comprising in potency all of its polyphonic developments.

Moreover, polyphonic composition symbolizes a concept of plurality which not only reconciles diversity and variety in unity, but also gives a multi-dimensional breadth (and therefore a significant enrichment in meaning) to the individual lines concurring in it. As Lippmann suggests, the interplay of two or more melodies intertwining in polyphonic music both challenges and delights the attentive hearer: the listeners' expectations "can be divided into two or three separately flowing channels of consciousness," which have also "intercommunication and mutual influence," so that "there is a unifying total consciousness along with the streams of individualized experience."[7] A polyphonic composition is thus an organic whole which both encompasses and transcends the single melodies, and at the same time partially transfigures them through their very interplay, which gives them new meanings and direction.

The architectural role of the *cantus firmus* was pivotal for the entire musical concept: even when the derivate parts were aurally equal to it, they remained causally secondary. This also applied to improvised polyphony. In the case of *super librum* improvisation (i.e., the extemporaneous addition of parts to the *cantus firmus*), the given plainchant constituted the fixed frame, the pillars of the work, which the added voices ought to respect, with which they had to conform, and which therefore largely determined their shape. According to Horsley, "The leading singer must know all the possible combinations at specific times over precise pitches, and those following him must have good ears and memories."[8] These techniques, as well as those regulating improvised variations, were extremely sophisticated

7. Lippmann, *Philosophy*, 59.

8. Horsley, "Improvisation" 2.2.1.

and allowed musicians to improvise together without tonal clashes, as "two, three, or even four singers could anticipate each other's moves."[9]

When the musicians who improvised polyphonically were particularly skilled, knew each other well, and employed the improvisation techniques properly, the result was impressive. It gave listeners the impression of an almost superhuman foreknowledge of each other's intentions.

This magical or transcendent feeling is conveyed in a treatise[10] (1274) by Elias Salomo (ca. 1229–1294), accompanied by an image that could have illustrated the Ainur's music. In Salomo's description (chapter 30), the four singers are led by a *rector* (conductor), and their parts all relate to the bass, entering in progression from the lowest to the highest; eye-contact is indispensable. The attached image shows the four singers disposed as to form a crescent ("*ad modum lunae*," thus with an explicit cosmological reference) around a choirbook where the *cantus firmus* is visible by all. As Ferand[11] points out, the visual arrangement is such "that they are—literally—'bound' by the rules and directions, laid down for the first time, for four-part singing." The singers in the image wear robes embroidered with crescents or stars, which emphasizes the cosmological imagery. Both the *cantus firmus* and the rules of the treatise constitute the net of references and models which makes improvised polyphony possible. These laws are not seen as a straightjacket forcedly imposed onto the singers' freedom, but rather as their chance to create, with their music, an aural equivalent of the cosmological order symbolized by their robes and position.

The Ainur's Song and the Harmony of the Spheres

The mention of Salomo's description and of its cosmological traits leads us to discuss how the theme of the harmony of the spheres intertwined with Christian beliefs about the unending song of the angels.

I will not summarize here the immense fortune and popularity of the Pythagorean theme of *harmonia mundi* and of the music of the spheres, whose relationship with the *Ainulindalë* has already[12] been studied, but rather limit myself to a few examples. In Plato's *Republic* (617b), the spheres revolve around Necessity: upon them, eight Sirens are seated, and sing each

9. Busse Berger, *Medieval Music*, 162.

10. Salomo, "Scientia."

11. Ferand, "Howling," 318.

12. See Eden, "Music of the Spheres."

a note, making harmony together.[13] In the *Timaeus*, on the other hand, the topic of harmony is inextricably tied to the presentation of the World-Soul. Ptolemy (*Harmonics* 3.3) locates harmony between Nature and Divinity, binding it to Reason: "For it belongs eternally to the gods, who remain forever the same."[14]

Among the many developments of this enormously successful theme, I will cite a few which seem relevant here. For example, Giorgio Anselmi (ca. 1386–1443) described the "holy throngs of blessed spirits," who "contend in song and in the ineffable beauty of their rivalling hymns."[15] Anselmi's description of the singing Seraphim, the highest order of angels, is very close to that of Tolkien's Ainur:

> They exceed all the other orders of angels in wisdom and power and bliss, and also in joy; they . . . are called 'burning' because, having a fuller participation in the divine light, they are vouchsafed a more intense flame of love and joy and perfection. . . . [Their sphere] is the realm of eternal heaven, inaccessible to any creature of a lower one. This circle truly includes the melody of all those beneath it, utterly excelling all harmony.[16]

For Anselmi, "The very soul of this great heavenly motion . . . will conform in its harmonious sound to those divine spirits, so that all the different consonant notes may combine with one another." Still, these consonances will be continuously varied, "sounding now a fourth, now a fifth, now an octave," and the angels, with whom he identifies the Platonic Sirens, sing songs which "sound grander and more beautiful by their very diversity."[17]

In Shakespeare's *Merchant of Venice* (5.1), the centuries-old image of the harmony of the spheres is evoked by the "orb" which "in his motion like an angel sings, / Still quiring to the young-eyed cherubins."[18] The harmony "is in immortal souls," but their being incrusted by a "muddy vesture of decay" makes them unable to hear it.

13. These Sirens are interpreted as gods by Macrobius, an author of the fifth century CE. He also writes that "It is natural for everything that breathes to be captivated by music since the heavenly Soul that animates the universe sprang from music" (Godwin, *Harmony of the Spheres*, 66–68).

14. Godwin, *Harmony of the Spheres*, 23.

15. Godwin, *Harmony of the Spheres*, 146.

16. Godwin, *Harmony of the Spheres*, 150–51.

17. Godwin, *Harmony of the Spheres*, 148, 150, respectively.

18. Shakespeare, *Merchant of Venice*, 169.

Edmund Spenser, who penned *An Hymn in Honour of Beauty*, also makes a deep and significant connection between music, love, celestial harmony and beauty. In this poem, outward beauty is the visible manifestation of a soul's goodness; the soul is seen as a "fair lamp," "which kindleth lovers' fire," and which shall retire "unto her native planet" after the end of mortal life. For the poet,

> Love is a celestial harmony / of likely hearts compos'd of stars' concent, / which join together in sweet sympathy, / to work each other's joy and true content, / which they have harbour'd since their first descent / out of their heavenly bowers, where they did see / and know each other here belov'd to be.[19]

Here love harmonizes the spiritual union of the souls, "likely hearts compos'd of stars' concent," whose "sweet sympathy" originates in heaven. This varied, harmonious and complex polyphony is also described by Johann von Dalberg (1760–1812), who portrays Urania's ruling of the "circling of the spheres," while "the silent night and the young day rejoice in the magic of her melodious voice." Directed by Urania, "the solemn melody of the creation sounds forth in antiphonal choirs," while both heavens and morality "are tones of the universal symphony," created, ordered and tuned by an "all-uniting Spirit."[20]

It is of course difficult to demonstrate that Tolkien knew any of these sources directly; however, it is worth mentioning that the harmony of the spheres was given a Christian interpretation by St. Athanasius,[21] whose writings were studied in depth and translated into English by Tolkien's mentor Cardinal Newman, and that Tolkien's Christian education largely took place under the influence of Newman at the Oratory in Birmingham.[22] Thus, it is rather unsurprising to read the following passage in one of Newman's *Oxford University Sermons*:

> Is it possible that that inexhaustible evolution and disposition of notes, so rich yet so simple, so intricate yet so regulated, so various yet so majestic, should be a mere sound which is gone and perishes? Can it be that those mysterious stirrings of heart, and keen emotions, and strange yearnings after we know not what, and

19. Spenser, *Poetical Works*, 300–301.

20. Godwin, *Harmony of the Spheres*, 336.

21. See Godwin, *Harmony of the Spheres*, 48–50.

22. Of course, the role of music in the theological and pastoral view of St. Philip Neri is possibly unequalled in the Catholic experience.

> awful impressions from we know not whence, should be wrought in us by what is unsubstantial, and comes and goes, and begins and ends in itself? It is not so; it cannot be. No; they have escaped from some higher sphere; they are the outpourings of eternal harmony in the medium of created sound; they are echoes from our home; they are the voice of angels, or the *Magnificat* of saints, or the living laws of Divine governance, or the Divine attributes, something are they beside themselves, which we cannot compass, which we cannot utter.[23]

Traces of the Christian understanding and interpretations of the harmony of the spheres can be seen here. Newman's observations about the temporal and atemporal quality of music, linked to those about the "eternal harmony" manifesting itself in the actual reality of the sounds are clearly consistent with the view expressed by Tolkien in the *Ainulindalë*.[24]

Polyphony in Dante's *Commedia*

The "eternal harmony," the "voice of angels" and the "*Magnificat* of saints" mentioned by Newman had been given an unforgettable poetic expression, in the fourteenth century, in Dante's *Commedia*, on which I will focus now. Here, the polyphonic dimension is particularly pronounced, and interwoven with theological symbolism.[25] In turn, the Christian interpretation of the "harmony of the spheres" constitutes a cornerstone in Dante's depiction of the heavenly realm. In the *Commedia* Dante organizes the presence of Music in an entirely consistent fashion, and it becomes an instrument for transmitting deep theological truths. In brief, music is seen as a symbol of love, as regards the mystical love of God for human beings and theirs for God, as well as the love/*agape* among human beings.

23. Newman, *Fifteen Sermons*, 346–47. See also Bellasis, *Cardinal Newman*, in which the following motto excerpted from a poem by Newman is found: "Music's ethereal fire was given / Not to dissolve our clay, / But draw Promethean beams from Heaven, / And purge the dross away." Moreover, Newman defined music as "the expression of ideas greater and more profound than any in the visible world," centered in Him "who is the seat of all beauty, order and perfection whatever" (Newman, *Idea*, 80).

24. I am very grateful to my friend Giuseppe Scattolini for having pointed out the Athanasius/Newman/Tolkien connection for me.

25. The theological import of music in the *Commedia* has been discussed principally by Schurr (*Dante e la musica*), De Benedictis (*Ordine e struttura*) and Ciabattoni (*Dante's Journey*). For further discussion on my views of their writings see Bertoglio, *Through Music to Truth*, 11–40; "Vedere il tempo."

Following the scheme suggested by Boethius, who divided music into the categories of *instrumentalis*, *humana* and *mundana*, Dante creates a progression of perfection in the three ultramundane realms. In Hell, we find a cacophony originating from the absence of love: souls and demons are bent on their own hatred, and condemned to an existence deprived of beauty, solidarity and empathy.[26] The only musical element which survives the infernal anguish is *rhythm*, a basic element of music, represented by the micro- and macro-rhythms of punishments and torments. In fact, even the extreme disharmony of hell is, for Dante, a component of universal harmony, since the punishment of evil is part of God's justice and order sustaining the construction of the universe. Here, the *instrumentalis* element of music is represented by the numerous mentions of musical instruments. It is also represented by the degradation of human beings, whose original vocation is to "become music," according to the full meaning of *musica humana*, but who instead are made to resemble musical instruments (for example in the case of Mastro Adamo, *Inferno* 30:49–132, whose "body" seems a lute but sounds as a drum).

In the *Purgatorio*, "*musica humana*" has an ambivalent function, similar to love itself: in Ciabattoni's opinion,[27] it is mostly an instrument for the "healing" of both the human soul and of society. Through the monodic singing of the liturgical repertoire—known as "Gregorian"—the penitent souls learn to "attune" themselves with each other. Instead of the attempts to overcome the other's voice and of the uncontrolled cries found in Hell, we find the effort to attune one's voice with that of the other, and to rebuild the unity of intentions, identified in the common desire for heaven, which characterizes and unifies the purgatorial society. Moreover, monodic chant is a symbol of penance not only by virtue of the exertion it requires (i.e., the attempt to listen and to accept the note of the others), but also of its liturgical function (during times of penance, it was the only musical form admitted in the church's rites).

In Paradise, where *musica mundana* is found, Dante employs the musical symbol of polyphony—a relatively recent practice at his time—to signify the perfect balance of love and freedom. Whereas during one's life (and partially also in Purgatory) misguided love could cause sin, and

26. It may be interesting to cite Screwtape's contempt for both music and silence in *The Screwtape Letters* by C. S. Lewis. See Lewis, *Screwtape Letters*, 102–3.

27. Ciabattoni, *Dante's Journey*, 97. The topic is further developed at various points of Ciabattoni's book.

consequently limit one's true freedom (i.e., the liberty to choose the ultimate Good), now love and freedom coincide. The individual melodic lines of polyphony obey the laws of counterpoint embodied in the limitations posed by each part to the others (and this symbolizes true love). At the same time, the listener must receive an impression of total liberty and fluidity, whereby the coordination of the melodic lines is not perceived as an artifice and appears as the result of an organic and creative thought.[28] Moreover, as we have seen, polyphony is a particularly rich symbol for the trinitarian mystery, in which there is distinction, communion and perfect beauty: from the "polyphony" of the Trinity originates the perfect society of heaven. The souls who have undergone the monodic purification of Purgatory and have learnt to attune themselves with each other are now enabled to intertwine their voices freely in the polyphonic praise to the perfect beauty of God.

In Dante, then, the Pythagorean and Platonic theme of the harmony of the spheres[29] acquires an exquisitely Christian nuance. It also relates to an epistemological point, which can be summarized as follows. The ability to *improvise polyphonically* in concord is the result of a combination of factors: the perfect knowledge of each other which the blessed spirits draw from their contemplation of God;[30] their will to "accord" themselves with each other; their acceptance of the limits that one's melody will pose to that of the other; their construal of these limits as a gift enabling the heavenly concert to come to life, rather than as a deprivation of the individual's autonomy.

Finally, as pointed out by Schurr,[31] Dante establishes a narrative scheme in *Paradiso*, whereby singing and music dovetail with the *vision* and *movement* (dance) of the blessed spirits. Similar to polyphony, dance implies the coordination "for the beautiful" of free wills which renounce their individual caprice in order to achieve the happiness of society as a whole. Dance parallels polyphony in *Paradiso* as a symbol for bliss and for a pacific society. Roger Scruton has memorably written that dance "shows freedom and discipline united in a single gesture, and at the same time

28. I would like here to recall the beautiful definition of polyphony penned by Martin Luther: "While one and the same voice continues in its course, several voices play, exult, and adorn it with the most delightful gestures all round it in wondrous ways, and so to speak lead a kind of divine dance" (Luther, *Schriften*, 373; Loewe, "Musica est optimum," 602).

29. See Godwin, *Harmony of the Spheres*; Spitzer, *Classical and Christian*.

30. See *ST* III q. 92.

31. Schurr, *Dante e la musica*, 47.

made subject to the demands of social order." In many societies of the past, dancing was "a picture of the ideal, in which freedom and order are perfected and reconciled."[32] If singing polyphony demands one's availability to listen and to welcome the music of the others, dancing together requires that one should "make room" for the other, in a free coordination of the wills.

Improvisation and Models

In particular, both Dante and Tolkien employed the musical image of collective, polyphonic improvisation to symbolize and signify the perfect concord of a heavenly society of blessed beings who contemplate God, and who derive their ability to improvise together from this contemplation. It is a powerful and efficacious image: it springs from familiar experiences—the pleasure of making music together and the freedom to improvise—but at the same time expresses, in the combination of the two, a reality which is impossible to realize in our earthly condition. In fact, while collective improvisation is practiced in a variety of historical and cultural contexts, it depends on models and rules in order to achieve aesthetically valuable results.

For example, a genuine collective improvisation is found in jazz music, when "some or all members of a group participate in simultaneous improvisation of equal or comparable 'weight.'" It "implies a degree of equality between all the players in the ensemble,"[33] different from the hierarchical concept of soloist and accompanist(s) which characterizes most improvisations in jazz music. As in the early polyphony discussed above, it is far easier to obtain an aurally satisfying result when only one musician is free to improvise, and the other(s) perform a known scheme, tune or harmony, upon which the improvised part can move relatively freely. When two or more musicians improvise together, and when there is equality between them, "no matter how intimately they know one another's work, some agreed decisions about the progress of a piece are normally necessary"; thus, "certain prearranged schemes, such as the sequence in which soloists should play and the signals by which players will communicate decisions, are usually followed."[34]

32. Scruton, "Lost Love."

33. Kernfeld, "Improvisation" 3.2.

34. Kernfeld, "Improvisation" 3.3.

Improvisation, according to Bjerstedt et al., can also foster the development of a different concept of the "now." In their view, the improviser experiments an "intensification of the present," and an "awareness of past-future dimensions," which they describe as "a need for *multidirectionality* in the musical improviser's attention."[35] This awareness of the "now" projects itself into the past and the future, encompassing them in an overall narrative. In consequence, the processes of (jazz) improvisation can be understood as a "storytelling perspective," with the improviser's imagination, according to Ed Sarath, working "both in a moment-to-moment manner and as a teleological (past-present-future) structure."[36]

The capability to navigate time, conceived as multidirectional and layered, and to coordinate past, present, and future as in storytelling enables improvisers to experience a different temporality through music. In the heavenly society portrayed by Tolkien and Dante, these processes happen effortlessly and spontaneously; in the musical experiences we are familiar with, improvisers need a shared language and an agreed structure.

In jazz music the improvising musicians constantly refer to "prearranged schemes," such as, for example, harmonic and chordal sequences. These can be considered as the *model* for their improvisation; as Nettl[37] puts it, a model is a "point of departure used as the basis of performance. No improvised performance is totally without stylistic or compositional basis. The number and kinds of obligatory features (referred to here as the 'model') vary by culture and genre." Since models may take a variety of shapes according to their historical-geographical context, one culture's concept of musical improvisation may be very different from another. In the case of Western medieval improvised polyphony, "the model may be a tune sung by one voice (against which the other is to improvise) and a set of allowable harmonic intervals as well as their characteristic sequences."[38]

The "model," whatever its nature, is therefore both a help and a limitation for the creativity of the improviser. The techniques used by musical improvisers in the Middle Ages are, for many aspects, akin to those employed by orators in classical antiquity, as shown by Busse Berger.[39] She established that the elaboration of speech, similar to that of musical

35. Bjerstedt et al., "Musical Present," 26.

36. Sarath, "New Look," 19.

37. Nettl, "Improvisation" 1.3.

38. Nettl, "Thoughts," 12.

39. Busse Berger, *Medieval Music*, 215.

improvisations, is based on the memorization of "a background grid of places, say an architectural structure," which is then visualized when the speech is delivered: "thus the art of memory is a kind of imaginary writing."[40] This combination of imaginary visualization, memory, creativity and aural result is highly relevant both to polyphonic improvisation (as, for instance, in faburden singing, with the "sights") and to the Ainur's music, where music and vision are intimately intertwined. If a visualized or otherwise retained model is indispensable for the creation, elaboration, and delivery of a verbal or musical composition which is not read contextually to its performance, the models for improvisation might also be seen as limits or limitations to the improviser's fantasy.

Polyphony and Relationship

In our society, which prizes autonomy and self-determination above most other values, limits and limitations have an inherently negative connotation. However, both in the "real" Middle Ages when polyphony was created and in the fictional epic past of Tolkien, limits are given to created beings for their own good, as the boundary within which they can flourish in fullness. Writing with reference to Dante's Ulysses, who defies the Pillars of Hercules which delimit human knowledge, Montemaggi argued that these Pillars are a gift. They are "a reminder that ultimate comprehension of the world is not even in principle available to human beings." All alternative construal of their reality implies that we misunderstand "what it means to say 'God', or the fact that God is love." Limits therefore prompt us to remember that the individual's "pursuit of knowledge" should "never lose sight of the proper dynamics of community."[41]

Completely free improvisation is possible only in the absolute absence of relationships. In fact, even a solo improviser who is singing according to his or her own fantasy will do so within a framework of rules (at least the rules guiding pitch and rhythm), and these will make his or her improvisation meaningful and therefore intelligible for the listeners. Absolute freedom implies incommunicability. The Ainur's improvisation must therefore take into account their relationship with Ilúvatar and with the themes ("models") he "declares" to them, and the contemporaneous musical intentions of their brethren.

40. Busse Berger, *Medieval Music*, 215.

41. Montemaggi, "In Unknowability," 73–74.

Polyphonic improvisation is therefore deeply relational. It is also a kind of game, where rules are given and accepted for the purpose of mutual enjoyment. Dante used the term "*gioco*" (play, game) to depict blessed life (*Purgatorio* 28:96; *Paradiso* 20:117). This "*gioco*" is the framework within which "the flourishing of virtue, of the dynamics of community" are made possible.[42] Music offers us the gratuitous enjoyment of beauty which characterizes play in its highest essence, and which can therefore be seen as a symbol for the contemplation of God. As Mazzotta[43] suggests, commenting on Dante, "As the creation of the soul is grounded in God's play activity, this view of God means that to play is to accept rules established by God; it also means that man is not to play God, but to be content with God's play as he lets the soul play." Playfulness, thus, transforms both rules and limits into gifts enabling creativity and freedom.

This perspective faithfully echoes Augustine's view of a perfect society: "The peace of the celestial city is the perfectly ordered and harmonious enjoyment of God and one another in God."[44] Augustine further develops the musical concept of harmony in its aural implications in the same work,[45] where he suggests that the concord of diversity is not just the actual reality of the heavenly city, but also the ideal model for a peaceful earthly society. This concept was developed throughout the history of the Christian thought, up to present-day. In fact, one of the greatest modern Catholic theologians, Hans Urs von Balthasar, defined Truth as being "symphonic," and described it in tones highly reminiscent of the Ainur's concert: "In his revelation, God performs a symphony, and it is impossible to say which is richer: the seamless genius of his composition or the polyphonous orchestra of Creation that he has prepared to play it . . . The unity of the composition comes from God." For Balthasar, in a fashion similar to the Ainur's at the beginning of their musical attempts, musicians tuning up their instruments before the concert "stand or sit next to one another as strangers"; but later "they realize how they are integrated. Not in unison, but what is far more beautiful—in *sym-phony*." And it is precisely by means of limits that the symphony is made possible: "Today's situation . . . is characterized by an impatient tugging at the framework of a unity that is felt to be a prison. Isn't it unjust that a melody is trapped within a triple fugue, and that the law

42. Montemaggi, "In Unknowability," 76.

43. Mazzotta, *Dante's Vision*, 227.

44. Augustine, *De Civitate Dei* 19.13; cf. *City of God*, 2:319.

45. Augustine, *De Civitate Dei* 2.21; cf. *City of God*, 1:74–77.

of the fugue governs how it shall develop—and even determines its original shape?"[46] In every polyphonic work, be it composed or improvised, the very fact of singing or playing together implies reciprocal limitations. These are, however, the necessary condition for all relationality and for the very existence of a polyphonic composition (such as a fugue, for instance).

This relational aspect—which is at the root of our discussion of collective improvisation—was conceived in musical terms by yet another great modern theologian, the Lutheran Dietrich Bonhoeffer, who maintained that our love for God should be the *cantus firmus* of our lives, with all other loves, relationships and interests constituting a counterpoint to it: "Where the *cantus firmus* is clear and plain, the counterpoint can be developed to its limits. . . . I wanted to tell you to have a good, clear *cantus firmus*: that is the only way to a full and perfect sound, when the counterpoint has a firm support and can't come adrift or get out of tune, while remaining a distinct whole in its own right."[47]

Limits, Limitations, and Freedom

Trying to understand the *Ainulindalë* within a theological perspective, this chapter has shown the following:

1. God's self-revelation is a gift freely bestowed on his creatures (Ilúvatar's declarations of his theme).
2. This revelation can only take place within the framework of a reciprocally and mutually loving relationship (the Ainur's knowledge of the "part of the mind" of Ilúvatar).
3. Through this revelation a creature not only learns something about God (by partaking in the Truth which He is), but also discovers the truth about him- or herself, as well as that about his or her brethren (the Ainur's listening to their brethren).
4. This revelation enables all creatures to realize their deepest vocation and to fulfil their potential (the Ainur's initial monodic singing).
5. When a created being contemplates the truth in God, he or she partakes in the knowledge of God's loving plan for the created world, in

46. Balthasar, *Truth Is Symphonic*, 7–8.

47. Bonhoeffer, *Letters*, 106.

which He wills the good of all creatures (the Ainur's learning of truths about Ilúvatar through their listening of their brethren).

6. When a created being fully and freely adheres to God's loving design about him or her, the creature's freedom is perfect, since we are really free only when we will what is good for us, and this coincides with God's will (the Ainur's adornment of the theme).
7. Therefore, the perfect society as willed by God is one where all are utterly free, all fully realize themselves, and all are in harmony with all others (the Ainur's polyphony and that depicted by Dante in the *Paradiso*).

This summary allows us to observe an important fact, i.e., that freedom does not coincide with arbitrariness and caprice, and that limits may be a gift. Tolkien was keenly aware of this truth, to the extent that he defined mortality as not only the Doom, but rather the "Gift of Men."[48] By establishing a boundary to our earthly life, death is what prompts us to create, to pro-create, to work and therefore to fulfil our potential. Similarly, in polyphonic music, the rules of counterpoint, strict as they may occasionally appear, are what enables the composer's creativity to blossom and flourish, and what ultimately creates the impression of coordinated freedom which characterizes contrapuntal music. By accepting Ilúvatar's theme as their *cantus firmus*, and the relationship with the other Ainur as the context of their musicianship, the heavenly musicians are enabled to create music at its most perfect and beautiful.

48. Tolkien, *Silmarillion*, xiv.

7

Discord and Dissonance

As readers of Tolkien's *Ainulindalë* will know, that state of perfect harmony was doomed not to last. Following once more the Christian theological tradition, and at the same time reinterpreting it creatively, Tolkien narrates the fall of the most perfect and gifted of the Ainur, Melkor/Morgoth. Similar to Lucifer/Satan, the creature on which the greatest gifts have been bestowed rebels against the divine will, out of pride and envy. Clearly the rebellious angel is not to be considered as a champion of free thought, who boldly dares to challenge a tyrannical being; rather, he is to be seen as someone who radically misunderstands the deep relationship binding God's gift of himself to his creatures, and the tie which unites knowledge, freedom, self-realization and acceptance of the other. As Edith Stein summarized it, "Though angels have an original store of knowledge, not acquired in the course of their existence but pertaining to their very being, they have nevertheless received this knowledge simultaneously with their being. A refusal to 'accept' amounts in this case to a rebellious opposition to their own true being."[1] By locating the origins of evil in this primeval disobedience, the Judeo-Christian tradition has acknowledged that intelligent beings can find their true happiness only in their joyful and free adhesion to God's will.

And this is one of the responses to some of the crucial questions which have given birth to all philosophy over the course of human history. Where does the world come from? What is the origin of evil? Why are suffering and death part of our world? Once the existence of one or more divine beings is posited, these questions may take a more direct and almost defiant

1. Stein, *Finite and Eternal Being*, 402.

shape. If there is an omnipotent *and* benevolent being, Why is the existence of evil tolerated? Why is there such a thing as evil?

One possible answer to these terrible questions affirms that the benign divine being is not absolutely omnipotent, but has to contend continually with one (or more) equally divine beings who are entirely evil (or who have some traits we identify as evil, such as bellicosity). This view has come to be identified with Manichaeism, but is also present in several religions and philosophies, and regularly resurfaces across time and space. History is therefore seen as the battle-field between the good and evil powers, and human beings frequently represent the (innocent) casualties of this divine war.

The Christian response to the problem of evil and suffering is both simple and complex. It is simple, since it is first and primarily an icon, rather than a theory: the icon of the crucified and risen Christ, whose paschal mystery embodied—in a surprising and powerful fashion—both the goodness and the omnipotence of God. It is complex since, beyond this immediate and visible answer, it admits several, sometimes deeply conflicting philosophical/theological accounts of *how* God's benevolence and omnipotence are shown in Christ's Passion and resurrection. One of the most compelling theological explanations of the origin of evil is that of St. Augustine, who worked out his philosophical and spiritual theology precisely in response to—and against—the Manichaean view, to which he had previously adhered. Simplistically summarized, this "evil" is in fact a non-entity, a non-being. It is to Being what darkness is to light, i.e., a lack of goodness.[2] Augustine understands that to materialize or personalize evil is to fall for prey to the Manichean heresy.

Augustine's view, although enormously influential in the history of Christian thought and of Western philosophy in general, was by no means the only response to the problem of evil. Actually, several theologies which acknowledged their common origin in his thought ended up with intensely divergent results. In particular, with the advent of modernity, a need for a "theodicy" made itself felt. Events such as the Lisbon earthquake of 1755 caused an intellectual and emotional scandal to arise and prompted some of the most prominent thinkers to set up God in the tribunal of reason, to ask Him to excuse himself for the unaccountable suffering of many innocents. "Theodicy" came to be seen as the "vindication" of God: although

2. See Milbank, *Chesterton and Tolkien*, 75–76, as concerns the Thomist theology of Tolkien (which in this instance is derived from an Augustinian model).

frequently assuming the form of an *ex-officio* defense of God's will, it also implicitly admitted the human beings' right to challenge God on the ground of the problem of evil. While this move is theologically problematic, since created beings are by definition incapable of "comprehending" the fullness of the mystery of God, it has an authoritative precedent in the Bible itself, where Job, a righteous man, requires from God an explanation for his suffering. The "theodicies" of Job's friends constitute a great part of the eponymous book, only to be ultimately discarded by God himself, who reveals his glory to Job alone. In this Old-Testament book, therefore, we find two different accounts of God's reaction to the challenges posed by human suffering. On the one hand, God seems to accept this confrontation, and is more favorable to Job's protest than to his friends' well-meaning justifications of God (Job 42:7). On the other hand, God's response to Job is an assertion of His omnipotence and of the inscrutable wisdom of His ways, which no created being can tread or understand (Job 38). From the Christian's point of view, Job's questions will have to wait until Calvary for the ultimate answer. And even at Calvary, it is debatable whether or not a purely "logical" account of the origin of evil can be provided. In other words, it is open to question whether any theodicy is sustainable, arguable, or even satisfactorily expressible.

What has been succinctly sketched here constitutes the core of some of the most important, pressing, and heated debates in the history of human thought. Tolkien's choice to represent the problem of evil through musical symbols is deeply rooted in this tradition, both theologically and culturally.

The Ainur's Polyphony

As we saw earlier, the enchantment of musical polyphony is due to the seeming freedom and independence of its various melodic lines, which ought to be independent and musically interesting on their own terms. However, the shape of each line is heavily conditioned and partly determined by the rules of good voice-leading, applied to the actual requirements of the specific individual lines which have already been composed.

Furthermore, with the affirmation of tonal language in music (sixteenth and seventeenth century), composers of polyphonic works had to think both "horizontally" and "vertically." "Horizontal" composition implies the successive and orderly elaboration of each individual melodic line, which has to be interesting, seemingly free and spontaneous, and yet has to obey the contrapuntal laws with reference to the other parts. In this way each part determines and is determined by the others. "Vertical" composition implies that the overall musical direction of the work corresponds to a harmonic chordal plan, with the "chords" created vertically by the simultaneous resonance of the various horizontal lines giving the listener an impression of purpose, musical teleology, and finality. Chords are the seemingly involuntary by-product of the seemingly haphazard meeting of seemingly independent melodic lines. Yet, the listener must feel a logic, a cogency, and sense the purposeful creation of the composer's mind and creative intention behind this game of intertwining voices.[3]

When the Ainur start to sing together they are enabled to improvise polyphonically by their increased and loving knowledge of their brethren's music, which represents an increased knowledge and love of their Creator. Their "harmony" arises from the reciprocal concord of their free wills and of their tunes, bearing witness to Ilúvatar's omniscience and goodness.

Melkor's "Music"

Melkor's fall is described in exquisitely musical terms in the *Ainulindalë*: "As the theme progressed, it came into the heart of Melkor to interweave matters of his own imagining that were not in accord with the theme of Ilúvatar; for he sought therein to increase the power and glory of the part assigned to himself."[4] Melkor's knowledge of his brethren is as perfect as possible for any created being ("he had a share in all the gifts of his brethren"[5]). However, his willingness to adjust his tune to those of the others decreases progressively as he starts to weave an accompanied monody, a soloistic melody to which the others create a musical background.

As we have seen, the Ainur's *cantus firmus* was the theme "propounded" to them by Ilúvatar, in its unadorned form;[6] Melkor wanted to replace Ilúvatar's theme with his own as the determining principle of musical

3. See Mersmann's definition: "Musical events take place in two dimensions: in the temporal succession of the tone sequences, which can be called horizontal in the applied use of the concept of space, and in the simultaneity of sound formations, which is conceptually linked to the vertical" (Mersmann, *Angewandte Musikästhetik*, 9).

4. Tolkien, *Silmarillion*, 16.

5. Tolkien, *Silmarillion*, 16.

6. As seen in the preceding chapters, most *cantus firmus* were sung in long note-values, while the upper parts were more richly decorated.

composition. If the presence of a model and of limits is the necessary condition for a successful collective improvisation, Melkor's failure to accept the "rules of the game" (i.e., the primacy of Ilúvatar's *cantus firmus* and of the model it represents) causes the disruption of the Ainur's polyphony.

Tolkien describes this tragic disorder: "Some of these thoughts he now wove into his music, and straightway discord arose about him, and many that sang nigh him grew despondent, and their thought was disturbed and their music faltered, but some began to attune their music to his rather than to the thought which they had at first."[7] Melkor has begun to transform polyphony into accompanied monody. The growth of the importance of his part begins to reduce the freedom of the others, and threatens their fullness and integrity of being. In Ilúvatar's plan, the musical space of everyone was harmoniously integrated with the others. By responding faithfully to Ilúvatar's call, each of the Ainur could express himself or herself in fullness, and this fullness of being simultaneously produced the most beautiful polyphony. By following Melkor, his disciples become accompanists instead of polyphonists, while all the others are forced to stay silent in puzzlement or to shout in the attempt to silence him. Melkor's disobedience destroys the delicate balance of the polyphonic game, and creates a deep chasm, which contradicts the ideal described by Cunningham:

> Polyphony could theoretically be either "harmonious" or "dissonant." Its chief attribute is simultaneous, non-excluding difference: That is, more than one note is played at a time, and none of these notes is so dominant that it renders another mute.[8]

Through Melkor's rebellion, the Music becomes discordant ("*discord* arose about him"[9]): I will now focus on this term. Some Tolkien scholars have understood "discord" to be synonymous with *dissonance*, even to the extent of replacing one with the other in their discussion.[10] Instead, as the following sections of this chapter will show, the two terms are not interchangeable, and their semantic history helps to shed light on the philosophical structure of the *Ainulindalë*. The role of dissonance, its dynamic function and its importance for musical composition have been the focus of "musical theodicy," whose history I will cursorily summarize. While I will not claim that

7. Tolkien, *Silmarillion*, 16.

8. Cunningham, *These Three Are One*, 129.

9. Tolkien, *Silmarillion*, 16 (my emphasis).

10. Naveh, "Tonality," 31.

Tolkien was familiar with any or all of the sources I will cite, I am persuaded that his use of the term *discord* (instead of *dissonance*) was purposeful, and corresponded to the cultural framework of its semantic history.

Discord and Dissonance

The linguistic histories of *discord* and *dissonance* (or rather of their positive homologues, *concord* and *consonance*) are, of course, deeply intertwined. In his fundamental study of *harmony* and its related terms, Spitzer demonstrates the connection between the Latin words *concordia* and *consonantia*.[11] For him, "Due to a particular coincidence not extant in Greek, there was in Latin a radical *cord-* susceptible to two interpretations: it could be connected not only with *cor, cordis*, 'heart' (which was the original meaning), but also with *chorda*, 'string.'"[12] The Latin *concordia* therefore had the double meaning of an agreement of hearts and of a harmony of (musical) strings.

Musically, however, these semantically related terms took on a distinct technical meaning,[13] as I will now proceed to demonstrate. The English word *chord*, derived from the family of *concordia*,[14] nowadays indicates the simultaneous sounding of three or more sounds disposed in thirds. Chords form the basis of *harmony* (here understood as another technical term, meaning the technique of putting chords in succession, the "vertical" form of composition). Chords are made of *intervals*, intervals being the difference in pitch between two sounds. And intervals have been traditionally classified as *consonant* and *dissonant*, even though historically there has been a fluctuation in the categorization of some, depending on various factors linked sometimes to aural feelings, in other cases to mathematical ratios.[15] In turn, chords can be *consonant* or *dissonant*. Traditionally, *triads* consisting of two thirds superimposed to each other and are consonant chords,

11. Spitzer, *Armonia del mondo*, 89.

12. Spitzer, *Classical and Christian*, 84.

13. Of course, I cannot demonstrate that Tolkien was aware of the technicalities of the musical lexicon. However, "dissonance" would have been the most obvious choice both musically and linguistically; moreover, my analysis discusses a literary work rather than its author's intentions. The use of *discord* in Tolkien's literary work seems, in my eyes, a significant and meaningful choice.

14. Spitzer, *Armonia del mondo*, 94.

15. Cazden, "Definition."

while chords with more than three sounds are dissonant (for example the seventh-chord, e.g., C-E-G-B). In traditional harmony and counterpoint, both dissonant intervals and dissonant chords are said to tend to the point of *resolution*, and this follows precise rules: for example, the dissonant interval F-B regularly tends to E-C. In this way dissonances operate as the propelling force of music. A dissonance creates expectations in the listener, and the composer plays with such expectations, either fulfilling or thwarting them.[16] Consequently, the creation of a musical dissonance is one of the guiding principles of musical harmonic writing. In musical terms, dissonance is indispensable for harmony.

However, the new Vulgar Latin verb **acc(h)ordare* lies both at the etymological root of the English *chord*, and of Neo-Latin words such as the Italian *accordare*, which has multiple meanings, including to tune an instrument ("*accordare uno strumento*"), to attune one's voice with those of the others (*accordarsi*), and to agree on something (*accordarsi*). As seen above, in Tolkien's narrative some of the Ainur start to "*attune* their music"[17] to Melkor's: in my opinion, Tolkien chose these words also by virtue of their technical meaning. Melkor does not simply insert *dissonances* into the Music, he wants to insert a new germinating principle, a new guiding logic, a new *idea* into the Music. On the contrary, music listeners understand the dynamic function of dissonances as fundamental components in the game of memory and expectation. They are part of the language of tonal music: they *make sense*. They are not simply tolerated as disruptions of an otherwise beautiful musical consonance; they give meaning to consonances, by linking them purposefully.[18]

In spite of this, the dynamic power of dissonance has frequently been seen to lie in its "displeasing" or "disagreeable" aural quality: dissonances lead to consonances precisely by exploiting the listeners' uneasiness in hearing them, and thus by making hearers wish that a state of quiet is achieved. While the pleasure (or lack thereof) of dissonances is a matter for disciplines such as the psychology of music, we may take these traditional statements at face-value, since they were commonly accepted at Tolkien's time. Given these elements, I will now proceed with a survey of literature to

16. See chapter 3.

17. Tolkien, *Silmarillion*, 16 (my emphasis).

18. It is interesting to compare this discussion with the terminology proposed by Stumpf with regard to intervals and chords: "Stumpf proposed that the terms concordance and discordance be applied to the embodiments of chordal actions that were perceived to operate on the higher level of functional harmony" (Cazden, "Definition," 151).

place the concepts of dissonance and discord in a larger historical context, in preparation for the discussion of musical theodicy.

The Fall and the Universal Music

As seen above, the idea of the universe as a *harmonious* entity, whose *symphony* mirrors its orderly structure, created by God, is an extremely ancient and pervasive concept with Pythagorean roots, and whose development has been traced in recent times by Godwin and Spitzer. What does not *accord* with this overall harmony of the cosmos—such as, for us humans, our own suffering and death—has frequently been seen as a disruption.

Honorius of Autun (ca. 1080–1154) likened the universe to a cithara created by God, in which He willed variety in order to create "manifold sounds." The harmonious consonance of those praising God is due to the lack of envy among the blessed spirits: all rejoice in their own glory, and none craves the gifts of others. However, free intelligent creatures such as angels and humans may opt for a lesser good rather than the supreme good, who is God. Honorius likens those who opt for a lesser good to "dissonant strings in the great cithara." By relegating them to a "lower place"—Honorius's word may indicate both a physical position and a low sound—God manages to re-establish an overall harmony. As symbolized by Tolkien's Ilúvatar, the Christian God may reweave even the disobedience of the "dissonant strings" within a greater harmony,[19] and as symbolized in Dante's cosmology, even hell constitutes a fundamental part of the order of the universe.

Much later, the English poet John Donne (1572–1631) wrote of the angels' fall in a manner close to Tolkien's musical mythology: "God made this whole world in such a uniformity, such a *correspondency*, such a *concinnity* of parts that it was an *Instrument, perfectly in tune*: we may say, the trebles, the highest strings were disordered first; the best understandings, angels and men, put this instrument out of tune."[20] Here, as in the *Ainulindalë*, the responsibility for the origin of evil is attributed to "the best understandings," "the highest strings." I find it significant that Donne, like Honorius, speaks of *strings* (*chordae* in Latin, *corde* in Italian) and of an *out of tune* (*scordato*, in Italian) instrument.

19. Honorius of Autun, *Liber XII Quaestionum* (*PL* 172) 2 (1179); 4 (1180).

20. Donne, *Sermons*, 2:170.

Later still, Louis-Claude de Saint-Martin (1743–1803) discussed the "origin of dissonance" in a similar fashion. He built his account on the commonly acknowledged definition of the triad as the perfect chord, frequently adopted as a symbol for the Christian Trinity.[21] Consequently, he suggested that the seventh-chord resulted from a "lack of perfection" in a triad. Considering a triad whose tonic is doubled at the octave (e.g., C-E-G-C), the upper C may "fail" to reach his perfection and remain below its goal (on the lower note of B), therefore producing an "imperfect" seventh-chord (C-E-G-B). It is important here to note that Saint-Martin is speaking of chords isolated from their musical context, such as a seventh-chord, which is perceived as "evil" because of its supposedly disagreeable sound. Saint-Martin wrote:

> If [the triad] had remained forever in its natural state, order and just harmony would have lasted perpetually, and evil would have been unknown because it would never have been born. . . . How then was it possible for the second Principle to become evil? How could evil have taken birth and appeared? Was it not because the superior and dominant note of the common chord, namely the octave, was suppressed, and another note introduced in its place?[22]

As in the *Ainulindalë*, the "second Principle"—i.e., the created being who resembled most closely the Creator—"became evil," and the note he was supposed to sing was replaced with another. A more complex and ambiguous stance was proposed a century later by the Franciscan Fr Peter Singer (1810–1882), who wrote:

> It seems that in these primordial intervals, still existing in the tone-world, the Creator has given us an eloquent picture of the original creation; for according to the most learned theologians, the original harmonies continued so long as sin had not entered into the world. Angelic and human nature were to have lived in recognition and love of the threefold primordial being without compulsion, in joyful recognition of their dependence and in free-willing realization of their final goal; they were to add their part to his outward glorification as they passed through their period of trial; then after their course was run, they would be taken up into

21. See Bertoglio, "Perfect Chord."

22. In Godwin, *Harmony of the Spheres*, 326. I have elsewhere argued that, in Bach's music, motifs "aiming" at a melodic interval of sixth but reaching it only by "sliding upwards" represent longing and desire, and thus embody a painful lack of perfection. See Bertoglio, *Through Music to Truth*, 107–78, esp. 141–50.

> eternal bliss—into the unmediated contemplation and the eternal joy of their highest and only good.[23]

Note that Singer links his argument to the symbolic value of the triad as an image of the Trinity ("the threefold primordial being"), and that he points out the "dependence" of the blessed spirits' music from God's and their "free-willing" acceptance of his plan as "their final goal." These correspond to my account of the role of polyphonic rules and of the limits they pose for individual melodies within it. Furthermore, Singer envisages a primeval and eschatological concert very similar to Tolkien's ultimate Great Music:

> Never since have the Ainur made any music like to this music, though it has been said that a greater still shall be made before Ilúvatar by the choirs of the Ainur and the Children of Ilúvatar after the end of days. Then the themes of Ilúvatar shall be played aright, and take Being in the moment of their utterance, for all shall then understand fully his intent in their part, and each shall know the comprehension of each, and Ilúvatar shall give to their thoughts the secret fire, being well pleased.[24]

Singer thus gave voice to what the created world might have been, had God's "harmonious" plan not been compromised by sin and fallenness. Naturally Singer's Christian view infuses his vision with nostalgic regret for a Paradise Lost, but foremost with the hope for a symphony of redemption to resound in the future *eschaton*. As Dostoevsky put it, "the Hosanna must be tried in the crucible of doubt."[25] The eternal symphony does not eschew the disagreeable dissonances of our earthly life, with its sin, doubts, the evil we have done and undergone. Similarly, though without referring explicitly to Christ's salvific mission in the reconciliation of the fallen world with God, the *Ainulindalë* prophesies a new Great Music, whose beauty will exceed that of the Ainur alone.

Responding to Discord

The Christian Paschal mystery does provide an answer to the question as to how a perfect music can arise from the fallen and suffering world we know; whereas, in the absence of this *crucial* event, the question remains open

23. Godwin, *Harmony of the Spheres*, 367.

24. Tolkien, *Silmarillion*, 15–16.

25. Dostoevsky, *Brothers Karamazov*, 732.

in Tolkien's *legendarium*. How will Ilúvatar respond to Melkor's music? If Melkor is truly capable of creating a music of his own without referring to Ilúvatar's theme, then does Melkor have a divine quality in competition with Ilúvatar's? If not—and if Melkor's music is, in its own fashion, a variation of the divine theme—then did Ilúvatar's original plan include the presence of evil?

Tolkien responds to some of these questions in an unambiguous fashion. Ilúvatar's reply is articulated in a series of actions. Firstly he *listens* ("Ilúvatar sat and hearkened"[26]): Tolkien's God respects the free will of his creatures. Then he rises, smiling, and lifts up his left hand: a new theme by Ilúvatar is heard, but Melkor strives against it and "there was a war of sound."[27] Ilúvatar arises again, with a "stern" expression, lifting up his right hand and creating a third theme: "there were two musics progressing at one time . . . and they were utterly at variance."[28] Ilúvatar's third theme is "deep and wide and beautiful, but slow and blended with an immeasurable sorrow, from which its beauty chiefly came";[29] against this, Melkor's music sounds "loud, and vain, and endlessly repeated"—reminiscent perhaps of a caricature of military music. The "most triumphant notes" of Melkor's music are "taken by the other and woven into its own solemn pattern."[30] Finally, Ilúvatar arises for the third time, with a "terrible" countenance, raising both hands, "and in one chord, deeper than the Abyss, higher than the Firmament, piercing as the light of the eye of Ilúvatar, the Music ceased."

Tolkien's narrative suggests some considerations. First of all, Ilúvatar's second and third theme originates from his "facial" expressions and from the gestures of his hands. Although it is never stated that Ilúvatar "sings" or makes music, the anthropomorphic description of Tolkien's God drives our attention to the relational quality of Ilúvatar's actions. He sits while he listens to the first disturbance introduced to the music by Melkor; then he arises, thrice, and by this "bodily" move he draws attention to his deeds and affirms his power. Then he responds by means of his "countenance" and hand gestures, which seem to be translated into sound. Every action of Tolkien's God is a Revelation of his Being: everything Ilúvatar does in the presence of the Ainur is a disclosure of his divine nature.

26. Tolkien, *Silmarillion*, 16.
27. Tolkien, *Silmarillion*, 16.
28. Tolkien, *Silmarillion*, 16.
29. Tolkien, *Silmarillion*, 17.
30. Tolkien, *Silmarillion*, 17.

Secondly, the narrative also shows that Ilúvatar does not try to avoid a direct confrontation with Melkor's music; indeed, it is "taken by the other and woven into its own solemn pattern."[31] Ilúvatar is shown as consistently transmuting Melkor's rebellious acts of defiance into something beautiful, which surprises the Ainur and reveals to them Ilúvatar's wisdom and omnipotence. For example, the disastrous frost with which Melkor seeks to destroy Ulmo's splendid realm of the waters[32] produces the enchantment of snow and ice through the combination of Melkor's evil glacial winds with Ulmo's water. Ulmo, in awe, acknowledges Ilúvatar's capacity to turn evil into something which exceeds in beauty and goodness the Ainur's original plan, saying: "Truly, Water is become now fairer than my heart imagined, neither had my secret thought conceived the snowflake, nor in all my music was contained the falling of the rain."[33] What is exemplified in this episode is generalized by Ilúvatar himself a few lines earlier: "And thou, Melkor, wilt discover all the secret thoughts of thy mind, and wilt perceive that they are but a part of the whole and tributary to its glory"; in fact "no theme may be played that hath not its uttermost source in me, nor can any alter the music in my despite. For he that attempteth this shall prove but mine instrument in the devising of things more wonderful, which he himself hath not imagined."[34]

Halsall comments that such views bespeak of a vision close to the paradoxical *felix culpa* of the Christian faith, in which sin can be blessed for having earned such a redemption as that realized by Christ on the cross. Halsall is careful to point out that "Ilúvatar did not plan for Melkor's rebellion, nor his temporal effect in Middle-earth via his discordant music becoming reality." Melkor's distorted use of free will "is but an opportunity for the greater diversity, plenitude and experience of grace in Creation as gift".[35] This view is inherently Augustinian, as maintained in the *City of God*: "It is true that wicked men do many things contrary to God's will; but so great is His wisdom and power, that all things which seem adverse to His purpose

31. Tolkien, *Silmarillion*, 17.

32. Tolkien, *Silmarillion*, 19.

33. Tolkien, *Silmarillion*, 19.

34. Tolkien, *Silmarillion*, 17. As Edith Stein put it, "[Satan] wants to be like God, and he therewith, even in warring against God, affirms divine being" (Stein, *Finite and Eternal Being*, 403).

35. Halsall, "Critical Assessment," 63.

do still tend towards those just and good ends and issues which He Himself has foreknown."[36]

It will be recalled that Melkor's rebellion takes place within the framework of a collective improvisation, and the dynamics described in the *Ainulindalë* resonate with the actual practices of improvisation. In fact, musicological studies on collective improvisation have highlighted the importance of "concepts of risk, competence, dealing with unexpected situations and making positive use of mistakes."[37] Ilúvatar seems to accept the "risk" of giving freedom to his creatures, and his second and third themes deal with the chaos created by Melkor's music. Ilúvatar makes "positive use" of the negative elements Melkor has inserted in the Music. As Augustine wrote in the *City of God*,

> When [God] foreknew that certain angels would in their pride desire to suffice for their own blessedness, and would forsake their great good, did not deprive them of this power, deeming it to be more befitting His power and goodness to bring good out of evil than to prevent the evil from coming into existence.[38]

Similarly, Tolkien presents evil as a transient aspect and as something which will ultimately contribute to the overarching symphony of creation. His narrative seems to imply that to consider evil as evil is almost an error caused by the creature's ignorance of God's mind. The lack of logical explanation for evil causes us to rebel against what we perceive as our unjust suffering; our failure to understand will, however, dissolve itself when the Great Music will resound, and we will be able to penetrate more deeply into the mysterious ways of the divine Being. Returning to the musical symbolism, we feel the music as disagreeable because we lack the capacity of perceiving the compositional logic of its harmony; it is as if we were able to apprehend one chord at a time, and would feel the dissonant chords as displeasing only because we are presently denied the experience of their resolution (more on this later).

This strongly suggests to me that Tolkien intended Ilúvatar's fourth "musical" intervention, which is a one-chord theme, to be not an

36. Augustine, *De Civitate Dei* 22.2; *City of God*, 2:474.

37. Nettl, "Improvisation" 1.1. The concept of risk applied to the Godhead in a context of salvation (soteriology) is found, for example, in Rowan Williams's interpretation of Karl Barth: "God, for our sakes, 'risks' his very identity" (Williams, "Barth on the Triune God," 130).

38. St. Augustine, *De Civitate Dei* 22.2; *City of God*, 2:474.

"interruption" of the Music, but rather a chord which brings it to a resolution. It may also be just an intermediate stage (similar, if the analogy is permitted, to the chord closing the exposition of a sonata-form on the dominant), but it is not an abrupt silencing of the Music: it is a provisional—though at the same time accomplished—resolution.[39]

Providence and Cacciaguida's Vision

In order to highlight how the idea of Providence intertwines with the subjects of God's eternal present and of the unfolding of his love in Time and history, I need to return to Dante's *Paradiso.* Approximately halfway through his itinerary across the heavenly realm, Dante meets with his most prominent ancestor, Cacciaguida, who died as a martyr in the Crusades. Along with Dante's main mentors (Virgilio, Beatrice and St. Bernard), Cacciaguida is the one single person who remains "onstage" for the longest time in the *Commedia.* He has the unwelcome task of explaining the meaning of some obscure prophecies overheard by his descendant in the previous *cantos*; the ancestor reveals to Dante that he will have to endure exile, perhaps for ever, from his beloved Florence. Counterbalancing this harsh fate, Cacciaguida also prophesies Dante's mission and vocation to poetry: artistic and literary creativity are fundamental components of what it means to be an intelligent being and a human person.[40] Given the importance of poetry as a vocation, Cacciaguida's *cantos* are interwoven with allusions to metaliterary/metatextual subjects such as communication, writing, language, and the ineffability of mystery. For example, Cacciaguida speaks in different languages, with the result that his descendant sometimes finds it difficult to understand him, while on other occasions Dante admires Cacciaguida's clear and precise discourse ("*preciso latin*": *Paradiso* 17:34–5). Moreover, just as Cacciaguida died as a martyr for his faith, so the "martyrdom of writing" will be the fate of his descendant.

Along with poetry, there is also a marked presence of music in these *cantos.* The episode takes place in the Heaven of Mars,[41] where music has a prominent role;[42] numerous details intersperse Cacciaguida's *cantos* with

39. Naveh seems to hold a view similar to that outlined here, though expressed in somewhat different terms (Naveh, "Tonality," 40, 47).

40. This subject will be explored in depth in the next chapter.

41. Cf. Ledda, "Canto XV," 432–33.

42. Dante explains this connotation of the Heaven of Mars in *Convivio* 2.13.20–26. (Alighieri, *Convivio*, 118).

music, and in the fifteenth *canto* the blessed souls are likened to a "sweet lyre," whose strings are loosened or tightened by the hand of God (an image which resonates with both the Ainur's concert and Honorius's idea of the cithara discussed above).

At the heart of Cacciaguida's *cantos*, a few *terzine* (*Paradiso* 17:36–45) stand out for their relevance to our argument. Cacciaguida's speech begins by discussing the connection between knowledge and necessity (following Boethius: see chapter 1): he affirms that God's foreknowledge does not imply that his will is constrained by necessity.

> Contingency, / while not extending past the book in which / your world of matter has been writ, is yet / in the Eternal Vision all depicted // (but this does not imply necessity, / just as a ship that sails downstream is not / determined by the eye that watches it).[43]

Here Cacciaguida significantly states that he can "read" the story and stories unfolding in time since they are "depicted" in a "book," i.e., in God's revelation of his thought.[44] Furthermore, Cacciaguida adds: "And from that Vision—just as from an organ / the ear receives a gentle harmony / what time prepares for you appears to me."[45] Dante scholars are still debating whether the Italian word *organi* should be understood here as meaning "organ" (the instrument) or "*organum*" (the polyphonic genre). Both can be supported: Dante's mention of a multi-voiced music at this point supports "organum," while the instrument is reminiscent of St. Augustine's theology. In his *Expositions on the Psalms* (150.5), Augustine explains the musical metaphor of the organ "to signify that [the saints] sound not each separately, but sound together in most harmonious diversity." Augustine believes that "even then [in heaven] the saints of God will have their differences, accordant, not discordant, that is, agreeing, not disagreeing, just as sweetest harmony arises from sounds differing indeed, but not opposed to one another."[46] The realization that "sweetest harmony"—an expression

43. *Paradiso* 17:36–42: "La contingenza, che fuor del quaderno / de la vostra matera non si stende, / tutta è dipinta nel cospetto etterno; / necessità però quindi non prende / se non come dal viso in che si specchia / nave che per torrente giù discende."

44. We may observe here that Cacciaguida's imagery resembles very closely that found in Jacques de Liège's *Mirror*, as discussed in chapter 5.

45. *Paradiso* 17:43–45: "Da indi, sì come viene ad orecchia / dolce armonia da organo, mi viene / a vista il tempo che ti s'apparecchia."

46. Augustine, *Enarrationes in Psalmos* 150.5; *Expositions*, 6:456.

found in both Dante and Augustine—may arise even from dissonance is one of the main points of Dante's spiritual experience and poetical mission.

In his condition as a blessed soul, Cacciaguida enjoys a perpetual Vision of God, in which he receives a revelation both of God's mystery and of the human realities known by God, as also happens to Tolkien's Ainur. This revelation possesses qualities such as immediacy, intuition and simultaneity, even though Cacciaguida (just as the Ainur or the angels) cannot fully understand, let alone "comprehend" God. Moreover, as we have seen, Cacciaguida's "vision" is likened to the reading of a book. Since he can see human time and history in a holistic and simultaneous fashion, through the contemplation of God, Cacciaguida can therefore appreciate their order, their harmony and the eventual "resolution" of the situations of suffering and tension. A similar view is offered by Mikhail Bakhtin, commenting on Dostoevsky's ability to write "polyphonically" (i.e., to "perceive the very stages [of literary development] themselves in their simultaneity, to juxtapose and counterpose them dramatically, and not stretch them out into an evolving sequence"). In Bakhtin's view, for Dostoevsky, "to get one's bearings on the world meant to conceive all its contents as simultaneous, and to guess at their interrelationship in the cross-section of a single moment."[47]

Therefore, Dante's choice to express an analogous vision musically is not a mere poetic device: music is a syntax of time, ordering the sound events not according to chance or caprice, but rather in an intelligible and logical fashion. Musical notation allows us to "see" music and recall it, but also to embrace, in a simultaneous gaze, the unfolding of successive musical events. Therefore, by writing music down we can visualize time and intuit God's eternal present, as well as understand that temporal events are disposed toward an orderly and harmonious resolution. I am not claiming that Dante's *terzina* (*Paradiso* 17:43–5) explicitly alludes to the notation of music (even though I am drawn to this interpretation); rather I believe that Dante's choice to use this particular musical metaphor is profoundly meaningful. It seems to affirm that were we able to contemplate history in the eternal present, just as we contemplate musical events unfolding in time in the simultaneity of music notation, we would then be able better to understand God's *pro-videntia* working in history, and the goodness and depth of God's judgments.

47. Bakhtin, *Problems of Dostoevsky's Poetics*, 28.

Bonaventure's Beautiful Song

The ultimate source for Dante's image is St. Augustine, who, in the *City of God*, affirmed: "For God would never have created any, I do not say angel, but even man, whose future wickedness He foreknew, unless He had equally known to what uses in behalf of the good He could turn him, thus embellishing, the course of the ages, as it were an exquisite poem set off with antitheses."[48] What has been translated here as "poem" is "*carmen*" in Latin, the very same word Augustine used when discussing the possibility of measuring time through a song.[49] A *carmen* is, in fact, poetry with music. Boethius,[50] who identified providence with God's thoughts, held a similar view, as Dubs summarized: "the unfolding of temporal as this is present to the vision of the divine mind."[51]

A later theologian, St. Bonaventure of Bagnoregio (ca. 1220–1274), compared the history of the world to a "most beautiful song," probably borrowing Augustine's image. In his *Breviloquium* (2.4), Bonaventure discussed the qualities of God's judgments, affirming that it is impossible to appreciate the beauty of a *carmen*, of a song, unless one can contemplate it in its entirety.[52] Since human beings cannot observe history from this supratemporal vantage point, Bonaventure suggested that Scripture, as the linguistic form of God's self-revelation, of his *Logos*, can be considered as a song in which the entire history of salvation is summarized.[53] Likening the world to a book (once more!), to a stair and to a song, Bonaventure employs a series of significant metaphors, which Dante would later adopt, mostly in the seventeenth *Canto* of the *Paradiso*. These images correspond to the numerous attempts to visually depict the structure of the world, of heaven and of the human body at Bonaventure's time (for example in cartography).

48. Augustine, *De Civitate Dei* 11.18; *City of God*, 1:457.

49. Augustine, *Confessiones* 11.26.33, 27.36; *Confessions*, 253–54, 256. See chapter 1 of this book.

50. Boethius, *Consolation* 4.6:88. It may be mentioned that, according to Shippey, Tolkien knew Boethius's *Consolation* in depth. Shippey, *Road to Middle-Earth*, 140–41.

51. Dubs, "Providence," 186.

52. As Martin Luther put it, "*in fine videtur cuius toni*": he aptly used a musical simile (the tone of a modal piece is revealed at the end) to signify God's ultimate and eternal judgement of the world, revealing His righteousness and His condemnation of the evil (Luther, *Vorlesungen*, 322).

53. Di Maio, "Rappresentazione," 16.

The success of such synthetic representations of reality seems to have encouraged a similar visualization of time and music through notation.

At this period, time had long been spatialized and "seen" in calendars, which mirrored the cyclic course of astronomic phenomena and of their influences on the daily experiences of human beings and nature. Similarly, the representations of lineages as family trees was common in the Middle Ages, and took inspiration from the biblical image of the Tree of Jesse.[54] If the Tree of Jesse symbolizes a cartography of time, a theological view could inspire even geographical maps. For example, the Ebstorf *Mappa Mundi*[55] (thirteenth century) represented the known world as a circle at whose center is the holy city of Jerusalem, where Christ rose from the sepulcher. The circle itself, however, stands for the Body of the risen Christ, whose head, hands and feet are depicted on the borders of the circumference. As Capuano put it, "in the world's very shape, as seen by medieval men, the history of salvation is inscribed, finding in Christ its point of departure and of arrival."[56] The world's shape and its story, known today in the study of history and geography, can be told *as an* (intelligible) *form* and *as a* (meaningful) *narrative* precisely because they are integral components of God's self-revelation. Creation, i.e., the visible form of nature, and the events taking place in Time, all combine to unveil and communicate the mystery of God's Being and of his Providence to human beings.

This view was also repeated by St. Bonaventure in his *Sententiae*,[57] where he forcefully affirmed that things are ordered to a finality, that they have a teleology. Therefore, the world and its history are defined once more as a "beautiful song" (*pulcherrimum carmen*), which unfolds according to "excellent consonances" (*decurrit secundum optimas consonantias*).

54. This very figure is clearly evoked in Cacciaguida's *cantos*, where the ancestor defines himself as Dante's "root," and his descendant as a "branch" (*Paradiso* 15:88–90). It can be argued that King David, Jesse's son, is one of Dante's ideals and models throughout the *Commedia*.

55. See https://www.raremaps.com/gallery/detail/46532/ebstorf-mappa-mundi-monialium-ebstorfensium-mappamundi-eckstein-stahle.

56. Capuano, *Segni della voce*, 197 (translation mine).

57. Bonaventure, *I Sent.*, d.44, a. 1, q. 3 co.

Jacopone's *Lauda LXIV*

Precisely at Bonaventure's time, a real song, a *lauda*, attempted to recount the unfolding of the history of salvation. Jacopone da Todi (ca. 1230–1306), one of the first poets to write in the Italian vernacular, put forward a view of the history of salvation and of redemption in a *lauda* about Christ's incarnation. Jesus's birth, he maintains, is a "new song," which "destroys the crying" of the fallen humankind. He symbolizes the height of the Logos's divine nature as a high-pitched note, where the song's "tune" is found, while Christ's *kenosis* is likened to a melody "suavely descending" to a low note, where "the Word resonates." This condescension causes a harmony unequalled in its "concord" (*concordato*). As in the Gospel narration of Christmas, Jacopone cites the choir of the "jubilant singers," i.e., the "holy angels," who sing around the "little child / who is God's Word / and whom I see incarnate." Jacopone also uses musical similes in a later stanza: "I see the divine note / written on parchment." What I have translated as parchment is called "*carta ainina*," "lamb's paper," by Jacopone. This curious expression alludes to the future Passion of Christ, the Lamb of God, on whose slain body we contemplate God's love for us. The song of redemption is inscribed on Christ's suffering body. "And God is the scribe / who opened his hand / to teach us the song":[58] Jacopone here combines the Guidonian hand, through which solmization was taught in the Middle Ages, with the equally famous depiction of the Father as an outstretched hand from which the Spirit is sent to the world. Jacopone understood that "those who are able to enter / will always find a song of love there. / It conforms to God / and takes the norm / of the good desire."

This extraordinary poem suggests that the history of salvation is a "written song," that is, a phenomenon unfolding in time, and yet engraved before the foundation of the world in the Lamb's skin.[59] Christ's incarnation is connected to his death and resurrection: through Christ's death, the Eternal mysteriously entered Time, while, through His resurrection, the

58. "En carta ainina / la nota diuina / ueggio ch'è scritta. // Là u'è il nostro canto / ricto & renfranto / a chi ben ci aficta, // E Dio è lo scriuano / ch'à 'perta la mano / che 'l canto ha ensegnato" (Ferri, *Laude*, 97).

59. Cf. Rev 13:8, of which two translations are possible: "Everyone whose name has not been written from the foundation of the world in the book of life of the Lamb that was slaughtered," or, alternatively, "Written in the book of life of the Lamb that was slaughtered from the foundation of the world." In the Vulgate, with which Jacopone would have been familiar, the latter version is found: "*in libro vitae Agni, qui occisus est ab origine mundi.*"

temporal was allowed to enter eternity, as God's mode of being. In God's "hand," the whole of the song of our world is already inscribed; it unfolds in time if we learn our own song by reading it on that very hand.

Dante and Providence

Jacopone, then, saw Providence as a song written on "lambskin"; Dante saw his story and his future as a song heard and contemplated by his ancestor Cacciaguida. This contemplation takes place in God's eternal present: "O my dear root, . . . since you rise so high / [you] can see the Point, in which all times are present."[60] The depiction of time as a line and of present as a point encourages us to imagine the eternal present as a point of extreme concentration. In the sixth century, Gregory the Great had similarly described a mystical experience: "in that vision . . . the whole and entire world was displayed before [St. Benedict's] eyes, as if it were gathered under a single ray of sunlight."[61] Approximately a thousand years later, the French musician Marin Mersenne stated that "Music has its sovereign perfection in God's intellect, which we may conceive as a luminous point which contains in itself an infinite light, and which darts its rays throughout the sphere of the universe."[62]

By gazing at that point, in God's eternal present, his ancestor can foresee Dante's future; the foresight (*pre-vision*) of a fact may help to understand it *pro-videntially*. "Providence" and "to provide" derive from *pro-video*; "prevision," just as "foresight," comes from *pre-video*; "improvisation" refers to *in-provideo*, i.e., something that cannot be "foreseen."

Viewing the totality of time enables us to understand and to make judgments about the song, by partaking of that "vantage point" outside time from which God, in Bonaventure's image, "observes" history. Time itself, in its past, present, and future form, is "revealed" to the blessed souls who, as in the case of Cacciaguida, can gaze directly into the mystery of God. Though such a contemplation takes place outside the human experience of temporality, Cacciaguida employs a musical simile to signify the *progress* in knowledge which the blessed souls continuously experience, without ever exhausting it. The "music" of God's revelation of Himself and of the Vision in which Time is also contained is an unceasingly unfolding harmony—or

60. *Paradiso* 17:13–4.

61. Gregorio Magno, *Vita di San Benedetto*, 99 (translation mine).

62. Mersenne, *Traité*, 59.

polyphony—composed of many intertwining voices which can be followed in parallel, both in their individual lines and in the resulting complexity.

This theme is resumed on another occasion in the *Commedia*; the connection between these two passages is highlighted by the use of an almost identical term (*quaderno* in *Paradiso* 17:37, *squaderna* in *Paradiso* 33:87; both refer to books). In Cacciaguida's canto, as we have seen, the world of contingency was likened to a closed volume, which is contemplated in its entirety by those whose sight can fix itself on God. In the very last *canto* of the *Commedia*, the same contemplation of the Triune God is likened to the observation of a book in which the universe and its history are bound:

> In its profundity I saw—ingathered / and bound by love into one single volume—/ what, in the universe, seems separate, scattered: // substances, accidents, and dispositions / as if conjoined—in such a way that what / I tell is only rudimentary.[63]

As previously mentioned, many books were read aloud at Dante's time, and thus even the written word possessed a temporality which today is no longer experienced. The union and contrast between the temporal dimension of reading aloud a written verbal text and the reality of a book in which the entire text is contained is even more present in the reality of musical books or scores, whose temporality is clearer, more pronounced, and proportionally organized.[64] Cacciaguida can "see" Time in God and in the "book" of the divine Providence, and yet experience this revelation as the unfolding of a harmonious music; Dante can see the totality of the created world and of its time in the "volume" of God's Grace. Mystically, the experience of music intensifies in parallel with Dante's ascent from heaven to heaven in the *Paradiso*. Aurally, however, as Dante progresses into the upper spheres, the hitherto unending and beautiful music seems to cease, in his ears: "and wherefore, say, / doth the sweet symphony of Paradise /

63. "Nel suo profondo vidi che s'interna, / legato con amore in un volume, / ciò che per l'universo si squaderna: // sustanze e accidenti e lor costume / quasi conflati insieme, per tal modo / che ciò ch'i dico è un semplice lume" (*Paradiso* 33:85–90). English translation by Allen Mandelbaum. This passage is fascinatingly studied and commented in Orsbon, "Universe as Book." Orsbon also underpins the etymological relation of "*quaderno*" with the Latin "*quattuor*" and the Italian "*quattro*," i.e., the number four, which frequently symbolized the universe and/or Earth with its four elements etc. (Orsbon, "Universe as Book," 93–94).

64. Messiaen's image of the chrysalis and the butterfly (Samuel, *Conversations*, 44; see chapter 3) is a modern counterpart of Dante's simile: for Messiaen, past and future seem to be contained in the chrysalis' closed wings.

keep silence here, pervading with such sounds / of rapt devotion every lower sphere?"[65]

On the one hand, Dante is told that his inability to hear the "sweet symphony" is due to his mortality, since the increasingly transcendent beauty of that singing would overcome his mortal senses. On the other hand, since this also happens as he nears the Prime Mover, it might be argued that the temporality of music ceases as the heavens approach their stillness in God's eternal present; and that music becomes an inaudible concentration of beauty, freed from its temporality and gathering in an infinite instant the fullness of time.

Dissonances in the Music of Providence

Dante is a mortal human being who has been granted the privilege of intuiting the beauty of the song of his own life. In spite of the harsh dissonances it contains (such as Dante's exile), it is ultimately a beautiful music as it is the loving song of God's providence. As Dubs writes, "although some events seem discordant or chaotic from our temporal perspective, they are not, because they remain subject to the order which proceeds from providence. It is our limited perception which is incapable of penetrating to the order which lies behind the apparent disorder."[66]

Similarly, in Tolkien, the discordant music by Melkor is encompassed by Ilúvatar's themes, and the Ainur can contemplate the temporal unfolding of Music in the simultaneous brilliance of a Vision: "Ilúvatar said to them: 'Behold your Music!' And he showed to them a vision, giving to them sight where before was only hearing";[67] McIntosh justly observes that the Vision wields "a greater theodical power . . . in comparison to the Music, providing the Ainur with a fuller disclosure of Ilúvatar's ability to bring about good from Melkor's evil."[68]

We have observed the surfacing of this perspective in Dante's poetry; however, the view that harmony can grow out of, and incorporate dissonance predates Christianity and is constantly found in the Western tradition. As Spitzer points out, Philolaus writes that "harmony is generally the

65. "E di' perché si tace in questa rota / la dolce sinfonia di paradiso / che giù per l'altra suona sì divota" (*Paradiso* 21:58–60). English translation by Allen Mandelbaum.

66. Dubs, "Providence," 186.

67. Tolkien, *Silmarillion*, 17.

68. McIntosh, "Ainulindalë," 60.

result of contraries; for it is the unity of multiplicity, and the agreement of discordances,"[69] while in Roman culture this concept was summarized as *concordia discors* (Horace[70]). These views were later infused with Christian theology, particularly by St. Augustine. In his *On Order*,[71] he asserted that even the facts which we deem as irrational are not outside reason. This is perceived as an understandable truth by the self-conscious spiritual beings who love God. Everything in creation is part of a harmonious and orderly structure. While no created being can encompass its governing logic, and thus fully understand the reason behind some bewildering aspects of the world, the *existence* of such a logic can be compellingly "felt" by those who are in communion with God.

Theological faith is the epistemological prerequisite which enables human reason to transcend itself. Indeed, as Mazzotta affirms, "in this abstract, metaphysical music on order we are explicitly told that nothing exists without reason and outside of God's order."[72] If Tolkien's Ilúvatar weaves Melkor's discordant music into his themes, then Augustine's Christian God has the power of turning even the evilest actions into something good:

> While foreknowing [that Lucifer] was going to turn out bad of his own free will, God still made him, not holding back his goodness in providing what was even going to be a noxious will with life and substantive being, at the same time foreseeing how much good use he was going to make of him by his own wonderful goodness and power.[73]

Augustine's view was later developed by John Scotus Eriugena (ca. 815–ca. 877), reinterpreting the idea of the *concordia discors* in terms of a musical theology of creation:

> Just as a melody consists of notes of different character and pitch, which show considerable disagreement when they are heard individually and separately, but provide a certain natural charm when they are combined in one or another of the modes, in accordance

69. Spitzer, *Armonia del mondo*, 11; cf. Diels, *Fragmente*, 252–53.

70. Horatius, *Epistulae* 1.12.12 (25).

71. Augustine, *De Ordine libri duo* 2.7.24 (83).

72. Mazzotta, *Dante's Vision*, 200–201.

73. Augustine, *De Genesi ad litteram libri duodecim* 11.22.29; *Literal Meaning*, 2:153. Halsall demonstrates that "Tolkien's 'aesthetic' approach to the problem of evil has a strong resonance with Augustine's 'aesthetic' theodicy" (Halsall, "Critical Assessment," 77).

> with definite and reasoned principles of musical science; so the universe, in accordance with the uniform will of the Creator, is welded into one harmonious whole from the different subdivisions of nature, which disagree with each other when they are examined individually.[74]

I will show later the implications of Eriugena's point for the interpretation of the *Ainulindalë*: elements which sound "disagreeably" if heard in isolation become harmonious when the entire melody is perceived. In his interpretation of Eriugena, Spitzer[75] writes that human wickedness can be understood as a dissonance whose presence enables the ultimate triumph of harmony and of the good.

Peter Abelard (1079–1142), who builds on Augustine's *De Ordine*, expresses a similar view: "as a picture is often more beautiful and worthy of commendation if some colors in themselves ugly are included in it, than it would be if it were uniform and of a single order, so from an admixture of evils the universe is rendered more beautiful and worthy of commendation."[76] Analogously, Alexander of Hales (1183–1245) compared the game of light and shadow in paintings to the moral errors which ultimately contribute to the universal beauty.[77] In the fourteenth century (1357), the music theorist Johannes Boen (d. 1367) admitted the use of dissonances in composition if their duration was sufficiently short so as not to "poison the hearing with its harshness. The ear lets itself be deceived in little things, but not in great ones." Moreover, he accepts that particularly disagreeable dissonances are tolerated by the ear if there are enough surrounding consonances to appease it.[78] It is important for Boen to find a balance of dissonance and consonance, so that the "little" displeasing things which "deceive" the ear are absorbed and partially neutralized by "great[er]" moments of musical pleasure.

74. Johannes Scotus Eriugena, *De divisione naturae*, in Hughes, *New Oxford History of Music II*, 273.

75. Spitzer, *Classical and Christian*, 41–42.

76. In *Epitome theologiae christianae* (*PL* 182), col. 1052, in Lovejoy, *Great Chain of Being*, 72.

77. Alexander of Hales, *Summa Theologiae* IIa, q. 16, V.i (Halensis, *Summa*), in Eco, *On Beauty*, 148.

78. Fuller, "Delectabatur," 474.

A Harmony with Dissonances?

In 1558, one of the greatest and most influential music theorist of the century, namely Gioseffo Zarlino (1517–1590), asserted the principle that "harmony is born not only from consonances, but also from dissonances": "for, when one of two opposites is found, it is necessary that the other be also found, and that both are equally known." He saw the task of good composers as the creation of "harmonies in which dissonances accord with each other, and sound together with a wonderful effect."[79] It is crucial for my argument that Zarlino thought it possible for dissonances to be in reciprocal "accord" and to "sound together" beautifully.

Zarlino's views were further developed by the learned Jesuit Athanasius Kircher (1602–1680), and by the German philosopher Gottfried Wilhelm von Leibniz (1646–1716). Kircher stated that "God has placed in heaven by his natural art two dissonant bodies, Mars and Saturn," who are responsible for all evil influences on Earth. To temper their power, God situated "the benign planet Jupiter" between them, and assigned to Mars "the most eccentric orbit of all" to keep its "virulence" as far as possible from the Earth. However, the evil behavior of Mars and Saturn should not lead us to accuse Mother Nature of being a stepmother, "as she well might be, by the highest and lowest counsel, for thus disposing matters," since "the world could not be maintained without them." Indeed, they act as a *pharmakon*, a beneficent poison, on the macrocosmic plane. "So," in Kircher's words, "there is nothing evil in the nature of things which does not eventually contribute to the good of all and the consecration of the universe." And, indeed, he wonders, "What else are Mars and Saturn but dissonances? Tied and syncopated by Jupiter in perfect consonance, they give to music not sweetness, exactly, but a great embellishment." Therefore, he concludes, "whoever will consider this a little more deeply will find that the seven planets sing with the Earth a perfect four-part harmony, in which dissonance is combined so artistically with consonance that it gives forth the sweetest chords in the world."[80] This harmony in diversity, which seems in fact to need diversity in order to be harmony, is guaranteed by the action of the "Harmost Nature," who distributes "celestial songsters in various choirs": while they are "different in sound," they "conspire in a consonant-dissonant union, ornamenting the

79. Zarlino, *Istitutioni harmoniche* 2.12, 79.

80. Godwin, *Harmony of the Spheres*, 273–74.

world with their diversity and witnessing to the ineffable wisdom of that super-mundane Harmost."[81]

In summary, the perfect order of God's creation keeps evil forces at bay, and uses their very power for the overall good of the universe. They are "dissonances" in the heavenly harmony, whose presence may be displeasing but may nevertheless contribute to the higher order of beauty. All planets, including the dissonant ones, are therefore indispensable for the "perfect harmony" of the universe. Kircher's discussion is strikingly close to Tolkien's *Ainulindalë* in that the behavior of Kircher's planets is morally evaluated and described in close relatedness with the traditional attributes of the corresponding pagan gods, and their contribution—albeit "dissonant"—to the Great Music is forcefully affirmed. Indeed, Louis-Claude de Saint-Martin later described universal history as a game or a struggle between consonance and dissonance: their very conflict is the source from which "all musical works are born."[82]

Kircher's perspective was further developed by Leibniz, who stated that "the most distinguished composers often mix dissonances with smooth harmonies in order to arouse the listener—to disturb him, as it were—so that he will be momentarily anxious about what is to happen, and will feel all the more pleasure when order is restored"; similarly, "small dangers" delight us, and we need bitter or sharp flavors "to stimulate our palate" and to appreciate "sweet things." Thus, "someone who hasn't tasted bitter things doesn't deserve sweet things, and indeed won't appreciate them! This is a law of delight: Pleasure doesn't come from uniformity, which creates disgust and makes us numb rather than happy."[83] In a letter, he also affirmed that "the imperfections which are found in the universe are as the dissonances in an excellent musical work, which contribute to make it more perfect, in the judgement of those who perceive well the connection [*ceux qui en sentent bien la liaison*, in French]."[84] As Boen and Eriugena stated, those capable of understanding—or at least intuiting—the "connection," the logic which orders the harmony of creation, will also understand or intuit the role of dissonances in music and in the spiritual world. But there is a new stress in Leibniz, which echoes writers such as Abelard: displeasing elements ultimately contribute to our pleasure, by adding interest and variety

81. Godwin, *Harmony of the Spheres*, 274–75.

82. Godwin, *Harmony of the Spheres*, 326.

83. Leibniz, *Philosophischen Schriften*, 7:306; *Ultimate Origin of Things*, 5–6.

84. Leibniz, *Philosophischen Schriften*, 3:521.

to what would otherwise be a predictable sequence of uniformly pleasant experiences. Saint-Martin stated that "if the ear were offered nothing but a series of common chords it would not be shocked, it is true; but aside from the monotonous boredom that would ensue, we would not find therein any expression, any idea."[85] Commenting on Leibniz's musical theodicy, Giorgio Erle writes that "the musical *ethos* is not just an *ars combinatoria*," but rather a creative and salvific undertaking, by virtue of which "a composer may make use of dissonances together with consonances," just as God, in consideration of the overall "architectural development" of the universe, "allowed good and evil to show themselves as indissolubly connected," in order to make the world "progress" and perfect itself.[86] In fact, for Leibniz,

> The apparent disorder is like certain chords in music which seem awkward when they are heard by themselves, but which a knowledgeable composer inserts in the piece because, *in joining them with other chords*, he enhances the music and makes the harmony more beautiful. And since what we now see is only a very small portion of the infinite universe, and because our present life is only a little portion of what will happen to us, we should not be astonished if all the beauty of things does not reveal itself at first sight.[87]

As in Bonaventure's "beautiful song," in the "sweet harmony" of Dante's life, and in Tolkien's Great Music to come at the end of all times, Leibniz suggests that the providential unfolding of history can only be observed from the outside, and is therefore not accessible through human intellect alone. Faith, as we have seen, may sustain the human reason in its struggle with the reality of evil. It is supported by the observation of the beauty of the created world and by the prayerful interpretation of our own past, which may reveal how God transformed in Grace even our sin, our suffering and our pain. For this reason, the final chapter of this book will focus on creation and subcreation.

85. Godwin, *Harmony of the Spheres*, 327.

86. Erle, *Leibniz*, 95.

87. Leibniz, *Philosophischen Schriften*, 7:545, in Coudert, *Leibniz and the Kabbalah*, 131 (emphasis added).

8

Creation and Sub-Creation

In Tolkien's *The Silmarillion*, Ilúvatar shows the Ainur their song in the form of a Vision, which in turn announces creation proper, the realization of the material world whose history was already contained in the Music and in the Vision. In this chapter, we will consider how the idea of a creation in music may influence our understanding of the History of salvation, of our own individual stories, and of our vocation as sub-creators.

Indeed, every human being on earth is arguably a "poet" inasmuch as he or she can perceive the beauty and wonder of the created world and feel its enchantment. The capability to translate this feeling of awe and amazement into words is poetry proper, which, at its zenith, may reach such heights that the reader is led to contemplate the world with new eyes, and perceive the mysterious greatness of creation beyond the customary appearance of things. If this enchantment for the created world may be considered as the first manifestation of a religious feeling among the human beings, then it may be argued that, by awakening our consciousness to the miracle and beauty of Nature, and thereby suggesting the hidden/revealed presence of the supernatural behind Nature itself, verbal and musical narrativity may act as a "pre-Gospel," as a kind of *euangelion*.[1]

Natural Theology and Myth

The Catholic perspective known as "natural theology" argues that there are certain theological truths which the human mind can grasp even in the absence of an explicit Revelation; and that the created world, in its harmony

1. Cf. Bassham, "Lewis and Tolkien," 11.

and beauty, is sufficient for leading us to acknowledge the existence of a Creator God. If the created world exists, there has to be a Creator; if the world is beautiful, the Creator has to be good.

However, many of our contemporaries tend to seek the ultimate cause of the world in purely material terms, by exploring through scientific means the material causes of natural phenomena—disregarding the fact that matter cannot have caused itself—and viewing religious or pre-religious interpretations of the world as fiction. This used to be the position of C. S. Lewis, who had abandoned Christianity in his youthful years; in 1929 he reluctantly came to accept the existence of God, without fully adhering to the Christian revelation. On September 19, 1931, Lewis, Tolkien and Hugo Dyson had a famous night stroll on Addison's Walk, in the grounds of Magdalen College, Oxford. Lewis expressed his skepticism of some Christian dogmas because of their similarity with archetypal narratives and mythological "tales" from earlier cultures. His thesis seems to have been that if a biblical episode or story appears to have literary models in other religious traditions, then the Bible is just a cultural product preserving interesting and sometimes fanciful interpretations of the "real" world rather than historical facts and "truths."

During that famous walk, and possibly on other occasions too, Tolkien helped Lewis to see matters differently. If a narrative sounds like a myth, it does not follow that it is a lie. There may be myths which cannot claim to represent "hard facts" in the same fashion as a chronicle, but may nevertheless speak real truths about the meaning of life; and there may be other "myths" which grow in the soil prepared by the myths, but nonetheless *do* represent "hard facts" which one can define as "true." Lewis summarized the gist of the belief after his debate with Tolkien and Dyson:

> The heart of Christianity is a myth which is also a fact. The old myth of the Dying God, *without ceasing to be myth,* comes down from the heaven of legend and imagination to the earth of history. It *happens*—at a particular date, in a particular place, followed by definable historical consequences. We pass from a Balder or an Osiris, dying nobody knows when or where, to a historical Person crucified (it is all in order) *under Pontius Pilate*. By becoming fact it does not cease to be myth: that is the miracle. . . . To be truly Christian we must both assent to the historical fact and also receive the myth (fact though it has become) with the same imaginative

> embrace which we accord to all myths. The one is hardly more necessary than the other.[2]

This is Lewis's personal interpretation and later reworking of what had been sown by Tolkien and Dyson, and so we cannot assume that this represents Tolkien's view precisely. What we do know, though, is what Tolkien himself wrote to Lewis shortly after that episode. Tolkien's ideas took the form of poetry ("Mythopoeia"), and of a philosophical essay ("On Fairy Stories"). Tolkien's concept of the relationship between human creativity (or *poesis*) and God's revelation are encapsulated in the following, which counters Lewis's earlier conviction that "myths were lies and therefore worthless, even though 'breathed through silver.'"[3]

> The heart of man is not compound of lies, / but draws some wisdom from the only Wise, / and still recalls him. Though now long estranged, / man is not wholly lost nor wholly changed. / Disgraced he may be, yet is not dethroned, / and keeps the rags of lordship once he owned, / his world-dominion by creative act.[4]

Tolkien's poetry is reminiscent of some passages from the biblical Book of Genesis. Here, the first divine attribute to be revealed is God's "creativity." The reader may intuit other qualities of the biblical Godhead (such as omniscience, goodness etc.), but they are not explicitly declared at first. Thus, when God creates human beings "in our image, according to our likeness" (Gen 1:26), human creativity shines forth as the primeval vocation of our species. Later, we will learn about God's omniscience (which encourages us to pursue knowledge, and in particular the knowledge of God), or about his goodness (encouraging us to charity), and so on. However, human beings are firstly called to fulfil their Creator's likeness by being "creative," or "sub-creative," as Tolkien would have put it.[5] Moreover, and as a consequence (Gen 2:19–21), Adam's very first action is to "give names" to God's creatures, corresponding in the Jewish tradition to a form of

2. Lewis, *Collected Works*, 343. See Lewis's letter to Greeves, September 22, 1931, expressing this viewpoint more succinctly but chronologically more closely to Lewis's conversion (Lewis, *Collected Letters*, 970). See also Lewis, *Surprised by Joy*, 222.

3. Tolkien, "Mythopoeia," 97.

4. Tolkien, "Mythopoeia," 98.

5. In Tolkien's own words, "Fantasy remains a human right: we make in our measure and in our derivative mode, because we are made: and not only made, but made in the image and likeness of a Maker" (Tolkien, "On Fairy-Stories," 50).

lordship over God's creation;[6] and this lordships is strictly bound to verbality, to the use of *words*. I think this is what Tolkien implies by mentioning the "throne," "lordship" and "dominion" granted by God to humans.

Called to Create

More explicitly, Tolkien evokes the poet's and author's vocation in other lines of the same poem: "Blessed are the legend-makers with their rhyme / Of things not found within record time . . . / I would that I might with the minstrels sing / And stir the unseen with a throbbing string."[7] As Caldecott puts it, Tolkien "believes that our capacity to create is part of our resemblance to God. In every act of creation—*poesis*—we echo the divine creation of the world itself. Tolkien believes that the creation of whole worlds in fantasy is the highest form of human creativity."[8] Tolkien explores these topics further in "On Fairy Stories," which may be considered the manifesto of his aesthetics and of his spiritual views. There is no opposition between the Story of Salvation and the tales narrated by human beings; rather, the pleasurable thrill we experience when a captivating tale manifests the providential design of God's love through the symbol of the *eucatastrophe*[9] is a resonance of our predisposition to receive the Good News of the Gospel. In Tolkien's words, "in the 'eucatastrophe' we see in a brief vision that the answer may be greater—it may be a far-off gleam or echo of *evangelium* in the real world";[10] moreover, "The Evangelium has not abrogated legends; it has hallowed them, especially the 'happy ending.'"[11] As we will later see, the same dynamics apply to the rules of music, of how it works on the human sensitivity, and may explain why Tolkien chose *musical* symbols in order to narrate the Creation of the world.

6. See also Caldecott, "New Light," 80, where it is stated: "Made in the image of the Creator, Man cannot but create, and thus attempt to continue the Creator's work. Imagination is the garden or landscape of the soul, and the Creator's command to tend and cultivate the land applied just as much to this interior world as it did to Eden."

7. Tolkien, "Mythopoeia," 99.

8. Caldecott, "New Light," 68.

9. A term by Tolkien, indicating the sudden turn of events by which a positive element reverses a character's tragic doom.

10. Tolkien, "On Fairy Stories," 84.

11. Tolkien, "On Fairy Stories," 84.

Far from being in competition with the Christian Revelation, Tolkien saw the (sub-)creation of mythical narratives (or "fairy-stories") as a privileged way of responding to God's primeval call to creativity, and to His vocation to transmit the truth of the Gospel to the other human beings.

However, human sub-creation is—in theological terms—an *analogue* of God's own creative activity. It is a creatural parallel to something which God possesses, is, or does on an utterly different plane (not just to a higher degree). Nonetheless it remains possible, through analogy, to state meaningful truths about God by likening them to human experience, and, to a certain extent, vice-versa. Thus, God's creation is from nothing, *ex-nihilo*, while human creativity is closer in kind to the "composition" of music: i.e., an artistic combination of (aural) materials bestowed on us so that we can make something beautiful and meaningful, in an activity mirroring God's creativity.

We have seen that God's life-giving activity is also a self-Revelation, a Gift, and a *kenosis*. It is within this framework that we should construe a Christian understanding of the process of Creation, and also of what human creativity may signify and imply. For a human being, to create is not to assert his or her individuality to the detriment of others, let alone exert a form of power or possession by means of the creative forces we have received; rather, it is a form of self-sacrifice, of oblation in which we give our innermost self in response to a divine calling.[12] Lewis may have glimpsed this sacrificial dimension when he stated:

> God, besides being the Great Creator, is the Tragic Redeemer. Perhaps the Tragic Creator too. For I am not sure that the great canyon of anguish which lies across our lives is *solely* due to some prehistoric catastrophe. Something tragic may . . . be inherent in the very act of creation.[13]

And this kenotic dimension is fully present, although frequently overlooked, in Tolkien's creation narrative. It is meaningfully embodied by his choice to represent Creation as a musical act. Moreover, it also impacts his

12. For instance, this concept underlies Sofia Gubaidulina's composition of *Offertorium*, a violin concerto dedicated to Gidon Kremer. In the composer's words, this work embodies "the sacrificial offering of Christ's crucifixion. . . . God's offering as He created the world. . . . The offering of the artist, the performing violinist. . . . The composer's offering" (Bannister, "Kenosis," 70).

13. Lewis, *Letters to Malcolm*, 91.

choice to give voice through his writings to the message of the incarnate Logos.

Seeds of the Word

Lewis was surprised by Tolkien's idea that myths may be an embryonic form of revelation. However, the roots of this concept are found in the earliest Patristic era; they also contributed to the extraordinary flowering of Christian theology resulting from the encounter between the Jewish tradition of biblical revelation and the Greek system of thought and practice called "philosophy." The first trace of such an inclusive attitude, which does not imply either syncretism or relativism, is found in Paul's Discourse of the Areopagus (Acts 17). Its development is attributed to Justin Martyr's *Apologies* (ca. 155 CE), where the idea of the Seminal Logos (*Logos spermatikos*) is discussed. Justin wrote that "Whatever things were rightly said among all men, are the property of us Christians,"[14] and since God's Logos exists outside Time and therefore "before" Time itself, "He was and is the Word who is in every man."[15] Thus, "all the writers were able to see realities darkly through the sowing of the implanted word that was in them."[16] This resonates with Tolkien's idea that "Only by myth-making, only by becoming a 'sub-creator' and inventing stories can Man aspire to the state of perfection he knew before the Fall. Our myths may be misguided, but they steer however shakily towards the true harbour."[17]

Tolkien saw creation myths not as the naïve attempt of pre-scientific people to explain (or explain away) those natural phenomena for which they did not (yet) have a convincing rational account, but rather as narratives "woven by us" and which, "though they contain error, will also reflect a splintered fragment of the true light, the eternal truth that is with God."[18] A similar expression is found in *Mythopoeia*, where Tolkien contemplates sub-creation as the refraction of light "splintered from a single White / to many hues, and endlessly combined / in living shapes that move from mind to mind."[19] These many "hues" which refract the "single White" are beauti-

14. Justin, *Second Apology* 13.
15. Justin, *Second Apology* 10.
16. Justin, *Second Apology* 13.
17. Carpenter, *Tolkien*, 147.
18. Carpenter, *Tolkien*, 147.
19. Tolkien, "Mythopoeia," 99.

fully paralleled by the idea of the Ainur adorning Ilúvatar's theme, each singing in his or her individual and personal style.

Consequently, Tolkien's study of creation myths and narratives far exceeded the dimension of an anthropological curiosity, and became a standpoint from which to contemplate a primeval form of revelation and from which to take inspiration for his own creation stories.[20] This may have happened, for instance, in the case of the Anglo-Druidic *Barddas*. Though it is considered by scholars to be essentially a forgery, Tolkien the author may have been fascinated by its imagery. It shows God, who, "alone in the universe . . . said His own name, and the voice was so beautiful that the universe burst into being with sound, light and form."[21] The "melodious sweetness" of God's voice makes "nonentity . . . rejoice into life."[22] Similar myths are found in the New Hebrides,[23] while Irish myths give order and ratio to the world through music and *poesis*.[24] The cultural connections between Britain and India may have favored Tolkien's knowledge of the Hindu tales of the god Prajāpati, which show significant analogies with the *Ainulindalë*,[25] and those of the *Gandharvas*, superhuman singers who have many points in common with the Ainur.[26] These creation myths built on "musical" narratives affirm the harmony of nature.

Generally speaking, creation myths express the enchantment we feel in the contemplation of the created world, and this is the source of a powerful religious feeling. In the biblical Book of Wisdom (13:1–9) it is argued that the enchanting beauty of the created world should have led the heathen to the Creator: "If through delight in the beauty of these things people

20. In the impossibility to ascertain which creation myth were known by Tolkien, I briefly mention some with which he might have been familiar. Since, however, my aim is not to reconstruct the sources of Tolkien's *legendarium*, but rather to frame it within a religious-cultural context, even an indirect knowledge may be relevant. For example, there are "musical" creation myths also in the Maya and Hopi cultures: Larsen, "Behold Your Music," 12. Fascinatingly, Kramer (*Time of Music*, 42) cites the Hopi culture as one "whose time conception is not linear," i.e., non-teleological. I find it very interesting, if this is actually the case, that the form in which their society narrates creation should be a musical myth.

21. Leeming, *Creation Myths*, 1:274; cf. Williams, *Barddas of Iolo Morganwg*, 1:47, 250–53, 259.

22. Williams, *Barddas*, 1:259.

23. Leeming, *Creation Myths*, 1:336.

24. Leeming, *Creation Myths*, 1:152.

25. Cf. Eggeling, *Satapatha Brahmana*, 3:143–64.

26. See Wilkins, *Hindu Mythology*, 362.

assumed them to be gods, let them know how much better than these is their Lord, for the author of beauty created them" (Wis 13:3). Similarly, also the continuing existence of the world constitutes a proof of God's benevolent will to sustain the universe.

In fact, if God's creative process should not be seen as a string of consecutive actions, conversely the creative act is not exhausted in "the making of" the world, but rather (in its temporal dimension) is to be conceived as a continuing process to which the universe owes its life and existence (cf. Hebr 1:3).[27] This benign and loving care which God bestows on the world and particularly on his children is therefore both an integral part of "creation" itself, and it is what we use to call Providence, the unfolding in time of the *eucatastrophe* par excellence which is the Story of Salvation.

Creation in Music

The roots of this story are found, once more, in the Book of Genesis; Christian theologians have frequently read it in musical terms. One of the early Church Fathers, Athanasius, employed musical similes to describe God's creative activity through his divine Logos. He wrote: "the single order and concord of the many and diverse shows that the ruler . . . is one"; just as the beautiful combination of varied tones on a lyre reveals the presence of a single and skilled musician playing it, so "the order of the whole universe being perfectly harmonious . . . it is consistent to think that the Ruler and King of all Creation is one."[28] Later, he describes the Logos's creative activity by employing once more musical terms:

> For just as though some musician, having tuned a lyre, and by his art adjusted the high notes to the low, and the intermediate notes to the rest, were to produce a single tune as the result, so also the Wisdom of God, handling the Universe as a lyre, and adjusting things in the air to things on the earth, and things in the heaven to things in the air, and combining parts into wholes and moving them all by His beck and will, produces well and fittingly, as the result, the unity of the universe and of its order, Himself remaining

27. It may be added that the following lines of Hebrews discuss the subordination of the angels to the divine Logos. Here too creation, revelation and the contemplation of God by the angels are strictly interrelated.

28. Athanasius, *Contra Paganos* 38.4.

> unmoved with the Father while He moves all things by His organising action, as seems good for each to His own Father.[29]

In the late seventeenth century, Angelo Berardi (ca. 1636–1694) cited Athanasius when describing God's creation of the world as a musical activity: "The supreme Archmusician, at the beginning of the world, filled everything with a wondrous harmony. . . . On these [modes, God] composed all of his works, which, like harmonious and well-concerted Madrigals, were invented with the art of his eternal wisdom, and written with the pen of his wonderful omnipotence." For Adam and Eve, God composed a beautiful two-part motet on the "tone" of their original innocence; "but, as soon as this music had begun, a third invidious Musician came, . . . and, with an off-key and harsh voice, he began singing a hellish song, *Eritis sicut Dij* [you will be like God]." God, "like a good chapel master," tried to reinstate them in their harmony; but Adam and Eve, ashamed, were expelled from "the Chapel of Heaven." Eventually, however, in the Empyrean "a new eternal symphony" will be sung, "with such a concord and harmony that this Music will never undergo discordance."[30] This account of God's creation, of his relationship with the intelligent created beings, of Satan's sin of pride and temptation of the progenitors, and of the "Great Music" to come is very similar to Tolkien's *Ainulindalë*.

Though I cannot claim that Tolkien was familiar with Berardi's writing and that it influenced his creation myth, the influence of John Milton (1608–1674) on *The Silmarillion* is known.[31] In his *Paradise lost*, musical imagery permeates the account of creation: "Nor passed uncelebrated, nor unsung / By the celestial choirs, when orient light / Exhaling first from darkness they beheld; / Birthday of heav'n and earth; with joy and shout / the hollow universal orb they filled, / And touched their golden harps, and hymning praised / God and his works."[32] Here, as in Augustine, the celestial beings contemplate the work of "God's hands," rejoicing for its beauty and expressing their amazement through music. Similarly, Samuel T. Coleridge

29. Athanasius, *Contra Paganos* 42.3.

30. Berardi, *Miscellanea musicale*, 1–2. See also his *Documenti armonici*, where he states: "The same Creator worked as a most skilled musician in the fashioning of the world, disposing everything as a well-ordered concord on a harmonious lyre. . . . Only the string of the human beings is frequently dissonant . . . but, if it is purged by penance and put in tune by contrition, it is changed from a harsh dissonance to a sweet and suave consonance" (Berardi, *Documenti armonici*, 10).

31. Cf. for example Sayer, *Jack*, 51; Hardy, *Milton*, 113–14.

32. Milton, *Paradise Lost* 7.253–59.

(1772–1834) in *The Eolian Harp* mentions the "soft witchery of sound / As twilight Elfins make," before invoking "the one Life within us and abroad, / Which meets all motion and becomes its soul, / A light in sound, a sound-like power in light, / Rhythm in all thought, and joyance everywhere." In these lines, we can recognize the Platonic theme of the World-Soul embodied by the image of the intertwining of light and sound. Coleridge then wonders whether "all of animated nature / be but organic Harps diversely framed / That tremble into thought" when they are animated by the "one intellectual breeze" which is "at once the Soul of each, and God of all." The pantheistic touch inherent in Coleridge's poetry is countered in the subsequent lines, where the terms employed are explicitly Christian and the poet humbly pleads for mercy.

Creation and Redemption

Creation in music and the mystery of redemption and forgiveness of sins are intertwined with each other also in *A Litany* by John Donne, who depicts "this universal quire / That Church in triumph, this in warfare here, / Warm'd with one all-partaking fire" (stanza XIV), which calls unto mind Tolkien's Imperishable Flame as well as the "integral view" seen in Bonaventure. Later (stanza XXIII), Donne beseeches the Lord to hear the sinners' prayer, since "to Thee / A sinner is more music, when he prays, / Than spheres' or angels' praises be / In panegyric alleluias."[33] Though Donne's language is explicitly Christian, we find a consistent use of musical metaphors to symbolize both the holy harmony and its disruption through sin. An analogous perspective, in which music is employed to symbolize not only the rupture of the heavenly harmony, but also its eventual reconstruction, is found in John Milton's *At a Solemn Music* where the mythical Sirens (alluding to the Christian angels) sing for "him that sits" on the "sapphire-colour'd throne," in the company of spirits and angels. The earthly beings join "with undiscording voice," as they "once . . . did, till disproportion'd sin . . . / broke the fair musick that all creatures made / To their great Lord." Notwithstanding the discordance brought in the music by evil, as by Melkor among the Ainur, Milton, similar to Tolkien, contemplates a greater music to come: "O may we soon again renew that Song / And keep in tune

33. Donne, *Poems*, 2:174–87.

with Heav'n, till God ere long / To his celestial consort us unite, / To live with him and sing in endles morn of light."[34]

Similar themes, with different and significant shades, are found also in more recent poems, such as *The Christ of Velázquez* by Miguel de Unamuno (1864–1936).[35] Here a meaningful itinerary connects Christ's incarnation, passion and resurrection to the unfolding of the harmonious song of Salvation. Just as in Jacopone's *lauda*, Christ's incarnation is seen as the intersection of the temporal and the eternal, whereby God's eternal present enters our history and our time. On the other hand, Unamuno reinterprets the Gospel account of Christ's transfiguration as another moment in which chronological time (theologically interpreted as the narrative time of the History of Salvation) intertwines with other temporalities (the past of Moses and Elijah, and the future of Christ's Passion) as well as with eternity (God's voice from heaven). It is also a moment so perfect that the apostles want it to last: they would remain in that experience of compresence of time and eternity, and make it last forever. So enchanting is Christ's transfigured body that "it invites us / to remain on the mountain, to pitch camp there / and drink in its whiteness." When the disciples hear the Father's voice,

> the snow-thick dawn of Your divine body / sings of resurrection from among the dead, sings /—not says—for Your divine body / is music, and this silent song / (its whiteness music for the eyes) / gives refreshment like the harp of David / to our souls when the spirit of the Evil / One is upon them, and at the sounds / of Your heavenly breast's harmony / our pain is laid to sleep, / in the nests of our hearts inhumed / by enchantment.

Christ's transfigured body is so white, of such an unearthly whiteness, that it becomes "music," "music for the eyes," being a prefiguration of his Resurrection. Indeed, the Paschal mystery will transform flesh into something suited for eternity (1 Cor 15:53–5): the bodily reality of temporal matter will be changed, just as the orderly sequence of our life's time will be embraced by God's Eternal Present. Therefore, the "whiteness" of Christ (prefiguration of the condition of the resurrected bodies) is "music for the eyes," as it allows us to behold the sense of time at a single glance. Unamuno continues: "You are the song without end or confine, / Lord, the sonorous

34. In Quiller-Couch, *Oxford Book*, 319–20.

35. Interestingly, this poem is inspired by a work of visual art: temporality, creativity and visualization of Time intertwine here too.

solitude, / and in the concert which links all beings / the epiphany. The spheres sing / through Your body, harp of the universe."[36]

Through Christ and his body, the communion of all the created world is made visible, it is manifested as an "epiphany." In Him, the mysteries of creation (the body), of temporality (his Passion and death), and of eternity (his Resurrection) are made one, thus revealing the harmony of the cosmos ("the spheres . . . harp of the universe"). In Christ, History and matter reveal their "harmony" and are contemplated in their causality, finality and providentiality as a history of salvation.

In both Unamuno's and Jacopone's poetry, the Paschal mystery is prefigured and seen, as if in transparency, behind Christ's Incarnation and his Transfiguration. The Paschal mystery, in turn, is strictly linked to the Eucharist: for Catholics, it re-presents and memorializes those historical events, so that Time is transcended once more on the altar.[37] Since Christ's Body is the bread of eternal life (John 6:54), in the sacrifice celebrated by the eternal priest who is Christ (Heb 7) the Eucharist mystically unites the eternal worship performed by the heavenly community outside of Time, the historical sacrifice of Christ on the cross, and the thanksgiving enacted in our times by the church. Thus, it can be said that the Eucharistic altar is yet another bridge connecting eternity and time. Music links time, eternity and the Paschal mystery in several artistic creations, among which I will cite a few of the most iconic. In Richard Wagner's opera *Parsifal*, Eucharistic symbolism is ubiquitous; just before the revelation of the Holy Grail, Gurnemanz sings: "Here time becomes space," thus representing a visualization of the eternal through music.[38] In visual art, we might recall the Ghent Altarpiece Jan van Eyck (ca. 1390–1441). Here, all revolves around the pivotal figure of the Lamb (as in Jacopone), from whose side the sacramental blood is poured into the chalice on the altar. Some of the surrounding angels display the instruments of Christ's passion, while others swing their

36. All quotes from *Christ of Velázquez* in Atwan et al., *Divine Inspiration*, 158–59. Eliezer Oyola has interestingly connected this fragment of Unamuno's poem to C. S. Lewis's account of creation in *The Chronicles of Narnia ("The Magician's Nephew")*, a work which has many points in common with Tolkien's *Ainulindalë* (Oyola, *Imagen y Palabra*, 85–86). I have compared Tolkien's and Lewis's creation myths in music in a forthcoming article (Bertoglio, "Lion and the Pitch").

37. See, for example, John Paul II, *Ecclesia de Eucharistia* 8; 21; 48. See also Vatican Council, "*Lumen Gentium*" 3; *ST* III, q. 83 r.

38. On the topic of Time and Space in Wagner, and of the theology expressed in his *Parsifal*, see Bell, *Wagner's Parsifal*, esp. 107, 226, 271–76, 308.

censers as happens in the Mass. Christ's incarnation is referenced in the Altarpiece through the depiction of the Annunciation, but this masterpiece is also interspersed with references to music. There are angels with musical instruments, a choir of singing angels, and some holy Popes singing from a book with musical staves, in a further example of musical notation as a symbol for the eternal present.

The same eternal act of thanksgiving portrayed by van Eyck is also evoked by the pre-Romantic poet Edward Young, to whom we owe one of the most impressive anticipations of Tolkien's *Ainulindalë*. In his *Night Thoughts*, Young describes "The song of Angels, all the melodies / of choral gods." Since angels, unlike humans, do not need redemption, the angels are paradoxically less blessed than the redeemed sinners: "View man, to see the glory of your God! / Could angels envy, they had envied here; / And some did envy; and the rest, though gods, / Yet still gods unredeem'd (their triumphs man, / Tempted to weigh the dust against the skies), / They less would feel, though more adorn, my theme. / They sung [sic] creation (for in that they shared); / How rose in melody, that child of love!"[39] Here, as seen in Jacopone, Unamuno and Wagner, the Paschal redemption opens up the gates of heaven, providing eternal life and admitting the fallen and mortal human beings to the rite of praise transcending Time.

In these last examples we have seen that the mystery of Creation (i.e., the birth of Time, and of things in Time, as a gift of the Eternal God), Incarnation (the entrance in Time of the Eternal Son of God), Redemption (through which the Incarnate Logos freed us from the bounds of time and gave us eternal life), and eternal praise in the heavenly worship are intertwined, and that music underpins their profound communion as a symbol of time and of the possibility of transcending it. Bearing this interwoven complexity in mind, we can therefore understand in a more complete and deep fashion the role of creation ("in music") and of subcreation.

Gathering, therefore, the most relevant threads of the current argument, a circular path starts to appear. From the one side, the contemplation of the created world leads human beings to search for the origins of that beauty, and therefore to awaken in them the first spark of a religious feeling. From the other side, by re-telling the process of creation, and/or by revealing the magic (or rather the mystery) hidden in the created world, the sub-creator opens the readers' eyes to a new appraisal of creation, which

39. Young, *Young's Night Thoughts*, 74.

ultimately translates into a prayerful praise.[40] This process does not imply that the beauty of creation may have originated religion by itself. Rather, the beauty of creation is an instrument used by God in order to reveal Himself to human beings, in a process which maintains an important dimension of mystery and unfathomability. The enchantment and joy we feel when we contemplate nature and life is best understood as a form of revelation of a God who gave Himself in the *kenosis* of Creation.

Shaping the Song

After contemplating the Godhead, singing together, overcoming the disruption of Melkor's discord, and beholding the Vision, Tolkien's Ainur (or Valar) are entrusted with the task of fashioning Arda, the material world. The contemplation of God's creativity elicits a similar response in the creatures. Their role is described by the author in his Letter to Milton Waldman:

> The cycles begin with a cosmogonical myth: the *Music of the Ainur*. God and the Valar (or powers: Englished as gods) are revealed. These latter are as we should say angelic powers, whose function is to exercise delegate authority in their spheres (of rule and government, *not* creation, making or re-making). They are "divine," that is, were originally "outside" and existed "before" the making of the world. Their power and wisdom is derived from their Knowledge of the cosmogonical drama, which they perceived first as a drama (that is as in a fashion we perceive a story composed by someone else), and later as a "reality." On the side of mere narrative device, this is, of course, meant to provide beings of the same order of beauty, power, and majesty as the "gods" of higher mythology, which can yet be accepted—well, shall we say baldly, by a mind that believes in the Blessed Trinity.[41]

It is particularly tantalizing to note Tolkien's emphasis that the Ainur have no authority of "creation, making or re-making," since their role in the shaping of Arda may seem very close to that of "creators." If we are to use Tolkien's language, however, even the Ainur are sub-creators rather than "Creators"; the molding of Arda is the embodiment of their adornment of those themes which have their only and ultimate origin in Ilúvatar. Melkor's

40. Cf. Bassham, "Lewis and Tolkien," 18. This experience is also beautifully described in Chesterton, *Orthodoxy*, 32–36.

41. Tolkien, *Letters*, 146.

"original sin" is precisely that of wanting "to bring into Being things of his own,"[42] and Ilúvatar clearly states to him that "no theme may be played that hath not its uttermost source in me."[43]

Tolkien's mention of Creation as of a "cosmogonical drama, which [the *Ainur*] perceived first as a drama," i.e., as "we perceive a story composed by someone else" is also worth noting. The idea of drama refers to such concepts as "plot," with its narrative overtones as concerns the presence of a dynamics of tension/distension, "struggle," "relationship"—and also its artistry and beauty. It should be noted in passing that the dramatic dimension is foundational for the entire theological perspective of Hans Urs von Balthasar, one of the greatest Catholic theologians of the twentieth century. In his *Theo-Drama*, he develops an interpretation of the immanent life of the Triune God and of the history of salvation by way of a powerful analogy, that of a drama written by an author, staged by a director and interpreted by an actor; God's action can then be seen as threefold, expressing the reality of the three divine hypostases. This view deeply resonates with the perspective of musical scores as a symbol for God's eternal present and for the history of salvation: the dimension of performance is inherent in both acting and playing music, and the script, similar to a score, embodies an unfolding narrative in a simultaneously existing written expression (just as happens with Tolkien's novel or Dante's poetry).[44]

Similar to actors who perform a script, or to musicians who play a score, the role of the Ainur, therefore, is first and foremost to *receive* Ilúvatar's theme (as "a story composed by someone else"), and to engage (sub-) creatively with it, by adorning it in an activity which, far from being passive, involves their personality in full, thus linking their self-realization with their acceptance of Ilúvatar's Gift. The Ainur are later involved in the "fashioning" of Arda, and they intervene (more or less directly) in many events recounted in *The Silmarillion*, occasionally committing blunders which have unforeseen and sometimes tragic consequences.

42. Tolkien, *Silmarillion*, 16.

43. Tolkien, *Silmarillion*, 17.

44. See Balthasar, *Theo-Drama*, 1.268–305 and 3.515–35. There is also more than an echo of Tolkien's "music of the Ainur" in Balthasar's view of the Truth as "symphonic." On Tolkien's possible influence on Balthasar, see Coutras, *Tolkien's Theology*, 14, and the works cited there.

Eucatastrophes

Indeed, the history of Arda, just as Dante's own story, and the history of humankind as a whole, are stories interwoven with joy and pain, good and evil, holiness and depravity, innocence and wickedness, feast and death. While the second terms of the preceding pairs are not willed by God, believers affirm that He can work them into the fabric of a providential song, the song of his love for us.

In one of his letters, Tolkien explicitly identified "the One" (i.e., Eru, Ilúvatar, the Godhead) as "the Teller" of a story; that story comes to being when he utters the creative "Let it Be": "Then the Tale became History, on the same plane as the hearers."[45] If Tolkien understood God as the One who tells the story of humankind, then the role of the sub-creators, of the poets, novelists, dramatists and musicians acquires a new meaning and a new significance.

By telling, or by being told a story, a myth, a narrative, or by composing or hearing a piece of music, we grasp or intuit the place and role of the negative elements of life. Dante's *Commedia*, literally a story with a "happy ending," narrates a human and spiritual itinerary which is interspersed with suffering but is ordered to a blissful and eternally joyful goal. Similarly, Tolkien, "a storyteller at heart," felt that "stories need conflict, just as humanity does. So the creation of dissonance is necessary," as it enables "humans to learn from their mistakes and to grow,"[46] as Jensen put it. As in a piece of music, where dissonances literally "lead" to consonances, Tolkien constructs his narrative in order to "provoke in us a longing for a happy ending that does not negate but fulfils the 'natural desire for the supernatural'" that, as Milbank put it, "both Augustine and Aquinas taught."[47] It is not by chance that Sam and Frodo, in *The Lord of the Rings*, converse with each other about "tales and songs" (i.e., narratives and music) which will ultimately recount their adventures. Their debate, expressed in simple and touching words, is in fact a poignant reflection about life, Providence, the capability to understand the events as a (God-given) story, as a *eucatastrophe*.[48]

45. Tolkien, *Letters*, 284.

46. Jensen, "Dissonance," 103.

47. Milbank, *Chesterton and Tolkien*, 112.

48. Cf. Tolkien, *Lord of the Rings*, 2:711–12.

Dissonance is needed not only in music, as we have seen, but also in narrativity. This can be observed even more clearly in the version of the *Ainulindalë* published in the *Book of Lost Tales*,[49] where sin will ultimately show itself to have made "the theme more worth the hearing, Life more worth the living, and the World so much the more wonderful and marvelous." As Naveh[50] observes, however, "it is hard to believe that any of Tolkien's characters would actually find themselves thinking of the deeds of Melkor, Sauron, or their agents in this way." Of course, along with all human beings inhabiting our post-lapsarian world, both the suffering characters and the empathic readers rebel against a vision of the evil or pain which considers them as "spicy" ingredients used to increase the pleasure of an eschatological banquet. Indeed, since Tolkien's *legendarium* was largely conceived during the most violent period of human history, his experience of life could hardly consider the two World Wars as mere piquant seasonings.

Tolkien's vision, and his use of the musical symbol, is however more complex and ultimately much more convincing. Narration, similar to music, is an attempt to insert the presence of evil within a discourse understandable by us fallen human beings. It gives us a key which renders pain at least partially intelligible by our reason, or, if this is impossible, leaves it in its condition of mystery while announcing its eventual and final "resolution." As we have seen, musical expectations are generated by the tension between dissonance and resolution, and—according to Meyer[51]—they are what creates musical emotion and meaning. In Schmuckler's synthesis of Meyer's thought, "expectation is the vehicle by which music becomes meaningful."[52]

This meaningfulness arises from our understanding of the temporality of music; indeed, along with chronological time and psychological time,[53] there may be yet another time, which is intensely theological. The Norwegian philosopher of music Arild Pedersen[54] has theorized what he calls "singing time," the time of religion and music. "Singing time" reveals the "formed project" behind the "charged" (i.e., meaningful, significant) moments, and, for him, is the source of religious and literary narratives,

49. Tolkien, *Book of Lost Tales*, 1:55.

50. Naveh, "Tonality," 39.

51. Meyer, *Emotion and Meaning*.

52. Schmuckler, "Expectations," 112.

53. See chapter 3.

54. Pedersen, *Singing Time*. See also Bjerstedt et al., "Musical Present."

as well as of music itself.[55] This concept may be woven within the account given here, inasmuch as Pedersen's "singing time" may be likened to the contemplation of the providentiality of time as a coordination of meaningful events. According to one of the greatest theologians of music, Jeremy Begbie,

> In musical experience we can enjoy a temporality which is in some measure incongruous with the extra-musical time(s) which we inhabit in our day to day lives. Something is happening which at its best might be described as music "taking" our time and "returning it" to us re-shaped in some manner. To share in music is to find a temporality in which—at least to some extent—past, present and future have been made to interweave fruitfully.[56]

What gives meaning to music, to narrative, and to life is the capability of seeing the connection behind the events; indeed, the very act of telling, of narrating a story, rests on the assumption that events are not casual by-products of random forces acting haphazardly in our world. As Milbank put it: "to tell a story is to affirm that there is meaning to life, and that experience is shaped and has an entelechy."[57] By giving a theological value to *poesis*, Tolkien suggests that the gratuitousness of aesthetics and the logic of narration are not opposing poles: logic has a theological beauty.

Beyond the Canticle

This goes some way towards explaining the crucial difference between dissonance and discord in the opening pages of the *Ainulindalë*. Dissonances are fundamental components of harmony, and the Great Music to come—as the latter themes of Ilúvatar—will embrace them in a "greater" symphony which all intelligent beings will sing to their God. Discord, on the other hand, is the "unredeemable" product of Melkor's pride. Ilúvatar's theme, given to all the Ainur so that they may decorate it, is also the principle which enables and facilitates their (musical) communication and their knowledge of each other; all of the Ainur's themes are variations of Ilúvatar's

55. This idea may also be enriched by a comparison with the concept of "chronotope" as proposed by Bakhtin in his discussion of literature: a time interspersed by meaningful events "thickens, takes on flesh, becomes artistically visible" (Bakhtin, *Dialogic Imagination*, 84). See the application of Bakhtin's ideas to music in Bjerstedt et al., "Musical Present," 25–26, to which this section is indebted.

56. Begbie, *Theology*, 150.

57. Milbank, *Chesterton and Tolkien*, 11.

original self-revelation. This linguistic and epistemological element is also the principle of their freedom, since it keeps together both their createdness (all have their common origin in Ilúvatar) and their creativity (their task is to decorate the theme).

Melkor's attempt to replace Ilúvatar's theme with his own as the leading and guiding principle of his brethren's music therefore diminishes the Ainur's capacity of communicating with each other. As in the biblical account of Babel's Tower (Gen 11), discord arises because of a lack of communication and mutual comprehension. Moreover, by factually denying his own createdness, Melkor reduces the space of creativity allotted to his brethren, and thus breaks the balance of createdness and creativity.

By choosing musical symbolism, rooted in a long literary and philosophical tradition of the Western thought, Tolkien is able to convey in the space of three or four pages an enormous depth of poetry and theology. Music, as the art of time, and as the art which demonstrates how dissonances can (and must) be part of harmony, is the perfect symbol for the redemption of the world, nourishing, as it does, our hope for the Great Music to come.

By demonstrating that musical events do not happen by mere chance, but rather are harmoniously, intelligently, and intelligibly organized in time, the composer gives meaning to our time, and encourages us to believe that also the factual events of our lives are not haphazardly combined, but rather part of a "story." By its structural and meaningful use of dissonance, music embodies a radical aesthetic theodicy, in which the order, reasonableness and beauty of the created world are believed in faith and asserted in the poetical experience. By giving form to our glimpses on eternity from the narrow window of time, it suggests that truth is larger than what we can grasp now, and yet will shine in its fullness when the entire symphony will be concentrated in a moment of eternal presence. Music, thus, is affirmed as a form of knowledge, of revelation, of creativity, which enables us to express reasonably and experientially our faith in the meaningfulness of life and in its ultimate beauty and goodness.

This in turn parallels the action of the author of fiction, of the "sub-creator," who announces the presence of a loving God by narrating a story which is intelligible as a sequence of causes and effects, and reveals a providential design behind the seeming chaotic events of our lives. Creation, as we have previously seen, is not something happening once and for all, but rather is the continuing life received as a Gift from God's eternal Will, from his benign and loving Providence.

Quodlibet

This book, similar to a fugue, has now reached its final stretto; all the subjects which have sounded throughout its pages should now combine with each other, in view of the final cadence. At first, we have considered the importance of Time in our experience: Time resists both an easy conceptualization and our yearning for a condition not entirely dependent on its laws. The reality of an omnipotent God must be free from such limits, and, at the same time, capable of entering into dialogue with our own temporal reality. Therefore, God's mode of being, as concerns His relationship with Time, has been conceived by Christian thinkers (such as Boethius and St. Augustine) as an "Eternal Present."

Both Boethius and Augustine are among the most influential thinkers about music in the early Christian era; logically, then, both reflect on Time and on the Eternal Present in musical terms, while also employing visual/spatial metaphors, symbols, and similes. Visual representations of Time, in fact, allow us to "observe" synchronicity and to "foresee" future events through recurring phenomena and patterns. Along with mathematical graphs, musical scores represent a valid, successful and pioneering example of how humans have depicted Time in a visual form.

By tracing the development of the notation of Western music, we find elements of synchronicity and an increasing degree of sophistication in their recording of time. In particular, new systems of notation were prompted and made indispensable by the needs of polyphonic music, and by the synchronism it requires. Musical notation found ways to express the "parallel" itinerary of multiple voices: the simultaneous movement of several parts suggests a form of multi-dimensional temporality, visually represented in spatial form through musical scores.

Possibly encouraged by notation itself, composers of polyphony pursued the utopian ideal of playing with time, creating retrograde and circular canons, which suggest alternative forms of conceiving Time (backwards or circularly). Later, the affirmation of the tonal language led to new challenges: composers such as Bach and Mozart purposefully elaborated on temporality. For Berger, Bach explicated in time a musical construction conceived in the "simultaneous" consideration of all compositional possibilities, while Mozart disposed musical events in an overtly teleological and temporally ordered succession.

Such a perspective is grounded on our capability, as human beings belonging in a certain culture and musical tradition, to perceive and "understand" the succession of musical events as constituting an ordered and intelligible structure. The rhythm of music mimics and rules our psychological time; its polyphony and harmony lead us to project expectations onto the future development of a piece, and retrospectively to interpret its musical events. This constitutes the uniquely musical form of a temporal narrativity whose "content" can rarely (and never univocally) be expressed in words, but which nevertheless is interpreted as a consistent and normally delightful "tale of sounds."

This aural and aesthetical experience is similarly lived by professional musicians and by those lacking musical literacy, albeit with different degrees of refinement and "understanding". However, the possibility of writing music made a major contribution to the very development of the Western musical culture. Some musical innovations of the twentieth century can be seen to spring from the interaction between the exploration of new aural effects and the stimuli offered by music notation itself.

Messiaen's view of the non-retrogradable (palindrome) rhythms as the musical embodiment of a butterfly is a case in point: a visual image (the butterfly) is understood as symbolizing a symmetrical rhythm which in turn allows the composer to imagine a bidirectional temporality. This kind of visualization largely depends on a musician's acquaintance with the conventions of notation. Through a long familiarity with scores, musicians acquire a habit for associating aural shapes with visual impressions. This in turn leads to the possibility of instantly recognizing the *Gestalt* and main musical features of a piece by observing a score. These same traditional conventions are exploited even in the case of unconventional notational forms, such as those of graphic scores, building on the musicians' familiarity with traditional notation, and deriving their forms from new interpretations of older schemes.

In many contemporary pieces (notated as graphic or more traditional scores), the visual idea may precede the aural "inspiration"; the spatialization of music may sometimes prompt its audible shape. This kind of interaction stimulated the imagination of several visual artists, such as Klee and Kandinsky, who visually reinterpreted the forms of musical notation. Here traditional boundaries seem to disappear, and it is difficult to classify musical compositions derived from graphical ideas, graphical translation of musical ideas, and visual art "proper." Frequently, such dialogues between aural and visual revolve around issues concerning the temporality of music, and the possibility of "beholding" a musical work in its entirety (in memory? on a score?) in spite of the dependence of performed music on sequential temporality.

Thus, the experiments of twentieth-century artists resonate with the intuition of visual artists from much earlier times. Visual artworks had frequently employed musical scores, in which a piece can actually be beholden, as symbols for temporality (in its fleetingness, but also in the effort of overcoming it). If the simple depiction of a musical score can symbolize Time in a painting, conversely musicians can gather substantial information about the musical features of a piece by observing its score. Moreover, familiarity with notational conventions permits the "navigation" of the piece's temporality. This exploration may happen in the mnemonic recalling of a known work, in the cursory observation of a score, and in the process of performance, whereby concurrent temporalities may be simultaneously present in an interpreter's consciousness. Studies in the psychology of music confirm the intuitions of practical musicians and of philosophers such as Bergson. Supported by the observation of scores, these studies affirm the mental compresence of different "flows of time" in the imagination of musicians.

This mapping of a musical piece normally involves its fundamental features rather than its smallest details. Similarly, although on a different plane, the notation of music is in itself a "mapping" of the musical events, since it translates a continuum into discrete indications, and leaves many spaces of indeterminacy whose actual embodiment in sound constitutes the interpreter's work. All these elements in Part One demonstrate that a musician's observation of a known score represents the almost instantaneous intuition of a temporal phenomenon. Therefore, this beholding constitutes an analogue for the Eternal Present, in which all Time may be embraced at a "glance."

This experience resonates with those described in Part Two, where Tolkien's *Ainulindalë* was taken as a filter for rereading the biblical narrative of Genesis. If "human" musical scores make Time present in an observable instant, conversely the contemplation of God by created beings outside Time may be likened to their observation of a musical score. This contemplation is their acceptance of the Godhead's revelation of Himself (the Logos) but also of their contextual calling, their "vocation": in God they can comprehend their own nature.

The Ainur's polyphonic improvisation represents Tolkien's reinterpretation of a long tradition rooted in the Pythagorean/Platonic theme of the harmony of the spheres. However, his description of the *processes* of listening, monodic improvisation, and polyphonic improvisation corresponds to the exquisitely Christian account of the angels' modes of knowledge in their intuition of God. The themes given by Ilúvatar to the Ainur are a form of *kenosis*, a calling, and an invitation to creativity. Ilúvatar's theme is akin to the *cantus firmus*, the sacred generating principle of polyphonic compositions, on which all parts depended, both individually and collectively. The Ainur's "adornment" of Ilúvatar's music is similar to their singing from a "score" (that of the Godhead's will) but also to an entirely free improvisation. When created beings behold the vision of God and wholeheartedly embrace the Gift bestowed on them, their individual wills cannot clash with each other but rather constitute an all-encompassing harmony.

Freedom also implies the possibility of refusing this gift and of destroying that harmony; this is what happens to Tolkien's Melkor and to Lucifer in the Christian tradition. Their rebellion can be musically understood as their desire to impose "their" theme to the created world; to trade the polyphonic concord for a despotic soloism; to spread discord and disharmony in the choir of creation.

By using musical similes, numerous authors encouraged a novel interpretation the problem of evil. In God's Eternal Present, Time and History are wholly encompassed, becoming part of the great "song" of the History of Salvation. This song reaches its climax in the events of Christ's life. In the Incarnation, Eternity entered Time and joined itself with the human experience of temporality. In the Transfiguration, the intuition of God's eternity led the disciples to wish for that moment to be turned into Eternity; there, the coincidence of past, present, and future encountered God's *voice* (an aural revelation in Time). In Christ's passion, death, and resurrection, the turning point of human history, the Eternal seemed to have undergone the destruction of mortality, but actually redeemed our temporality by making it capable of eternity. And this history of salvation is still unfolding itself in the life of the church, in the Eucharist which bridges the chasm between Time and Eternity, and in our individual lives. Providence, the temporal dimension of God's creative, life-giving, and redemptive activity, is still acting in the History of Salvation: those able to contemplate its unfolding in the Eternal Present can see how the greater and lesser dissonances in the music of Time will ultimately be subsumed and "saved" by God's loving will.

This reality, which presently eludes our condition as fallen creatures, is however beholden by angels and saints. In Tolkien's *Ainulindalë*, history unfolds in the Ainur's song, is contemplated in their Vision and is enacted in the Being of Arda; in Dante's *Commedia*, the protagonist's human life is "seen" in the vision of God, and "heard" as a polyphony by his ancestor Cacciaguida. As in a "comedy," a tale with a "happy ending" (a "Gospel," a *eucatastrophe*) the ultimate resolution of all dissonances in the harmony of God's will is contemplated by those outside time, and believed in faith by those living in time.

This faith sometimes requires an almost heroic effort. At the same time, the very *quest* for a meaning and a "sense" in History and in our story expresses our belief that such a meaning exists. On the one hand, then, the sub-creative telling of tales or myths and musical composition are the human response to the primeval vocation to creativity bestowed on them by their Creator. On the other hand, they are an act of faith and a faith-sustaining act. If even God's creation of the world can be understood in "musical" terms (by Tolkien, in myths, and also in Christian reinterpretations of Genesis), then the creation of music is a "religious act" in the highest meaning of the term. By giving a beautiful form and an intelligible order to the aural events in time, musicians proclaim that events are part of a (musical) story; when this story can be observed at a glance, on a score, we may intuit "providence." We instantaneously behold how musical events develop in time, eventually to reach their point of stasis, their Tonic.

Listening to music and reading novels rehearses our belief in the final cadence, in the *eucatastrophe*. It encourages us to keep searching the meaning of life, and to try to gather, from the "clues" found in the score, where the Fugue is pointing to. By looking backwards to the years of our past life, we observe the musical score of our very own song, or of that of Salvation; we are allowed to see the pages which have already been turned, and to study them. This analysis shows us the underlying logic, though this process requires continuously to be reinterpreted, refreshed, and renewed as the appearance of new themes gives a new meaning, in retrospect, to those musical events we have already heard.

Faith allows us also to glimpse some elements (few, but crucial) of the pages to come. We are told that the final chord will definitely resound; that all the seemingly conflicting subjects of the Fugue will ultimately display their "accord"; that the Composer is a true master of his art, and that he is building, with us and for us, a marvelous concert. We are also led to believe that the score has already been conceived, in the Creator's mind, and that it is eternally present to his loving gaze and to his providence. Furthermore, we are encouraged to see that the song unfolding in time is just a part of a much larger composition. More precisely, the present song is to eternity not only as a movement is to a symphony, but rather as a square to a cube: an anticipation, a representation, happening however on an utterly different plane.

After today's music, or rather beyond it, there will be a music of eternity, which actually is already being sung, outside Time, by the firstborn of creation and by the blessed spirits. There, the "Score" will shine in our eyes; we will immediately see its infinite beauty, and will love it; because our part, it will be revealed, is precisely the one we would have given anything to sing—just better. Thus, our "improvisation," the spontaneous expression of our innermost being, will also be our singing from the Score. Our song will be, at the same time, the one we always longed to sing and the one lovingly written by God for us.

Encore

When I was about three or four years old, my father took me to hear a piano recital given by a famous musician. I loved it, even though it was slightly too long for me. At the end, during the enthusiastic clapping applause, my father whispered in my ear: "Look, perhaps he will *grant* us an encore." I remember feeling rather puzzled, because, in the opinion of my younger self, we had already had too much of a good thing, and an encore was a threat rather than a treat. I hope, therefore, that this final encore will not be met with a similar reception by my readers.

These last pages are called "encore" because they are an *ad libitum*, prompted by a kind suggestion of one of my dearest friends. After reading the first draft of this book, she told me that she had missed "my" voice, in the polyphony of the preceding pages, and that possibly someone might want to know more about my background and why I had the idea to write this book.

These last pages are therefore unapologetically personal. In the two main parts of this book, I have sought "knowledge" through research, reflection, and representation. In this Encore you will read something about the "knowledge" which comes from my experience. I share it here in the hope that the grain of truth may nourish a fellow traveler on the path of life.

Dante would say that I am currently *"nel mezzo del cammin di nostra vita,"* halfway through a reasonable life expectancy, though, of course, I cannot know how far along the way I am. What I can say is that the vast majority of years behind me have been spent in the company of my piano and my books. Practicing and performing, reading, thinking, and writing have filled my days. Sometimes, these activities dovetailed with each other; they were always informed by my deeply felt interest in spiritual life as a Christian. I decided to complement my studies in piano and musicology with theology, and this book is the result: an intersection of my three main areas of interest—music as performance, music as research, music as prayer.

Some years ago, I was giving concerts for an Italian charity which organizes musical events in the oncological wards of public hospitals. It is an activity I have always done most gladly, because I have been blessed with good health, and I consider it my duty and my pleasure to share that gift and the gift of music with those who are less fortunate than me. These moments are also among the most cherished of my experience as a musician, because—contrary to many "normal" concerts—there is deep, heartfelt feedback from the "audience," and the sense that the music is having a positive impact on the lives of those hearing it.

I also loved talking with the doctors and psychologists who had encouraged these musical activities. I remember with gratitude two mind-opening dialogues, one in Bolzano and one in Brescia, with two doctors who expressed the same concept albeit in different forms. They explained that while every activity and stimulus that has a therapeutic value and promotes the patients' well-being is most welcome, music is the most efficacious of all arts for an oncological patient. "When they are diagnosed with cancer," I remember one of them saying, "their time is suspended. Their past (with their jobs, holidays, pastimes) seems to belong to the life of somebody else; their future is utterly unforeseeable, to a much greater extent than before. The present alone remains: and music, the art of time, helps them to give a meaning to this present."

These ideas fell on fertile ground in my mind, imagination and reflection, and can be considered as the germinating principle of this book.

My experience as a performing musician taught me a special kind of concentration in the present. While the musician's concentration must project itself toward what is to be played in the future and to look back at the past minutes, what really matters is the quantity and quality of the attention one is capable to give to the present moment. As I unceasingly repeat to my students, one should play as with blinkers: without reproaching oneself for errors or faults just made, and without worrying for a difficult passage one has yet to face, musicians must concentrate uniquely on what is, quite literally, "at hand." Sometimes, this concentration may cause problems, particularly when playing from memory. For example, the extreme focus on every note (a focus which is rarely achieved during practice and rehearsals, and which normally happens only on stage) may lead one to notice a detail that had escaped attention during practice, and this can undermine the automatic responses upon which the performance of music is grounded. My experience shows me how fundamental it is to try and attain that same kind of concentration before the concert, and that this is best achieved when one "journeys through" the piece without reading the score itself and without actually playing on a musical instrument. It is an entirely mental journey, in which all details of the piece must be recalled, and which unfailingly highlights those minimal aspects frequently overlooked in mechanical practice.

The habit formed by such concentration provides musicians with a particularly keen feeling for time and tempo. Feeling for time is expressed in the capability to measure with precision the time of daily activities; feeling for tempo regards the "pace" of life, and the possibility of evaluating objective time with respect to one's psychological time. Inexperienced musicians tend to perform in public much more quickly than at home as they are unconsciously accustomed to measure rhythm by their heartbeats, and so they translate a quickened heartbeat into a quicker performance.

These practical aspects may seem to affect only music performance but that is not the case. They have an impact on one's consciousness, on one's perception of the self, of life, of the meaning of life, at least in my own experience. Music makes us hyper alert to the present, and, at the same time, it teaches us the fleetingness of time, and the seeming non-recoverability of the moment. There is no "undo" button in a musical performance. And there is no "undo" button in life. At the same time, even the best performance comes to an end, and once it is over, it disappears. The same happens in life. I have seldom experienced a perfectly joyful moment without being acutely aware of its doom—to disappear in the abyss of time, and to remain, as a pale shadow, in memory. That shadow not only fails to recover the original joy, but frequently brings us at least as much nostalgia and sadness as it brings smiles.

This yearning to find a way to preserve the best moments in the music of life has lived with me for many years. And then, quite unexpectedly, the sadness and anguish of this longing lightened. I ceased fearing the loss of the moments of happiness precisely at a time when I was closest to losing many of them. I began to truly enjoy and savor those moments precisely because they were so precious few.

A few days before Christmas 2019, a beloved member of my family entered the ranks of those oncological patients for whom I had played so often. Our time, as a family, became that suspended time I had been told about by my medical friends. We lived day by day, simply loving each other as much as possible, without escaping the experience we had been called to, but without picturing all possible scenarios.

The day my relative came back from the hospital, after undergoing surgery, I began playing an Impromptu by Schubert. I wanted to play it as a lullaby, as a musical caress. I had played that piece innumerable times, and always when a performance was particularly meaningful for me—as an encore. I had played it for other oncological patients. I had also played it for a young child with a severe form of autism, who used to kick everybody who came near him, but who, upon hearing that Impromptu, sat on my lap while I kept playing. I played that Impromptu with my relative in the adjacent room; both, unnoticed by the other, began to cry. We cried for the physical and psychological pain of those days; we cried for relief, since the surgery had been successful; we cried because that music meant hope, and it embodied our love for each other.

And immediately afterwards came COVID-19, which hit Italy with particular strength, almost destroying our social life, annihilating the possibility to play in public, and creating a clear "before" and "after" in my own life, and in those of my family, my country, and globally. The virus swept away all the things I loved most, and which used to give meaning and beauty and happiness to my life: going to church, making music, meeting people, walking in nature. The weeks succeeded each other, as a bubble surfacing over the sea of my previously hectic life, and without the metronome of the daily activities. And yet in spite of being plunged in the most painful time of my entire life, I began to feel the present… as a present, as a gift.

And I now understood the profound truth of what I already believed, knew, and proclaimed, without having truly experienced it. It was a truth I believed as one believes what has the unmistakable ring of verity, a truth one trusts, but which did not really belong to me. I learned from the inside that the only way we have for preserving something forever is by loving it. Love bridges the chasm between time and eternity, because Love is the matter of which God Himself is made, and it is an experience which permeates every moment of our life. By infusing the moments of life with Love with a capital L—self-giving love, *agape*—they are projected into God's Eternal Present, which is their very source. "We love because he first loved us" (1 John 4:19); eternity permeates time through love, and thus turns immanence into transcendence, turns what passes into what remains.

When the pillars upon which we build our existence, self-consciousness, and identity start to crumble, I began to experience (as I had previously read in Chesterton's book on St. Francis) that the world, in truth, is upside down; that Life sustains those pillars, not the other way around. And this may happen because Life is sustained by an unending love, the life-giving, life-supporting, *living* love of God.

My temporal worries gave way to a much deeper desire for eternity; I no longer desired the impossible lengthening of a happy moment, but rather the eternal present where all beauty, all happiness, all truth are gathered and live forever.

And I realized afresh that if our story is written in letters of gold in God's heart, then the music of our life is also inscribed there. Just as a musician reads, interprets, contemplates and remembers the music on a score, so human beings can glimpse the meaning of their lives even in the here and now, by trying and fixing their gaze in God. In eternity, however, we will be able to see and understand this meaning in an immensely more joyful and perfect way.

In the score of God's love, not a single note of our lives will be missing; and I believe and hope that when the music of life on earth will have reached its final chord, the true symphony will begin. Franz Liszt summarized the sense of *Les Préludes*, a poem by Lamartine found in his *Nouvelles méditations poétiques* as follows: "What else is our life but a series of preludes to that unknown Hymn, the first and solemn note of which is intoned by Death?" It is not Death, however, that intones the Hymn; Death is just the upbeat, that very special moment when all members of an ensemble draw a breath together, before diving into the performance. By that breath they are made one; it synchronizes one of the fundamental functions of their life in order to create a new organism, a performing ensemble. This, I believe, will be the Eternal Present: a symphony of people, freely loving each other, freely playing their parts, freely improvising at will, and freely fixing their gaze into God's Eternal Present.

Bibliography

Adlington, Robert. "Musical Temporality: Perspectives from Adorno and de Man." *Repercussions* (1997) 5–60.

Adorno, Theodor W. *Gesammelte Schriften XIII*. Edited by Gr. Adorno and R. Tiedemann. Frankfurt am Main: Suhrkamp, 1971.

———. *Towards a Theory of Musical Reproduction. Notes, a Draft and Two Schemata*. Translated by Wieland Hoban. Cambridge: Polity, 2006.

Alighieri, Dante. *The Convivio of Dante Alighieri*. Translated by Philip H. Wicksteed. London: J. M. Dent, 1903.

———. *The Divine Comedy of Dante Alighieri: A Verse Translation La Divina Commedia*. Translated by Allen Mandelbaum. Berkeley: University of California Press, 1982. Online. https://digitaldante.columbia.edu/dante/divine-comedy.

Aquinas, Thomas. *Summa Theologiae*. Translated by Fathers of the English Dominican Province. London: Burns Oates & Washbourne, 1920. Online. http://newadvent.org/summa.

Athanasius. *Against the Heathen*. Translated by Archibald Robertson. Buffalo, NY: Christian Literature, 1892. Online. https://www.newadvent.org/fathers/2801.htm.

Atwan, Robert, et al., eds. *Divine Inspiration. The Life of Jesus in World Poetry*. Oxford: Oxford University Press, 1998.

Augustine. *The City of God*. Translated by Marcus Dods. 2 vols. Edinburgh: T&T Clark, 1871, 1913.

———. *The Confessions of St. Augustine*. Translated by J. G. Pilkington. Garden City, NY: International Collectors Library, 1900.

———. *Expositions on the Book of Psalms*. Translated by Silvano Borruso. South Bend, IN: St. Augustine's, 2007.

———. *The Literal Meaning of Genesis*. Edited and translated by Johannes Quasten et al. Mahwah, NJ: Paulist, 1982.

———. *On Free Choice of the Will*. Translated by Thomas Williams. Indianapolis: Hackett, 1993.

———. *On Order*. Translated by Members of the English Church. Vol. 6. Oxford: John Henry Parker, 1857.

Babbitt, Milton. "The Synthesis, Perception and Specification of Musical Time." *Journal of the International Folk Music Council* 16 (1964) 92–95.

Bakhtin, Mikhail. *The Dialogic Imagination: Four Essays*. Edited and translated by C. Emerson and M. Holquist. Austin: University of Texas Press, 1981.

———. *Problems of Dostoevsky's Poetics*. Edited and translated by C. Emerson. Minneapolis: University of Minnesota Press, 1984.

Balthasar, Hans Urs von. *Theo-Drama: Theological Dramatic Theory*. 5 vols. Translated by Graham Harrison. San Francisco: Ignatius, 1988.

———. *Truth is Symphonic: Aspects of Christian Pluralism*. Translated by Graham Harrison. San Francisco: Ignatius, 1987.

Bannister, Peter. "Kenosis in Contemporary Music and Postmodern Philosophy." In *Contemporary Music and Spirituality*, edited by Robert Sholl and Sander van Maas, 54–81. Abingdon: Routledge, 2017.

Barce, Ramón. *Fronteras de la música*. Madrid: Real Musical, 1985.

———. "Grafización." *Sonda* 2 (1968) 11–18.

Barnes, Jonathan, ed. *The Complete Works of Aristotle*. Rev. Oxford Translation. Princeton, NJ: Princeton University Press, 1991.

Barry, Barbara. *Musical Time: The Sense of Order*. Stuyvesant, NY: Pendragon, 1990.

Begbie, Jeremy. *Theology, Music and Time*. Cambridge: Cambridge University Press, 2000.

Bell, Richard H. *Wagner's Parsifal: An Appreciation in the Light of His Theological Journey*. Eugene, OR: Cascade, 2013.

Bellasis, Edward. *Cardinal Newman as a Musician*. London: Kegan Paul, 1892.

Bent, Margaret. *Magister Jacobus de Ispania, author of the Speculum musicae*. Farnham: Ashgate, 2015.

Berardi, Angelo. *Documenti armonici*. Bologna: Giacomo Monti, 1687.

———. *Miscellanea musicale*. Bologna: Giacomo Monti, 1689.

Berger, Karol. *Bach's Cycle, Mozart's Arrow: An Essay on the Origins of Musical Modernity*. Berkeley: University of California Press, 1997.

Bergson, Henri. *Duration and Simultaneity. With Reference to Einstein's Theory*. Translated by Leon Jacobson. Kansas City: Bobbs-Merrill, 1965. Online. https://archive.org/details/durationandsimultaneityhenribergson.

———. *Durée et simultanéité. À propos de la théorie d'Einstein*. 7th ed. Paris: Les Presses Universitaires de France, 1968. Online. http://classiques.uqac.ca/classiques/bergson_henri/duree_simultaneite/duree_et_simultaneite.pdf.

Bertoglio, Chiara. "Dante, Tolkien, and the Supreme Harmony." In *Tolkien and the Classics*, edited by Giampaolo Canzonieri et al., 83–96. Zürich: Walking Tree, 2019.

———. "Dissonant Harmonies: Tolkien's Musical Theodicy." *Tolkien Studies* 15 (2018) 93–114.

———. "High Scores: The Notation of Music, Time and the Eternal Present." *Logoi.ph*, 5.14 (2019) 59–122.

———. "The Lion and the Pitch." In *The Songs of the Spheres*, edited by Łukasz Neubauer and Guglielmo Spirito. Zürich: Walking Tree, forthcoming.

———. "Musical Scores as Symbols for the Eternal Present." *Culture e fede—Pontificium Concilium de Cultura* 27.1 (2019) 6–13.

———. "A Perfect Chord: Trinity in Music, Music in the Trinity," *Religions* 4 (2013) 485–501.

———. "Polyphony, Collective Improvisation and the Gift of Creation." In *Music in Tolkien's Work and Beyond*, edited by J. Eilmann and F. Schneidewind, 3–28. Zürich: Walking Tree, 2019.

———. *Reforming Music: Music and the Religious Reformations of the Sixteenth Century*. Berlin: De Gruyter, 2017.

———. *Through Music to Truth. Music and Theology in Dialogue with Italian Culture.* Turin: Effatà, 2016.

———. "Vedere il tempo in una dolce armonia: la profezia di Cacciaguida in *Paradiso* XVII e l'eterno presente." In *La musica e Dante* (provisional title), edited by Stefano Leoni, 91–102. Milan: Rugginenti-Volontè, 2021.

Bjerstedt, Sven, et al. "The Musical Present: A Polyphonic Philosophical Investigation." *Nordisk Musikkpedagogisk Forskning: Årbok* 17 (2016) 9–39.

Bodley, Lorraine Byrne. *Goethe and Zelter: Musical Dialogues.* Abingdon: Routledge, 2009.

Boethius, Severinus Anicius. *The Consolation of Philosophy.* Translated by Victor Watts. London: Penguin, 1999.

Bolpagni, Paolo. "Musica visiva / colori immateriali. Tentazioni sinestesiche e prospettive intermediali negli anni Sessanta–Settanta." *Medea* 1.1 (2015). Online. http://ojs.unica.it/index.php/medea/article/download/1818/1531.

Bonaventure of Bagnoregio. *Commentaries on the Four Books of Sentences, Book One: On the One and Triune God.* Translated by a Franciscan Brother. Mansfield, MA: Franciscan Archive, 2014.

Bonhoeffer, Dietrich. *Letters and Papers from Prison.* Edited by Eberhard Betge. London: SCM, 2017.

Boulez, Pierre. *Il paese fertile. Paul Klee e la musica.* Translated by Guillemette Denis. Milan: Leonardo, 1989.

———. *Le pays fertile.* Edited by Paule Thévenin. Paris: Editions Gallimard, 1989.

Busoni, Ferruccio. *The Essence of Music and Other Papers.* London: Rockliff, 1957.

Busse Berger, Anna Maria. *Medieval Music and the Art of Memory.* Berkeley: University of California Press, 2005.

Cage, John. *Silence. Lectures and Writings.* Middletown, CT: Wesleyan University Press, 1961.

Caldecott, Stratford. "A New Light: Tolkien's Philosophy of Creation in *The Silmarillion.*" *Journal of Inklings Studies* 4.2 (2014) 67–85.

Capuano, Gianluca. *I segni della voce infinita. Musica e scrittura.* Milan: Jaca, 2002.

Carpenter, Humphrey. *Tolkien: A Biography.* Boston: Houghton Mifflin, 1977.

Carswell, John M. *Tolkien's Overture. Concerning the Music of the Ainur.* Franklin, TN: True Myths, 2018.

Carter, Elliott. "Music and the Time Screen." In *Current Thought in Musicology*, edited by John W. Grubbs, 63–88. Austin: University of Texas Press, 1976.

Cazden, Norman. "The Definition of Consonance and Dissonance." *International Review of the Aesthetics and Sociology of Music* 11.2 (1980) 123–68.

Chesterton, Gilbert K. *Orthodoxy.* Edinburgh: CrossReach, 2017.

Ciabattoni, Francesco. *Dante's Journey to Polyphony.* Toronto: University of Toronto Press, 2010.

Cioran, Emil. *Syllogismes de l'amertume.* Paris: Gallimard, 1952.

Clifton, Thomas. *Music as Heard: A Study in Applied Phenomenology.* New Haven: Yale University Press, 1983.

Coudert, Allison P. *Leibniz and the Kabbalah.* Dordrecht: Kulwer Academic, 1995.

Coutras, Lisa. *Tolkien's Theology of Beauty. Majesty, Splendor, and Transcendence in Middle-Earth.* New York NY: Palgrave MacMillan, 2016.

Craig, William Lane. "The Eternal Present and Stump-Kretzmann Eternity." *Reasonable Faith*, n.d. Online. https://www.reasonablefaith.org/writings/scholarly-writings/divine-eternity/the-eternal-present-and-stump-kretzmann-eternity.

Cunningham, David S. *These Three Are One: The Practice of Trinitarian Theology*. Oxford: Blackwell, 1998.

Da Vinci, Leonardo. *Thoughts on Art and Life by Leonardo da Vinci*. Edited and translated by Maurice Baring. Boston: Merrymount, 1906. Online. https://archive.org/details/thoughtsonartlifooleon.

David, Hans T., et al., eds. *The New Bach Reader. A Life of Johann Sebastian Bach in Letters and Documents*. New York: Norton, 1998.

Davies, Stephen. "Notations." In *The Routledge Companion to Philosophy and Music*, edited by Theodore Gracyk and Andrew Kania, 70–79. London: Routledge, 2011.

De Benedictis, Raffaele. *Ordine e struttura musicale nella "Divina Commedia."* Fucecchio: European Academic, 2000.

Della Seta, Fabrizio. "Idee musicali nel *Tractatus de configurationibus qualitatum et motuum* di Nicola Oresme." In *La musica nel tempo di Dante. Quaderni di Musica/Realtà*, edited by Luigi Pestalozza, 222–56. Milan: Unicopli, 1988.

Di Maio, Andrea. "La rappresentazione della natura in Bonaventura da Bagnoregio." *Przegląd Tomistyczny* 25 (2019) 143–70.

Diels, Hermann. *Die Fragmente der Vorsokratiker*. Berlin: Weidmannsche Buchhandlung, 1903.

Donne, John. *The Poems of John Donne*. London: Lawrence & Bullen, 1896.

———. *The Sermons of John Donne*. Edited by George Potter and Evelyn Simpson. Berkeley: University of California Press, 1953–1962.

Dostoevsky, Fëdor. *The Brothers Karamazov*. Translated by Constance Garnett. Uttar Pradesh: Om International, 2018.

———. *Notes from the Underground*. Translated by Constance Garnett. Indianapolis IN: Hackett, 2009.

Dreyfus, Laurence. *Bach and the Patterns of Invention*. Cambridge, MA: Harvard University Press, 2004.

Dubs, Kathleen E. "Providence, Fate, and Chance: Boethian Philosophy in *The Lord of the Rings*." *Twentieth Century Literature* 27.1 (1981) 34–42.

Dürr, Alfred. *Johann Sebastian Bach's "St. John Passion": Genesis, Transmission, and Meaning*. Oxford: Oxford University Press, 2000.

Eco, Umberto. *On Beauty*. Translated by Alastair McEwen. London: Secker & Warburg: 2004.

Economopoulos, Harula. "Lionello Spada (Bologna 1576–Parma 1622). 27. Concerto." In *Colori della Musica. Dipinti, strumenti e concerti tra Cinquecento e Seicento*, edited by Annalisa Bini et al., 68. Milan: Skira, 2000.

Eden, Bradford Lee. "The 'Music of the Spheres': Relationships between Tolkien's *The Silmarillion* and Medieval Cosmological and Religious Theory." In *Tolkien the Medievalist*, edited by Jane Chance, 183–93. New York: Routledge, 2013.

Elders, Willem. *Composers of the Low Countries*. Translated by Graham Dixon. Oxford: Clarendon, 1991.

Eliot, Thomas Stearns. *Four Quartets*. Orlando FL: Harcourt, 1943.

Erle, Giorgio. *Leibniz, Lully e la Teodicea. Forme etiche dell'armonia musicale*. Padua: Il Poligrafo, 2005.

Farago, Claire J. *Leonardo da Vinci's "Paragone": A Critical Interpretation with a New Edition of the Text in the "Codex Urbinas."* New York: Brill, 1992.

Ferand, Ernst Th. "The 'Howling in Seconds' of the Lombards: A Contribution to the Early Polyphony." *The Musical Quarterly* 25.3 (1939) 313–24.

Ferneyhough, Brian. "Die Taktilität der Zeit." *Musik Texte* 35 (1990) 14–17.

Ferri, Giovanni, ed. *Laude di Frate Jacopone da Todi.* Rome: La Società, 1910.

Ficino, Marsilio. *All Things Natural. Ficino on Plato's Timaeus.* Translated by Arthur Farndell. London: Shepheard-Walwyn, 2010.

Flieger, Verlyn. *Interrupted Music: The Making of Tolkien's Mythology.* Kent: Kent State University Press, 2005.

Flotzinger, Rudolf. "Discant I. Discant in France, Spain and Germany. 4. Discant in Three and Four Voices." *Grove Music Online.* Online. https://www.oxfordmusiconline.com/grovemusic/view/10.1093/gmo/9781561592630.001.0001/omo-9781561592630-e-0000007839.

Fubini, Enrico. "Sufficienza e insufficienza della notazione musicale. All'origine del problema interpretativo." In *Musica e interpretazione. Soggettività e conoscenza nell'esecuzione musicale*, edited by Luigi Attademo, 27–37. Turin: Trauben, 2002.

———. "Temporalité de la musique et notation musicale. A l'origine du problème de l'interprétation." *Musicae Scientiae Discussion Forum* 3 (2004) 21–35.

Fugelso, Karl. "Music as (Im)mortality in Leonardo's 'Portrait of a Man.'" *Source: Notes in the History of Art* 30.1 (2010) 24–28.

Fuller, Sarah. "'Delectabatur in hoc auris': Some Fourteenth-Century Perspectives on Aural Perception." *The Musical Quarterly* 82.3–4 (1998) 466–81.

Godwin, Joscelyn. *The Harmony of the Spheres. A Sourcebook of the Pythagorean Tradition in Music.* Rochester: Inner Traditions, 1992.

Goethe, Johann Wolfgang von. *Faust.* Translated by David Luke. Oxford: Oxford University Press, 1994.

———. *Goethe's Literary Essays. A Selection in English Arranged by J. E. Spingarn.* New York: Harcourt, Brace and Company, 1921.

Goldman, David P. "Sacred Music, Sacred Time." *First Things*, November 2009. Online. https://www.firstthings.com/article/2009/11/sacred-music-sacred-time.

Goolsby, Thomas W. "The Parameters of Eye Movement in Vocal Music Reading." PhD diss., University of Illinois at Urbana-Champaign, 1987.

Grant, Edward, ed. *A Source Book in Medieval Science.* Cambridge, MA: Harvard University Press, 1974.

Gregorio Magno [Gregory the Great]. *Vita di San Benedetto e la Regola.* Translated by the Benedictine Fathers of Subiaco. 1975. Reprint, Rome: Città Nuova, 2006.

Guido d'Arezzo. *Micrologus.* Rome: Desclée, Lefebvre et S. Edit. Pont., 1904. Online. http://ks4.imslp.info/files/imglnks/usimg/a/ae/IMSLP270547-PMLP438314-39087009494248text.pdf.

Halensis, Alexander. *Summa universis theologiae (Summa fratris Alexandri).* Edited by Bernardino Klumper and the Quaracchi Fathers. 4 vols. Rome: Collegii S. Bonaventurae, 1924–1948.

Halsall, Michael J. *Creation and Beauty in Tolkien's Catholic Vision. A Study in the Influence of Neoplatonism in J. R. R. Tolkien's Philosophy of Life as "Being and Gift."* Eugene, OR: Pickwick, 2020.

———. "A Critical Assessment of the Influence of Neoplatonism in J. R. R. Tolkien's Philosophy of Life as 'Being and Gift.'" PhD diss., University of Nottingham, 2015.

Hanoch-Roe, Galia. "Scoring the Path: Linear Sequences in Music and Space." In *Resonance: Essays on the Intersection of Music and Architecture*, edited by Mikesch Muecke and Miriam Zach, 77–145. Ames, IA: Culicidae Architectural, 2007.

Hardy, Elizabeth Baird. *Milton, Spenser and The Chronicles of Narnia: Literary Sources for the C. S. Lewis Novels*. Jefferson, NC: McFarland, 2007.

Harley, Anne-Maria. "Musique, espace et spatialisation." *Circuits* 5.2 (1994) 9–20.

Haskins, Rob. "John Cage's Organ Music (Mode 253–4, 2013)." *RobHaskins* (blog), March 15, 2015. Online. https://robhaskins.net/2015/03/15/john-cages-organ-music-mode-253-54-2013.

Hepokoski, James. *Sibelius: Symphony No. 5*. Cambridge: Cambridge University Press, 1993.

Higgins, Kathleen Marie. "Visual Music and Synesthesia." In *The Routledge Companion to Philosophy and Music*, edited by Theodore Gracyk and Andrew Kania, 480–92 London: Routledge, 2011.

Horace [Quintus Horatius Flaccus]. *Epistles I*. Cambridge: Cambridge University Press, 1956.

Horsley, Imogene. "Improvisation. II. Western Art Music. 2. History to 1600. i. Ensemble improvisation." *Grove Music Online*. Online. https://www.oxfordmusiconline.com/grovemusic/view/10.1093/gmo/9781561592630.001.0001/omo-9781561592630-e-0000013738.

Houghton, John William. "Augustine and the Ainulindalë." *Mythlore* 21.1 (1995) 4–8.

Hughes, Anselm. *The New Oxford History of Music II*. London: Oxford University Press, 1954.

Husserl, Edmund. *Ideas for a Pure Phenomenology and Phenomenological Philosophy: First Book*. Translated by Daniel O. Dahlstrom. Indianapolis IN: Hackett, 2014.

Illiano, Roberto. "Musical Notation and Figurative Arts." In *Music and the Figurative Arts in the Twentieth Century*, edited by Roberto Illiano, ix–xv. Turnhout: Brepols, 2016.

Ingarden, Roman. *Ontology of the Work of Art: The Musical Work, The Picture, The Architectural Work, The Film*. Translated by R. Meyer and J. T. Goldthwait. Athens: Ohio University Press, 1989.

———. *Untersuchungen zur Ontologie der Kunst*. Tübingen: Niemeyer, 1962.

———. *The Work of Music and the Problem of Its Identity*. Translated A. Czerniawski. Berkeley: University of California Press, 1986.

Isidore of Seville. *Isidori Hispalensis Episcopi Etymologiarum sive originum libri XX*. Edited by W. M. Lindsay. Oxford: Clarendon, 1911.

Jensen, Keith W. "Dissonance in the Divine Theme: The Issue of Free Will in Tolkien's *Silmarillion*." In *Middle-Earth Minstrel. Essays on Music in Tolkien*, edited by Bradford Lee Eden, 102–13. Jefferson, NC: McFarland, 2010.

John Paul II. "Ecclesia de Eucharistia." Encyclical given April 17, 2003. Online. http://www.vatican.va/holy_father/special_features/encyclicals/documents/hf_jp–ii_enc_20030417_ecclesia_eucharistia_en.html.

Johnson, Julian. *Out of Time: Music and the Making of Modernity*. Oxford: Oxford University Press, 2015.

Justin. "The Second Apology." In vol. 1 of *Ante-Nicene Fathers*, edited by Alexander Roberts et al., 188 93. Translated by Marcus Dods and George Reith. Buffalo, NY: Christian Literature, 1885. Online. http://www.newadvent.org/fathers/0127.htm.

Kandinsky, Vasilij. *Point and Line to Plane. Contribution to the Analysis of the Pictorial Elements*. Translated by Howard Dearstyne and Hilla Rebay. Bloomfield Hills: Cranbrook, 1947. Online. https://archive.org/details/PointLineToPlaneKandinsky.

———. *Punkt und Linie zu Fläche. Beitrag zur Analyse der malerischen Elemente*. Munich: Albert Langen, 1926. Online. http://bibliothequekandinsky.centrepompidou.fr/imagesbk/RLPF728/M5050_X0031_LIV_RLPF0728.pdf.

Kernfeld, Barry. "Improvisation. III. Jazz. 2. Solo and Collective Improvisation." *Grove Music Online*. Online. https://www.oxfordmusiconline.com/grovemusic/view/10.1093/gmo/9781561592630.001.0001/omo-9781561592630-e-0000013738.

Kierkegaard, Søren. *Either/Or, Part I*. Translated by H. V. Hond and E. H. Hong. Princeton NJ: Princeton University Press, 1987.

Klee, Paul. *Das bildnerische Denken*. Basel: Schwabe & Co., 1956.

———. *Diaries*. Translated by R. Y. Zachary and Max Knight. Berkeley: University of California Press, 1964.

———. *The Thinking Eye*. Vol. 1 of *Paul Klee Notebooks*. Translated by Ralph Manheim. London: Lund Humphries, 1961.

———. *Tagebücher 1898–1918*. Edited by Wolfgang Kersten. Stuttgart: Gerd Hatje, 1988. English translation in Paul Klee, *Diaries*. Translated by R. Y. Zachary and Max Knight. Berkeley: University of California Press, 1964.

Koechlin, Charles. "Le Temps et la musique." *La Revue musicale* 7.3 (1925) 45–62.

Kramer, Jonathan. "Studies of Time and Music: A Bibliography." *Music Theory Spectrum* 7 (1985) 72–106.

———. *The Time of Music*. New York: Schirmer, 1988.

Labberton, Robert Henlopen. *Outlines of History; with Original Tables, Chronological, Genealogical and Literary*. Philadelphia: Claxton, Remsen & Haffelfinger, 1872.

Laloy, Louis. "M. Henri Bergson et la musique." *Comœdia*, February 19, 1913. 3.

Lamartine, Alphonse Marie Louis. *Nouvelles meditations poétiques*. Paris: Urbain Canel, 1823.

Langer, Susanne. *Feeling and Form*. New York: Scribner, 1953.

Larsen, Kristine. "'Behold Your Music!': The Themes of Ilúvatar, the Song of Aslan, and the Real Music of the Spheres." In *Music in Middle-Earth*, edited by Heidi Steimel and Friedhelm Schneidewind, 11–28. Zürich: Walking Tree, 2010.

Ledda, Giuseppe. "Canto XV. Dante e Cacciaguida nel Cielo di Marte: I modelli, il martirio, la città." In *Cento Canti per Cento Anni. III. Paradiso*, edited by Enrico Malato and Andrea Mazzucchi, 430–58. Rome: Salerno, 2015.

Lee, Sherry D. "' . . . Deinen Wuchs wie Musik': Portraits, Identities, and the Dynamics of Seeing in Berg's Operatic Sphere." In *Alban Berg and his World*, edited by Christopher Hailey, 163–94. Princeton: Princeton University Press, 2010.

Leeming, David. *Creation Myths of the World: An Encyclopedia*. Santa Barbara: ABC CLIO, 2010.

Leibniz, Gottfried W. *Die philosophischen Schriften von Gottfried Wilhelm Leibniz*. Edited by C. I. Gerhardt. 7 vols. Hildesheim: Olms, 1978.

———. *The Ultimate Origin of Things*. Edited and translated by Jonathan Bennet. Online. http://www.earlymoderntexts.com/assets/pdfs/leibniz1697b.pdf.

Leijonhufvud, Susanna. "Sångupplevelse—en klingande bekräftelse på min existens i världen. En fenomenologisk undersökning ur första-person-perspektiv." PhD diss., Stockholms Universitet, 2011.

Lewis, Clive Staples. *The Chronicles of Narnia*. London: HarperCollins, 2001.

———. *Family Letters 1905–1931*. Vol. 1 of *The Collected Letters of C. S. Lewis*. New York: HarperCollins, 2004.

———. *The Collected Works of C. S. Lewis*. New York: Inspirational, 1996.

———. *Letters to Malcolm*. London: HarperCollins, 2017.

———. *The Screwtape Letters*. New York: Collier, 1961.

———. *Surprised by Joy*. London: HarperCollins, 2010.

Ligeti, György. "Metamorphoses of Musical Form." *Die Reihe* 7. London: Universal, 1965.

Lippmann, Edward A. *The Philosophy & Aesthetics of Music*. Lincoln: University of Nebraska Press, 1999.

Loewe, J. Andreas. "Musica est optimum. Martin Luther's Theory of Music." *Music and Letters* 94.4 (2013) 573–605.

Løgstrup, Knud Ejler. *Skabelse og Tilintetgørelse*. Copenhagen: Gyldendal, 1978.

Lorenz, Alfred *Das Geheimnis der Form bei Richard Wagner*. Berlin: M. Hesse, 1924.

Lovejoy, Arthur O. *The Great Chain of Being*. Cambridge, MA: Harvard University Press, 1978.

Luther, Martin. *Schriften 1536/39*. Vol. 50 of *Kritische Gesamtausgabe*. WA 50. Weimar: Böhlau, 1914.

———. *Vorlesungen über die Stufenpsalmen und Ps. 90 1532/35; Vorlesungen über Jesaja 9 und 53 1543/44; Auslegung von Hosea 13 1545*. Vol. 40.3 of *Kritische Gesamtausgabe*. WA 40.3. Weimar: Böhlau, 1930.

Machaut, Guillaume de. *Poésies Lyriques*. Edited by V. Chichmaref. Paris: Champion, 1909.

Mann, Thomas. *The Magic Mountain*. Translated H. T. Lowe-Porter. New York: Knopf, 1982.

Marino, Giovanni Battista. *Dicerie sacre*. Edited by Erminia Ardissino. Rome: Storia e Letteratura, 2014.

Mazur, Barry. "On Time (in Mathematics and Literature)." March 8, 2009. Online. http://www.math.harvard.edu/~mazur/preprints/time.pdf.

Mazzotta, Giuseppe. *Dante's Vision and the Circle of Knowledge*. Princeton: Princeton Legacy Library, 1993.

McIntosh, Jonathan. "*Ainulindalë*: Tolkien, St Thomas, and the Metaphysics of Music." In *Music in Middle-Earth*, edited by Heidi Steimel and Friedhelm Schneidewind, 53–74. Zürich: Walking Tree, 2010.

Melzi, Francesco, ed. *Trattato della Pittura*. Manuscript. Codex Urbinas 1270, Biblioteca Vaticana, Rome. Online. https://digi.vatlib.it/view/MSS_Urb.lat.1270.

Mersenne, Marin. *Traité de l'harmonie universelle*. Paris: Guillaume Baudry, 1627.

Mersmann, Hans. *Angewandte Musikästhetik*. Berlin: M. Hesse, 1926.

Messiaen, Olivier. *Music and Color: Conversations with Claude Samuel*. Translated by E. Thomas Glasow. Portland, OR: Amadeus, 1994.

Meyer, Leonard. *Emotion and Meaning in Music*. Chicago: University of Chicago Press, 1956.

Meyer, Stephen C. "From the Music of the Ainur to the Music of the Voice-Over. Music and Medievalism in *The Lord of the Rings*." In *The Oxford Handbook of Music and Medievalism*, edited by Stephen C. Meyer and Kirsten Yri, 611–35. Oxford: Oxford University Press, 2020.

Milbank, Alison. *Chesterton and Tolkien as Theologians*. London: T&T Clark, 2009.

———. "In a Dark Wood: Tolkien and Dante." Paper presented at School of English, Trinity College Dublin, September 21–22, 2012.

Miller, Clement A. "Erasmus on Music." *The Musical Quarterly* 52.3 (1966) 332–49.

Milton, John. *Paradise Lost: Book 7*. 1674. Online. https://www.poetryfoundation.org/poems/45743/paradise-lost-book-7-1674-version.

Mitchell, William J. T., ed. *The Language of Images*. Chicago: University of Chicago Press, 1980.

Montemaggi, Vittorio. "In Unknowability as Love. The Theology of Dante's *Commedia*." In *Dante's* Commedia: *Theology as Poetry*, edited by Vittorio Montemaggi and Matthew Treherne, 60–94. Notre Dame, IN: University of Notre Dame Press, 2010.

"Music and Eye Tracking." Special issue of *Journal of Eye Movement Research* 11.2 (2018). Online. https://bop.unibe.ch/JEMR/issue/view/793.

Musica Hogeri. Musica enchiriadis. Scholica enchiriadis. Commemoratio brevis. Manuscript. Cambridge, Corpus Christi College, MS 260. Online. https://parker.stanford.edu/parker/catalog/fc475fd2528.

Napolitano Valditara, Linda M. *Lo sguardo nel buio*. Rome: Laterza, 1994.

Naveh, Reuven. "Tonality, Atonality and the *Ainulindalë*." In *Music in Middle-Earth*, edited by Heidi Steimel and Friedhelm Schneidewind, 29–52. Zürich: Walking Tree, 2010.

Nettl, Bruno. "Improvisation. I. Concepts and practices. 1. Concepts." *Grove Music Online*. Online. https://www.oxfordmusiconline.com/grovemusic/view/10.1093/gmo/9781561592630.001.0001/omo-9781561592630-e-0000013738.

———. "Thoughts on Improvisation: A Comparative Approach." *The Musical Quarterly* 60.1 (1974) 1–19.

Newman, John Henry. *Fifteen Sermons Preached Before the University of Oxford*. London: Longmans, Green and Co., 1909.

———. *The Idea of a University*. London: Longmans, Green and Co., 1907.

North, John. *The Ambassadors' Secret*. London: Orion, 2004.

Oehlmann, Werner. "Musik in Zeit und Ewigkeit." *Der Tagesspiegel* 2223 (1.1.1953).

Orsbon, David Allison. "The Universe as Book: Dante's *Commedia* as an Image of the Divine Mind." *Dante Studies* (2014) 87–112.

Owens, Jessie Ann. *Composers at Work. The Craft of Musical Composition 1450–1600*. New York: Oxford University Press, 1997.

Oyola, Eliezer. *Imagen y Palabra: En torno a "El Cristo de Velázquez" de Unamuno*. Bloomington, IN: Palibrio, 2012.

Paddison, Max. "Performance and the Silent Work." *Filigrane*, May 27, 2011. Online. http://revues.mshparisnord.org/filigrane/index.php?id=147.

———. "Performance, Reification, and Score: The Dialectics of Spatialization and Temporality in the Experience of Music." *Musicae Scientiae Discussion Forum* 3 (2004) 157–79.

Pater, Walter Horatio. "The School of Giorgione." In *The Renaissance: Studies in Art and Poetry*, edited by D. L. Hill, 102–22. Berkeley: University of California Press, 1980.

Pedersen, Arild. *Singing Time: Meaning, Music and Interpretation—quasi una prelude and fugue*. Oslo: Unipub, 2011.

Petersen, Nils Holger. "Carolingian Music, Ritual and Theology." In *The Appearances of Medieval Rituals: The Play of Construction and Modification*, edited by N. H. Petersen et al., 13–31. Turnhout: Brepols, 2004.

———. "Time and Space in W. A. Mozart's *Ave Verum Corpus* (1791): Transcendence and the Fictive Space of the Musical Work." In *Transcendence and Sensoriness*, edited by Svein Aage Christoffersen et al., 287–325. Leiden: Koninklijke Brill, 2015.

Pickover, Clifford A. *Time: A Traveler's Guide*. Oxford: Oxford University Press, 1998.

Plato. *The Republic*. Translated by B. Jowett. Oxford: Clarendon, 1888.

———. *Timaeus*. Translated by Francis M. Cornford. New York: MacMillan, 1959.

Poirier, Alain. *André Boucourechliev*. Paris: Fayard, 2002.

Priestley, Joseph. "'A Description of a Chart of Biography' and 'A Description of a New Chart of History' (1769)." In vol. 24 of *The Theological and Miscellaneous Works of Joseph Priestley*, edited by John Towill Rutt, 463–515. 25 vols. London: G. Smallfield, 1817.

Quiller-Couch, Arthur Thomas, ed. *The Oxford Book of English Verse*. Oxford: Clarendon, 1912. Online. https://archive.org/details/cu31924011997909.

Reiner, Thomas. "A Chameleon Called Musical Time: Some Observations about Time and Musical Time." *Context* 5 (1993) 19–24.

Restagno, Enzo, ed. *Xenakis*. Turin: EDT/Musica, 1988.

Ricoeur, Paul. *Time and Narrative*. Translated by K. McLaughlin and D. Pellauer. Vol. 1. Chicago: University of Chicago Press, 1984.

Rink, John. "Analysis and (or?) Performance." In *Musical Performance: A Guide to Understanding*, edited by John Rink, 35–58. Cambridge: Cambridge University Press, 2002.

Rosenberg, Daniel, and Anthony Grafton. *Cartographies of Time: A History of the Timeline*. New York: Princeton Architectural, 2013.

Rössler, Kalmut. *Contributions to the Spiritual World of Olivier Messiaen*. Translated by Barbara Dagg and Nancy Poland. Duisburg: Gilles & Francke, 1986.

Rousseau, Jean-Jacques. *The Confessions of Jean Jacques Rousseau*. London: Reeves and Turner, 1861.

Salomo, Elias. "Scientia artis musicae." In vol. 3 of *Scriptores ecclesiastici de musica sacra potissimum*, edited by Martin Gerbert, 16–64. 3 vols. Hildesheim: Olms, 1963.

Samuel, Claude. *Conversations with Olivier Messiaen*. Translated by Felix Aprahamian. London: Stainer and Bell, 1976.

Sarath, Ed. "A New Look at Improvisation." *Journal of Music Theory* 40.1 (1996) 1–38.

Satapatha Brahmana, Part III. Translated by Julius Eggeling. Delhi: Motilal Banarsidass, 1894. Online. https://archive.org/details/in.ernet.dli.2015.22480.

Sayer, George. *Jack: A Life of C. S. Lewis*. Wheaton, IL: Crossway, 1994.

Schadel, Erwin. *Musik als Trinitätssymbol*. Frankfurt: Peter Lang, 1999.

Schelling, Friedrich Wilhelm Joseph von. *Philosophie der Kunst*. Stuttgart: Cotta, 1859.

Schenker, Heinrich. *Der Tonwille. Pamphlets in Witness of the Immutable Laws of Music*. Translated by Ian Bent et al. 5 vols. Oxford: Oxford University Press, 2004.

Schmuckler, Mark A. "Expectations in Music: Investigation of Melodic and Harmonic Processes." *Music Perception: An Interdisciplinary Journal* 7.2 (1989) 109–49.

Schönberg, Arnold. *Style and Idea: Selected Writings of Arnold Schoenberg*. Edited by Leonard Stein. Translated by Leo Black. Berkeley: University of California Press, 1984.

Schopenhauer, Arthur. *The World as Will and Representation*. Translated by E. F. J. Payne. New York: Dover, 1969.

Schumann, Robert. "Rules for Young Musicians." *Junior Keynotes* (Winter 1985) 33–35. Online. http://jmm.people.si.umich.edu/blog/schumann%27s_rules_for_young_musicians.pdf.

Schurr, Claudia Elisabeth. *Dante e la musica. Dimensione, contenuto e finalità del messaggio musicale nella Divina Commedia*. Perugia: Università degli Studi di Perugia, 1994.

Sciarrino, Salvatore. *Le figure della musica da Beethoven a oggi*. Milan: Ricordi, 1998.

Scruton, Roger. "The Lost Love of Dancing." *Roger Scruton* (blog), n.d. Online. https://www.roger-scruton.com/about/music/understanding-music/173-the-lost-love-of-dancing.

Shakespeare, William. *The Merchant of Venice*. Cambridge: Cambridge University Press, 2003.

Shippey, Tom. *The Road to Middle-Earth*. Boston: Houghton Mifflin, 1983.

Sloboda, John A. "The Eye-Hand Span: An Approach to the Study of Sight Reading." *Psychology of Music* 2.2 (1988) 4–10.

Söhngen, Oskar. *Theologie der Musik*. Kassel: Johannes Stauda, 1967.

Solomos, Makis. "The Complexity of Xenakis's Notion of Space." In *Komposition für hörbaren Raum. Die frühe elektroakustische Musik und ihre Kontexte. Compositions for Audible Space. The Early Electroacoustic Music and its Contexts*, edited by Martha Brech and Ralph Paland, 323–37. Bielefeld: Transcript, 2015.

Souvtchinsky, Pierre. "La Notion du temps et la musique." *La Revue Musicale* (1939) 70–80.

Spenser, Edmund. *The Poetical Works of Edmund Spenser*. vol. 5. Edinburgh: James Nichol, 1859.

Spitzer, Leo. *L'armonia del mondo*. Bologna: Il Mulino, 2009.

———. *Classical and Christian Ideas of World Harmony*. Baltimore: Johns Hopkins Press, 1963.

Stachó, László. "Mental Virtuosity: A New Theory of Performers' Attentional Processes and Strategies." *Musicae Scientiae* 22.4 (2018) 539–57.

Stein, Edith. *Finite and Eternal Being*. Translated by Kurt F. Reinhardt. Washington, DC: ICS, 2002.

———. *Potency and Act*. Translated by Walter Redmond. Washington, DC: ICS, 2009.

Sternfeld, Frederick, ed. *History of Western Music*. New York: Praeger, 1973.

Stockhausen, Karlheinz. "Structure and Experiential Time." Translated by Leo Black. *Die Reihe* 2 (1959) 64–74.

Stravinsky, Igor. *Poetics of Music. In the Form of Six Lessons*. Translated by Arthur Knodel and Ingolf Dahl. Cambridge, MA: Harvard University Press, 1947. Online. https://monoskop.org/images/6/64/Stravinsky_Igor_Poetics_of_Music_in_the_Form_of_Six_Lessons.pdf.

Struik, Dirk J., ed. *A Source Book in Mathematics, 1200–1800*. Cambridge, MA: Harvard University Press, 1969.

Stuckenschmidt, Hans Heinz. "Short Operas." *Musikblätter des Anbruch* 10 (1928) 204–07.

Stump, Eleonore and Norman Kretzmann. "Eternity." *Journal of Philosophy* 78.8 (1981) 429–58.

Taruskin, Richard. *Text and Act: Essays on Music and Performance*. New York: Oxford University Press, 1995.

The Didascalicon of Hugh of St Victor: A Medieval Guide to the Arts. Translated by Jerome Taylor. New York: Columbia University Press, 1991.

Teixeira, William, and Silvio Ferraz. "The Performance of Time (Or the Time of Musical Performance)." *Performance Philosophy* 4.2 (2019) 490–509.

Terribile, Claudia. "La musica nella cultura figurativa veneta del XVI secolo." In *Colori della Musica. Dipinti, strumenti e concerti tra Cinquecento e Seicento*, edited by Annalisa Bini et al., 89–94. Milan: Skira, 2000.

Tolkien, J. R. R. *The Book of Lost Tales, Part One.* (The History of Middle-Earth 5). Edited by Christopher Tolkien. London: Unwin Hyman; Boston: Houghton Mifflin, 1987.

———. *The Letters of J.R.R. Tolkien.* Edited by Humphrey Carpenter with Christopher Tolkien. London: George Allen & Unwin; Boston: Houghton Mifflin, 1981.

———. *The Lord of the Rings.* London: George Allen & Unwin; Boston: Houghton Mifflin, 2002.

———. *A Middle English Vocabulary. Designed for Use with Sisam's Fourteenth Century Verse & Prose.* Oxford: Clarendon, 1922.

———. "Mythopoeia." In *Tree and Leaf*, 97–101. London: Unwin Hyman, 1988; Boston: Houghton Mifflin, 1989.

———. "On Fairy-Stories." In *Essays Presented to Charles Williams*, 38–89. London: Oxford University Press, 1947.

———. *The Silmarillion.* Edited by Christopher Tolkien. London: George Allen & Unwin; Boston: Houghton Mifflin, 1977.

Trippett, David. "Composing Time: Zeno's Arrow, Hindemith's *Erinnerung*, and Satie's *Instantanéisme*." *The Journal of Musicology* 24.4 (2007) 522–80.

Truitt, Frances E., et al. "The Perceptual Span and the Eye-Hand Span in Sight Reading Music." *Visual Cognition* 4.2 (1997) 143–61.

Vatican Council. "*Lumen Gentium*: Dogmatic Constitution on the Church." November 21, 1964. Online. https://www.vatican.va/archive/hist_councils/ii_vatican_council/documents/vat-ii_const_19641121_lumen-gentium_en.html.

Villa-Rojo, Jesús *Notación y grafía musical en el siglo XX.* Madrid: Iberautor/SGAE, 2003.

White, Hayden. *The Content of the Form: Narrative Discourse and Historical Representation.* Baltimore: John Hopkins University Press, 1987.

Wilkins, William Joseph. *Hindu Mythology, Vedic and Purānic.* Calcutta; Simla: Thacker, Spink, 1913.

Williams, John [Ab Ithel]. *The Barddas of Iolo Morganwg.* Llandovery: Roderic, 1862.

Williams, Rowan. "Barth on the Triune God." In *Wrestling with Angels: Conversations in Modern Theology*, edited by Mike Higton, 77–85. Grand Rapids: Eerdmans, 2008.

Winternitz, Emanuel. "La musica nel 'Paragone' di Leonardo da Vinci." *Studi Musicali* (1972) 79–99.

Wittgenstein, Ludwig. *Tractatus logico-philosophicus.* Translated by C. K. Ogden. London: Routledge & Kegan Paul, 1955.

Whobrey, Megan A. M. "From *Ainulindalë* to Valhalla. J. R. R. Tolkien's Musical Mythology and its Eddaic Influences." PhD diss., University of Central Oklahoma, 2013.

Wolff, Christoph. *Johann Sebastian Bach: The Learned Musician.* New York: Norton, 2000.

Wu, Jean Marie. "Mystical Symbols of Faith: Olivier Messiaen's Charm of Impossibilities." In *Messiaen's Language of Mystical Love*, edited by Siglind Bruhn, 85–120. New York: Routledge, 2012.

Xenakis, Iannis. *Musique, Architecture.* Tournai: Casterman, 1971.

Young, Edward. *Young's Night Thoughts.* Edited by George Gilfillan. Edinburgh: J. Nichol, 1853.

Zarlino, Gioseffo. *Le istitutioni harmoniche.* Venice: De Franceschi, 1573. Online. https://ks.imslp.net/files/imglnks/usimg/3/37/IMSLP106837-PMLP156553-le_istituzioni_harmoniche.pdf.

Zuckerkandl, Victor. *Sound and Symbol.* Translated by Willard R. Trask. Princeton, NJ: Princeton University Press, 1969.

Subject/Name Index

Scripture Index

OLD TESTAMENT

NEW TESTAMENT

www.ingramcontent.com/pod-product-compliance
Lightning Source LLC
LaVergne TN
LVHW050632100826
845148LV00011B/1841

* 9 7 8 1 7 2 5 2 9 5 0 2 5 *